Heavenly Fragrance

Cooking with Aromatic Asian Herbs, Fruits, Spices and Seasonings

by Carol Selva Rajah

foreword by David Thompson
photographs by Masano Kawana
styling by Christina Ong and Magdalene Ong

PERIPLUS EDITIONS
Singapore • Hong Kong • Indonesia

COOKING WITH AROMATIC ASIAN SPICES   136

Cardamom * Cinnamon and Cassia * Cloves * Coriander Seeds * Cumin * Fennel
Galangal * Ginger * Pepper and Sichuan Pepper * Saffron * Star Anise * Turmeric

COOKING WITH AROMATIC ASIAN SEASONINGS   196

Chinese Black Vinegar * Fermented Soybean Pastes * Fish Sauces * Hoisin Sauce * Mirin * Oyster Sauce
and Abalone Sauce * Rice Wines * Plum Sauce and Lemon Sauce * Sesame Oil * Shrimp Pastes * Soy Sauces

TAPPING INTO DELICIOUS MEMORIES

I have been fortunate enough to have eaten Carol's food many times, sometimes with Carol sitting next to me telling me the most marvelous tales of her family, her Amah and her childhood in Malaysia. I sat mesmerized as she wound her stories around her food—until I was not sure which was the more alluring. But I was always left wanting more, and I was not alone in this as I know many who have been held in the same thrall of her charm and her cooking.

"We cooked for pleasure," she told me. "We forgot which community we belonged to and we cooked to feed and to please our friends—whether they were Malays, Chinese, Tamils, or later Australians." And such hospitable charm fills this book.

Heavenly Fragrance is an account of these stories and their dishes—a dance through her childhood, tapping into delicious memories with the steady, rhythmic clunk of the granite pestle pounding the spices and filling our senses with the pungent aromas that still hold such a powerful sway over her and her cooking. The garden of her youth was filled with lemongrass, galangal, roseapples and durians. Her Amah's Chicken Curry skips straight out of her rich, happy past. I can imagine it served with Fragrant Pandanus Coconut Rice (*nasi lemak*), or on special occasions with Roti Jala, the lacy pancakes of Malaysia. Flaked Fish Salad with Spices and Coconut was a dish which her husband, Selva, insisted on preparing himself to ensure the proper seasoning, while her "lethal weapon" of Babi Tayu (*Tau Yew Bak*)—Sweet Soy Pork with Mushrooms and Star Anise—packs an Amah's love!

This book is not just based in the vivid but somewhat distant past. It is a collection of the author's memories throughout her life—and it contains many recipes that are not just Asian. They are her own authentic recipes reflecting her life's journey. Carol's Leek and Potato Vichyssoise with Lemongrass captures the change in food that occurred around the time she arrived in Australia, when cooks began to dabble with spices to color their otherwise dull cuisine. Carol's version adds lemongrass and she even suggests a dash of chili pepper too! Her Barbecued Beef Steaks with Sweet Onion Jam tells of her experiences in Australia with her family. Settled and firmly planted now in Sydney, I can see her—and hear her—preparing a spicy Shrimp with Tropical Coconut Laksa Gravy and a Mint Vodka Collins with Watermelon Fingers with Lyndey Milan making a screamingly good tipple in the background.

Heavenly Fragrance evokes more than just memories—it excites the imagination and fills the senses with the possibilities of pungent fragrances and tastes that create new memories. It articulates the past and present of a talented cook in the very best way—with wonderfully delicious recipes!

David Thompson
Winner of the James Beard Award
and IACP Finalist for *Thai Food*

FRAGRANT MEMORIES FROM MY YOUTH

by Carol Selva Rajah

Fragrance evokes memories. If you have ever entered a bread shop while cinnamon buns are baking or passed someone's kitchen at Christmas and whiffed the spicy aromas of a Christmas cake or breathed deeply as you walked through a pine forest after a spring rain, then you will share some of my passion for fragrance in food and its ability to stir up memories of the past. This phenomenon has been most famously described by French author Marcel Proust, as he sipped a cup of tea and ate a soggy madeline biscuit. This simple and almost mundane act of eating and drinking set off a chain reaction of fragrance, awakening long-lost memories and indeed becoming the inspiration for one of the greatest of all literary works—his classic novel, *Remembrance of Things Past* (*A la recherche du temps perdu*). Simple, humble tastes and smells have the power to project us back to our childhood and remind us of a forgotten event or moment faster and more effectively than almost anything else; and always remind me of Proust's madeline.

My own childhood, spent in Malaysia and Singapore, abounds with fragrant memories which have inspired the recipes in this book and built up my appreciation for fragrant home-cooking. Walking through the tropical spice gardens of Bali, Penang or Sri Lanka, your senses are overwhelmed by a combination of distinctive aromas as you stop and mentally attempt to separate them into what is culinary and what is purely floral. For me it is like a dance through my childhood and a mental game of guessing

the origins of each aroma. I have found that in Asia the ingredients from gardens, kitchens and floral markets overlap as they are all used in cooking, conjuring memories of a mouth-watering curry from a street stall in Chiang Mai or Singapore's Newton Circus. With this book I hope to inspire you to create new "food memories" with simple, deliciously fragrant recipes drawing upon the vast rainbow of aromatic produce one finds in traditional Asian kitchens.

When I was growing up in Malaysia, beautiful scents were all around us, pervading our lives. I lived with my family on a large sprawling property planted with a jumble of fruits and herbs. Mango and rambutan trees framed my window, the aroma of mango flowers brushing past the mosquito netting, spreading their light caramel-like fragrance around my room. Now whenever I bite into a juicy Bowen mango from Queensland, I close my eyes and am immediately transported back to the warmth and comfort of my childhood bedroom. Stalwart jackfruit trees stood like soldiers along the back fence, producing meter-long fruits which resembled spiky green

ABOVE: Drawing of the family home and garden in Klang near Kuala Lumpur. To the left of the old colonial bungalow was the attached kitchen with herb garden beds and badminton court. On the right were orchids and various fruit trees. In front of the house stood the bougainvillea bower and the fish pond underneath it (as shown in the diagram). **OPPOSITE:** My father and mother when they were very young sitting in the garden by the side of the house. By the time I had grown up this garden was filled with rambutan, mango, jambu, roseapple, and jackfruit trees.

balloons hanging ponderously from the stems. As these fruits slowly matured, they gave forth a spicy, pineapple-honey scent that enticed everyone passing the open breezeway to the kitchen and the chili beds beyond. These beds were only chili in name—in fact they were littered with the distinct lemon-oil scents of lemongrass and galangal and the pungent, oily turmeric, yielding a tousled jumble of aromatic citrus and rose whenever disturbed, especially on a hot afternoon. These herbs and spices were gathered and tossed together on occasion into a beautifully tart jackfruit salad—colorful, fragrant and deeply satisfying, having come straight from our own garden.

Our garden was a place where you ate with your eyes and your nose before you even got to the dining table. There was perfume everywhere. In front of the house was a high metal planter that supported scarlet bougainvillea and delicate white flowers of orange blossom and red hibiscus which were thrown into juicy Sri Lankan sambols. Under this impressionist splash of color sat a circular fish pond with darting blue fighting fish, watched benignly by the resident tortoise. Nearby was a mass of blue pea flowers that colored our Nonya cakes and gave off a delicate perfume. Behind the house, an old roseapple or *jambu ayer* tree struggled for survival, laced with pale lichen and crawling with giant red ants, all headed for the special juicy sweetness in the fruit that we, as children, all craved. These beautiful juicy roseapples had the aroma of peaches and were used in our family Rojak salad—their sweetness contrasting with the spice of chili and pungent shrimp paste.

On one side of the house we had curry leaf bushes which gave off peppery aromas that ended up in my father's hot Ceylonese curries and a famous sour, salty Mulligatawny soup known as *rasam* in India. The subtle, newly-mown grass scent of the pandanus palm

pervaded our garden and glamorized our coconut rice cakes. Father's bud-grafted trees, gnarled and bent with heavy green pomelo fruits, with pink pockets of lemony-sweet fruitiness on the inside, jostled with the lime trees whose fruit was indispensable in the kitchen. Everytime my father was annoyed, my Amah would produce her Pomelo and Shrimp Salad to placate him with its soothing colors and aroma, often involving the *jambu ayer* roseapple and several herbs from the garden. The kalamansi lime bushes with their cherry blossoms of dark green that spurted orange-sweet juice that was used for the ubiquitous lime cordials—so loved for their thirst-quenching properties, was a necessity in the tropical heat. Nothing was wasted—the spent fruit, rind and all, was massaged into scalps to create squeaky-clean, lime-perfumed and shampooed hair, again a strong Proustian channel to childhood innocence.

Central to all of this was the kitchen, tucked onto the back of the house yet the pivot of the home. The kitchen was divided into two areas: the "wet-kitchen" where pounding, grinding and slicing of spices and herbs was done each morning in preparation for a meat or fish curry, close to a running tap so that everything could be splashed clean. The other "dry-kitchen" was for cooking—where the old wood and coal stove sat squat across from the sink and wash area, and on it, a huge pot bubbled quietly with a joint of mutton for a curry or filled with chicken bones for stock inside. A vast wok sat on top of the stove almost permanently where a special dry chicken curry would be slowly sautéed, full of potatoes, tomatoes, chili and plump chicken pieces. I remember being drawn to the kitchen by the sharp, nose-tickling spike of the chili as it splattered into the hot oil, burning my eyes and nostrils until the onion and the soothing garlic were thrown in and left to mellow slowly in the wok. Amah, my "other mother," would be there, stirring the mixture

My Cantonese Amah dressed in her white Chinese samfu top and black pyjama pants holding me on my second birthday.

calmly, adding the soft citrus and gingery aromatics—the lemongrass and galangal and the earthy, fecund shrimp paste—finally converting it all miraculously into a composite of satisfying aromas, flavors and colors.

Amah was a natural cook, a master of flavor and aromatic patterns. As part of my multicultural extended family, she observed and learned the Jaffna Tamil and Malay influences of our country and added it to her own store of cooking and Chinese herbal lore. She was Cantonese but her and our food heritage was from everywhere. Sri Lankan fish and shrimp curries with their soul-satisfying coconut soupy sauces followed the spicing rules of my father's people. For Chinese cuisine, we adhered to the strong herbal and saucing traditions of Amah, intertwined with my mother's early Hokkien and Nonya food experiences in Penang, where her first loves were the hot and spicy shrimp pastes and chili heat of the Nonya Laksa and Mee Siam. There were other influences of course, like the Malay dishes that friends and neighbors prepared

and the formal European dinners that were given by my mother's colonial associates and missionary friends. These recipes were all eagerly borrowed, recorded and tested again and again at our home until they gradually became our own, carefully recorded in old broken-spined school exercise books.

Every morning before school, under Amah's expert tutelage, I learned to pick and portion the herbs. In one instance lemongrass, galangal, chili and turmeric would evolve into a mouth-watering curry paste for her unique Sambal Shrimp (see page 66). We would start first with a collection of chopped onion and garlic and pounded shrimp paste and tamarind puree. Working on the grinding stone, she would grind the chili, pulverize the onion and garlic, then add the rock-hard turmeric—so difficult to judge, coloring everything it touches with a saffron stain—until it splinters and releases its rose-musk fragrance. Lemongrass would go in next. As more herbs were added, they actually made the grinding easier. From her I learned the secret of layering ingredients when cooking, adding first the garlic and waiting for it to release its enticing aromas, then adding the next ingredient and then the others in their turn so that the oils and fragrance in each spice was released separately to build on the flavor of what came before. The Sambal Shrimp that finally emerged was a mixture of all these perfumed ingredients and remains an indelible memory of my ancestral home.

While we went to our gardens frequently for the aromatic herbs and spices for the grinding stone, it would be off to the jostling, noisy market for our fresh produce—always at dawn before the sun wilted away the best ones. Crisp green beans and jelly-like tofu—shaking as we picked it up from its aromatic banana leaf container—and the fresh scents of *kailan* (chinese broccoli), and mustardy *choy sum* (flowering cabbage) with its peppery yellow flowers, jewel-like eggplants and bright green, knobbly bitter gourds—all of these would be carefully selected, wrapped and dropped into our bulging shopping basket.

Asian markets are tumultuous, exciting places. Some are mere collections of tiny little thatched lean-tos. Others are rambling, colorful and well-stocked. How lavish the brightly-colored mix of the vegetable stalls always seems. Pyramids of fresh green wing beans—I salivate at the thought of using them for a quick,

Shopping for aromatic herbs and vegetables in Sydney's Asian market at Cabramatta, where the largest concentration of Asian migrants live, grow their market produce and serve an amazingly eclectic range of Asian foods.

crispy stir-fry with dried shrimp and slowly carameliz-ing onions. Orange and saffron-colored bananas, bright red tomatoes, towers of food looking so neat yet so precarious. What hilarity to see them accidental-ly scattered amongst the regal purple brinjals (egg-plants) and the jungle-green bittersweet drumstick beans! The sweet fragrance of coconut, reminiscent of ripe cucumber, cream and pandan is a Proustian link to palm trees and beaches, so familiar to us all, and a unifying element amongst all the wonderful countries and cuisines of the tropics.

Markets smell different in Asia than elsewhere. Enter one and you are met with an onslaught of fragrances: musky, fishy, yeasty, nutty. The salty tang of fresh fish in large, musty-wet bamboo baskets—I picked up some whiting so fresh it almost leapt at me! The trevally is particularly tempting and the snapper always inviting because of its pink shiny scales. Further down, there are the caramel-like smells of roasting chicken satay. The pungency of chili powder being ground; the clean aromas of galangal and warm nut-meg; the sweet scent of cardamom and cassia perfumed tea, poured out in a tall, thin stream to create a magnificent, spicy froth. Asian markets are always a beehive of activity with people jostling and carrying baskets—busy, busy everywhere.

Aromas alone can announce the culture and the nationality of a market. Indian markets are suffused strongly with the pungency of curry leaves, cumin and coriander. The magical dry-roasting of these spices creates completely new aromas, such as those found in a vegetarian dal dish cooked with tomato and garnished with black mustard seeds and frying onions. And everywhere in India there is the faint lingering aroma of cardamom and chocolaty cinnamon.

Chinese markets announce their presence by the squawking of live ducks and chickens and row upon row of pork butchers. Herbal concoctions boil in vats and onion-mustardy smells emanate from rows of stalls selling *choy sum*, bok choy, *een choi* and various

other cabbages piled in pyramids with other greens. In another area one finds assorted pickles and preserves in large earthenware jars, close to stalls with charcoal braziers where pork is slowly roasted, yielding the arresting sweetness of *hoisin*, and the ever-enticing caramel aromas of *char siew* pork and anise-glazed ducks which hang on hooks like soldiers in a row.

Every country has its characteristic aromas: the Balinese ones are best represented by the delicately perfumed ginger flower chopped into the *babi guling* roast pork salad; Thailand by its coriander and lemongrass with peppery chili and the lemony tang of its Tom Yam Soup and Mee Krob; Vietnam by the herbal fragrance of perilla in its beefy Pho soups.

The importance of aroma

Over three quarters of what we taste in fact comes from smell. When we put food in our mouth, its aromas travel to the back of our throat and up to the nose. To demonstrate this to my students, I have them eat a few grains of strong, aromatic cumin, fennel and sugar while their nose is blocked with a clothes pin. They get nothing—no sensation of taste or smell. Then I have them remove the clothes pin. Whoa! Smell and taste return with surprising force.

Max Lake, the famous food and wine critic and my personal mentor and friend, has reinforced and influenced a great deal of my own understanding of aroma and taste. He writes that olfactory memories are strong because the nose is connected to the primitive brain, and thus connected to our sensual drives. Perfumers and sommeliers have long been aware of this relationship. His analysis of how the part of the brain devoted to smells affects our enjoyment of food and wine serves to confirm what I have learned through personal experience—that the emotional and physical functions of the brain are conjoined via the nose.

Because they are so closely tied to personal and cultural memories, aromas affect different people in very different ways. The smells of a ripe durian and of a ripe blue cheese are equally strong, yet they evoke either repulsion or greedy anticipation in a person depending upon whether their upbringing is Asian or Western. However, a look at the long queues at a bread shop or an Italian pizza shop redolent with roasting garlic, will also confirm that many aromas are universal.

ABOVE: Elegant star anise pods—an aromatic star-shaped spice with the fragrance of cassia and anise. **OPPOSITE:** Fresh garlic chives not only look attractive, they pack a garlic punch when added to a tossed noodle dish or a chili crab dish (see Chili Crabs with Ginger and Garlic Chives—page 64).

I feel that taste memory—the ability to perceive and differentiate between aromas—is always present in a person, but requires training through cultivation and practice. I recall Amah's natural ability to use her taste and smell memory to recreate flavors in a dish quite foreign to her. Once she tasted something, her own senses would guide her through a personal library of ingredients and formulae, enabling her to cook from intuition rather than from a written recipe. Even if the ingredients were not quite right, as when she tried a new curry recipe (she was not Indian, but Cantonese), she managed to arrive at the desired flavor anyway by adding other ingredients—for example a thick soy sauce. Friends often wondered why Amah's curry had such powerful flavors. This ability to recreate flavors from memory is one of the most desirable gifts that all good chefs the world over possess.

This leads me to the concept of *yin* and *yang*. Another attribute of Asian cooks is the ability to achieve a

FRAGRANT MEMORIES FROM MY YOUTH

ABOVE: Pickled garlic can be truly surprising when used in salads and meat dishes and can be easily made at home.
OPPOSITE: Perfect for a summer lunch that speaks of rarefied paradise (see Black Pepper Lobster Tails with Garlic Butter—page 183) with a glass of your favorite bubbly.

balance in their cuisine between the opposing energies of *yin* (earth, darkness, cold and receptivity) and *yang* (sunlight, heat and activity). In food this is important because some foods are known to be cooling (*yin*) and others heating (*yang*). This relationship is encouraged and fostered in both aroma and flavor, and has little to do with actual temperature, but more with creating heating and cooling sensations in the body with dishes and their ingredients.

Yin aromas have a calming effect on the *chi* (life force or human energy). Examples of this are the delicate, almost feminine perfumes of the grassy pandanus and green teas, the citrusy lemongrass, the floral bouquets of the ginger flower or the delicate *keng hua* (cactus flower). *Yang* aromas are warm and stimulating. Examples are pepper, ginger, chili and the musky and nutty aromas of spices and some meats. Do not turn down a cup of "heaty" ginger tea offered to you when you have a cold coming on—the aromas will clear the sinuses and the

ginger will warm your chest.

I have often felt homesick for the tastes and smells and that little chili patch back home, and for the Asian kitchens which always beckon with their spicy, intriguing aromas that change each day as the daily menu changes. Living in Australia, I slowly came to realize that in the West herbs are subtle and gentle, whereas the herbs used by Asians are intense and fiery, and clash together as they cook in the wok. Moreover, the spices that are strong in their own right, such as cumin, coriander and fennel, are often dry-roasted to give them added punch. This represents a major difference in our cultures. Our cuisine in the East is so aromatic because that is what is most important to us. Good Asian cooks are trained to bring out the aromas of each individual spice or herb. Garlic aromas are teased out in woks, and curry pastes are slowly cooked until they became aromatic. The abundance of perfumed ingredients makes it easy to create such food once you understand this simple point. To this day I live by one of my Amah's major tenets: "*Ahh, ho heong, ho sek mah!*" which means "Good smell, good to eat!"

Friends who travel with me to Asia are enraptured. One friend, a television producer, used to looking at things through the confining lens of a camera, turned to me in the midst of filming a market and remarked that he wished he had a "smell-a-vision" camera. Canadian and Australian friends repeatedly walk into my kitchen and are seduced by the aromas, immediately heading for the stove and lifting up the lids to breathe deeply of their contents, trying to analyze each of the dozen herbs and spices I had painstakingly layered into a tender rich Rendang. An Australian diplomat who had lived in Asia for many years once walked into my home and immediately asked whether I had forgotten he was coming to dinner. Prior to his arrival, I had cleaned the kitchen thoroughly and sprayed it with air freshener to extinguish the curry smells and he assumed there was nothing cooking! I never did that again. Today I bask in the aromas of my food and its glorious flavors, and my kitchen remains a proud outpost of my native land.

This book was born from a discovery that Asian flavors and aromas are simple to recreate in your kitchen. Follow my Amah's rule "If it doesn't smell good, it will not taste good!" Just go ahead and have fun with these aromas.

'Asian herbs brazenly provoke the taste buds— speaking to you in louder terms than the thymes and the bergamot of the west ...'

Cooking with
aromatic asian herbs

If your childhood memories are stirred by the gentle aromas of parsley, sage, rosemary and thyme, as well as by a Simon and Garfunkel ballad, then you are clearly a child of the West. If, on the other hand, memories of your mother's kitchen are summoned by the citrusy perfume of kaffir lime, the freshness of Chinese celery, the peppery blast of basil, the comforting softness of coriander, and the pepper and lemony aromas of curry leaves and sweet lemongrass, then you are a child of the East. It is the variety of herbs, the leaves and flowers of plants, that separates the cuisines of Europe and Asia.

I think the place to understand the strident tones that tropical herbs create is in an Asian market. Everything is loud, colorful and "in your face" here. A gaggle of geese, ducks in cages, the flower lady advertising her wares in her loudest voice—hoping to drown out the hot tofu seller next door. Walk past the fish stall, and above the cacophony of market calls you will hear the screech of the auctioneer. Stand still and breathe deeply. There is nothing subtle about this at all. It is raw and vocal. So are the herbs—strong, pungent, perfumed, aromatic and unforgettable—there is nothing bashful about the herbs of the tropics. You are reminded of countless curry meals in the roadside stalls of Thailand and the fried *kway teow* hawkers cooking their noodles with abandon in the night markets of Malaysia. Bunches of herbs are plucked hastily and thrown into a *mee krob* salad, or into a biting-red chili crab dish.

The Asian cook blends many ingredients together to make a dish. Imagine the cook as a builder starting from the foundation and working upwards, with garlic and hot oil forming the base of the structure. From there, as each ingredient is browned and releases its fragrance, other contrasting ingredients such as onion or chili are added. And so different aromatic layers and enticing flavors are added—one on top of the other—to provide an extraordinary blend.

In the West, flowers are cut for decoration and their perfumes waft through the house. In the East, flowers are more likely than not cut for the kitchen, and their fragrance is distilled and decanted into foods and dining rooms. It is true that in the West one might find candied violets by a grandmother's bedside, or peppery-tasting nasturtium leaves in the salads of Vogue readers—but the former is rarely seen these days and the latter is subject to the whims of fashion. In Asia, banana blossoms and ginger flowers release their floral grassy or cinnamon-like gingery scents, always distinctive, into fish sambals and krabu herbal salads on a daily basis. These dishes are as commonplace and as widely prepared as a Western Caesar Salad, a Salad Nicoise or a Lebanese Tabouli.

A wise cook once told me that the main difference between spices and herbs is that you go out to buy spices whereas you grow herbs in your garden. In other words, herbs are more accessible and freshly available if you grow them in a pot or devote a tiny garden bed to your most commonly used varieties. I believe the most beautiful herb in the world is the statuesque "Jerry Hall" of herbs—the ginger flower, locally known as *bunga kantan*. It grows tall and straight, blossoming out and facing toward the sun, then curving inward again, like hands cupped in prayer. The aroma is unbelievably subtle—containing the perfume of ginger and roses, slightly peppery, with a touch of cinnamon, jasmine and sweet chilies. The ginger flower has a stunning cherry-colored heart that slowly lightens into pink, fading into warm creamy-yellow petals.

A shrimp sambal or a salad cooked with chopped ginger flower makes all these wonderful aromas come alive at once in the mixture. I have witnessed an amazing Balinese salad called *babi guling*—roast suckling pig with many herbs and vegetables including chopped ginger flower. The ginger flower perfume was so infused into the dish that diners couldn't resist bending forward to inhale the wondrous scents as the dish was served. Now wouldn't you think a ginger flower is something worth exploring?

Lemongrass grows in a prolific clump like tall grass. The root clump divides into many individual stalks and each one produces a fat, juicy, lemony, fragrant bulb that can be harvested and used to perfume your curries, or ground into aromatic sambals, drinks and teas. Vietnamese mint grows like the Triffids spreading their minty, peppery roots into any available space! You will find that most herbs can grow in a semi-tropical or Mediterranean climate, and when disturbed by the wind, gives you that wonderful aroma evocative of the Tropics, that is certainly worth cultivating if you can.

Fresh herbs, especially the trusty lemongrass and ginger, are unbelievable in their aroma, intensity and staying power. Even after being cooked, a sauce or sambal made with fresh herbs can always be picked out and a trained palate can always distinguish between the crunch of lemongrass or the bite of curry leaf or even the sweet, suffering touch of pepper-like Vietnamese mint.

Although I may wax lyrical about fresh herbs, I realize that in many communities, and even in the large cities, they may not be available, especially in winter. So feel free to use dried herbs if you must, making sure you check the use-by date. It's better to use a dried herb than no herb at all. Enjoy an herbal experience whenever you can and enjoy their perfumes in your food and in your life!

Asian basils ~

On my first trip to Thailand many years ago, I attended a class with Charlie Amatyakul, the chef at the Oriental Hotel Cooking School. Charlie's set-up was ideal—small groups of students, an extensive working space and exclusive attendees. While I wondered what I would be doing, in came the ingredients in large bowls and we started touching, feeling, smelling and sorting them. Soon the whole classroom turned into an aromatic atrium filled with the fragrances of aniseed, mint, citrus and rose. It was a shock to the system although I had used most of these herbs in my cooking before. But never in such profusion or variety. Basil was the first herb I picked up and held to my nose with my eyes closed. The scent of the leaves was comforting, sharp and almost healing—I had never taken notice of such a strong aroma from this herb. I looked

Thai Basil

Holy Basil

again; this was what Charlie called Thai basil: red veins giving way to dark purple florets and firm green leaves. This was the beginning of my own love affair with Thai basil, the herb that is used whenever Thai food is cooked. The bite of the leaf produces a surprising flavor and aroma at the back of the throat; pleasant and memorable.

A bunch of fresh dark green basil sprigs held in your hands and pressed to your nostrils to release the peppery aniseed aroma is about as close as you can get to the aroma of hospitality. It is one of the oldest herbs in cultivation, used by many of the world's cooks both in Europe and Asia. There are many different basils used in different regions of the world. The European basil is slightly different, with hairier stems and droopy leaves.

Asian basils come in three different varieties. The most common of the three has an intense aroma and is generally known as Thai basil (*horapa* in Thai; *daun kemangi* in Malaysia and Indonesia). Lemon-scented basil (*manglak* in Thai) is usually cooked rather than eaten raw. Holy basil or *kaprow* in Thai has a strong, sharp aroma and is used only in a few dishes. It is so called because the Hindus consider it sacred. A basil plant brought to a new home brings blessings, said a Croatian friend of mine when she walked into my new house—a good indication that traditions of herbs in food are found both in the East and West dating back to ancient times.

Purchasing: Look for brightly-colored, fresh basil with leaves that stand firm, without any hint of wilting. If you press a leaf between your fingers, this should release a strong aroma.
Culinary uses: Used in stir-fries, in salads with each leaf picked and tossed together with other ingredients, or as a garnish for steamed fish. A **Basil Pesto** is easy to prepare: process 1 cup (40 g) of chopped fresh basil, $1/2$ cup (125 ml) of olive oil, 2–3 cloves of garlic and 2 green finger-length chili peppers (deseeded) with 6 macadamia nuts in a food processor until smooth, then season with salt and pepper to taste. This Pesto may be used as a stir-fry starter with garlic and ginger, or added to a curry paste for an extra "bite," or served as a dip with cheese and yogurt.

Preparation: Wash and dry the leaves well. Tender leaves can be used but separate the leaves from the harder stems.
Storing: Wrap the leaves (still on the stems) in paper towels and refrigerate in a covered container or sealed plastic bag for 2–3 days. If the stems droop, refresh them in ice cold water for a couple of hours before using.
Substitutes: European basil is a good substitute though it may not have as much bite and aroma as the Asian basil. And you may have to use more than the required amount or grind it for more aroma and flavor.

Banana leaves, flowers and stems ～

Every part of the banana plant can be used: the leaves, flower, fruit and stems. The banana leaf—dark green and about 3 feet (1 meter) long—grows like a long and wide palm leaf and is commonly used to cover or wrap foods in Asia. It has a light grassy and wax-like aroma that transfers to any food cooked in it and is used as the natural "aluminum foil" of the East. In Asian homes, banana leaf is a sensual steaming wrapper for rice, fish or meat smeared with some lemongrass, garlic and other herbs. The steaming cooks the food and imparts the subtle perfume of the light, grassy leaf which adds an unmatched aroma.

A common dish of rice cooked with coconut milk and garnished with curried shrimp, then folded and steamed in a banana leaf has an unmistakable perfume that is irresistible to the diner. The many aromas of this dish, called *nasi lemak*, coalesce to form an unforgettable moment of sensory indulgence. By contrast, the unopened male flower of the banana plant is a popular vegetable throughout tropical Asia, like a fragrant cabbage. It can be found in specialty stores outside Asia, particularly those stocking Vietnamese and Thai ingredients.

Purchasing: Both banana leaves and flowers are obtainable from Asian markets. Look for the leaves wrapped in large bundles. They are usually sold by weight, with the thick center ribs removed and the leaf portions folded. The flowers should be fresh and firm, without any wilting.

Culinary uses: Because of their natural wax content, banana leaves make ideal wrappers for food and are even used to provide a wax coating on irons, to make ironing easier! They are also used as decorations for the table and as plates. In Indian vegetarian homes and restaurants, banana leaves are the preferred service platters because no meat has previously touched them. According to Indian etiquette, the rib edge should be placed at the head of the table setting, away from the diner. After eating, the leaf is folded away to indicate that you have finished eating. If you fold it the other way it means you want a second helping. Cooked banana flowers are often made into salads in Southeast Asia. Blanched fine shreds can be added to dressings and soups, or simmered in seasoned coconut milk.

Preparation: Remove and discard the thick central rib of the banana leaf and use only the flat leafy part. Before using it to wrap food, blanch the leaf in a basin of boiling water for a few seconds or heat it directly over a flame to make it pliable for easy folding. A toothpick or skewer threaded through the end is often the only thing needed to hold wrapped parcels together. To prepare the banana flower, pull off the outer petals and the long, narrow yellow blossoms until the pinkish white inner heart is revealed. Then use the heart as instructed in the recipes.

Storing: The leaves and flower will keep in a loosely packed plastic bag in the refrigerator for up to 1 week.

Substitutes: Bamboo shoots or cabbage can be used in place of banana flower for a crunchy texture. A good substitute for wrapping purposes is lotus leaf or aluminum foil.

Coriander leaves ~ cilantro

The coriander leaf, almost mandatory in Asian cooking, has the most complex of herb flavors: it is spicy, citrusy with hints of lime, and almost pungent and curry-like, all at the same time. Fresh coriander leaves are invigorating—warm and minty in flavor and perfume—although the roots are peppery and bitter.

Someone not familiar with the aroma of coriander leaf may find it overpowering. When I was a child, we used it copiously in our home, but I would shy away from the aroma. The warm and minty herb reminded me of the stinkbug, and as I later found out, the name "coriandrum" indeed means stinkbugs, which perhaps explains the aversion I had to the herb!

It is a popular herb used in all types of Asian dishes, from soups to salads. It's a useful herb to have in the garden and is readily available in both Eastern and Western markets since the Thai, Vietnamese, Chinese, Indian and Mexican cuisines all use it copiously. All parts of the coriander plant are used. The leaves are used as a garnish or in curries, the seeds are used in curry pastes in Creole and Mexican cooking, and the pungent roots are mainly ground into Thai curries. This was the original heat enhancer for "spicy" foods along with ginger and pepper before chili peppers came to Asia.

To sniff deeply of a coriander plant is a refreshing experience as the aromas of pepper and lime combine with the lingering aroma of aniseed. I have noticed that a simple steak cooked with a bit of garlic and onion is transformed into something special when a few coriander leaves are thrown into the pan just before the meat is done. The same goes for chicken dishes. There is a lightness in coriander leaves that lifts the meat. Yet when it is used with seafood, a different kind of aroma is produced, raising an awareness of lemon this time. Perhaps this happens unconsciously, as we often think of mixing lime and lemon with seafood. However when I add coriander stems, leaves and ground roots to a green shrimp curry, the final result always astonishes my guests.

Purchasing: Always buy the whole plants with roots attached, as they keep better that way. The leaves should be fresh and bright, not droopy, and the stems should be firm.

Culinary uses: Fresh leaves are often chopped and added to salads and fillings in Asia cuisines, or ground and added to spice pastes in Thailand, Laos and Cambodia. They are also commonly used as an edible garnish in soups and noodle dishes. To use the leaves, do not chop them unless you want the flavors to diffuse with the cooking. They are best added just before the end of the cooking as the leaves are the most pungent and flavorsome then. Try not to use the stems. When stems are ground into a curry, especially green curry, David Thompson refers to the result as "muddy." The Thais use the roots in their curries because of its pungent peppery flavor.

A simple recipe for **Coriander Leaf Pesto:** Process 2 cups (80 g) chopped coriander leaves, 1–2 deseeded green Asian finger-length chili peppers and 1 cup (100 g) grated coconut to a smooth paste in a food processor, then season with the juice of 1 lime and add sugar and salt to taste. Use it as you would a regular pesto, or turn it into a sauce for steamed or baked fish by adding some coconut milk to it.

Preparation: Wash and dry the leaves well, then use them either whole, chopped or ground, as instructed in the recipes.

Storing: Wrap the plants loosely in paper towels and store in the vegetable compartment of the refrigerator. Store any left-over leaves or roots in the freezer in foil. To refresh a droopy plant, soak it in ice water before using. In a mild Mediterranean climate, it is possible to grow this herb in pots which can be picked fresh for your enjoyment as needed.

Substitutes: Dried coriander leaves do not have the wonderful flavor and aroma of fresh ones, although they can be used.

Curry leaves ~

A relative of the orange blossom, these leaves have a distinctive lemon-pepper fragrance with tinges of lime and ginger that may contribute to the impression that it is "curry-like." It is today associated with South Indian and Southeast Asian curries, especially in combination with coriander, cumin, fennel, ginger and chili peppers.

The curry leaf plant grows only to the height of a small bush in equatorial Malaya, but can grow much taller in more temperate regions. I remember being quite confused as a child when I read about explorers traveling through the forests of north India. Their elephants reached up to chew on some aromatic branches which filled the forest with the perfume of curry, lime and pepper. It was difficult to imagine this as our curry leaf plant at home in tropical Malaysia barely reached 2 feet (60 cm)! It was only when I grew a curry leaf plant in my backyard in Sydney that I realized the plant positively thrives in temperate climates, perfuming the surrounding area with its seductive aroma.

There are different ways to use the curry leaves to vary their aroma and flavor. Dried curry leaves have very little flavor compared to fresh leaves, and should only be used when fresh leaves are unavailable. Reconstitute the dried leaves by soaking them in warm water, then add them to curries, omelets and salads. Another way to heighten the flavor is through the Indian trick of heating some oil and frying the curry leaves very quickly so they crisp and infuse the oil with flavor. When they are shallow-fried with onions and added to omelets and other dishes, they release a different flavor, which is just as effective, yet lighter in aroma.

Purchasing: Fresh almond-shaped leaves are generally sold on the stem, and are sometimes picked and packed in plastic bags. Look for green and firm, fresh-looking leaves.
Culinary uses: Curry leaves may be chopped or ground into a simple pesto (page 30) and are used in many traditional Southeast Asian and Indian dishes. To enhance the flavor of curry leaves, cover them with 2 teaspoons of oil and microwave or fry for 2 minutes until crisp. These crispy-fried leaves are ideal as a garnish for curries, salads and Indian dal recipes.

Preparation: Wash and dry the sprigs, then pull the leaves off the stems before using.
Storing: Wrap in several layers of damp paper towels and refrigerate in a covered container for up to 2 weeks. Freeze in the same way as coriander leaves.
Substitutes: Dried curry leaves, though not as fragrant, can be used, or substitute fresh coriander leaves instead.

Garlic chives ~

Also known as Chinese or Asian chives, this vegetable is indigenous to Siberia, Mongolia and northern China. As its name implies, garlic chives have a strong garlicky aroma and flavor. Regular garlic chives resemble coarse, flat blades of dark green grass. An exception to this is flowering chives, which have an unopened flower or bud at the tip of their long, slender stalks.

Sliced garlic chives, with a hint of garlic and grassy flavors with a peppery edge, are the perfect addition to any noodle dish. For an awesome aromatic hit, uncover noodles which have "sweated" in a wok full of garlic chives, and you will be struck by a wave of grassy garlic and crisp-frying onion aromas.

My favorites are the dark-green, flat-stemmed garlic chives, which are quite unlike the tiny, round-stemmed chives common in Western cooking. Their garlicky aroma, the main ingredient in the Malaysian *char kway teow* noodle dish and Chili Crabs, makes this an invaluable herb in my vegetable garden. Light green garlic chives are cultivated by covering the plant with black plastic bags to prevent the sunlight from reaching them. This reduces the chlorophyll in the plant and produces a lighter color, but does not affect the flavor.

Garlic chives can be domestically cultivated in large pots if you find yourself as addicted to the herb as I do. The chives may be used instead of green onions in any dish. I use them finely chopped in omelets instead of fried garlic and onion. Garlic chives also form the aromatic basis for many Chinese dim sums such as pork dumplings, which are commonly found in *yum cha* trolleys, and in the chive pancakes cooked in northern China.

Purchasing: Garlic chives are normally sold in bunches. Look for bright green ones. They should be firm and dry, with crisp lower ends that snap if bent. Avoid any that have rotted and become "slimy."

Culinary uses: Garlic chives are used mainly in Chinese and Korean cooking. They have a strong flavor when raw but become more delicate after cooking. The pale, golden type called yellow chives, are prized for their delicate flavor. They are often added to soups, noodles and stir-fries, or minced and added to dumpling fillings. Flower chives are stir-fried and used as a garnish because of their decorative appearance.

Preparation: Take the whole bunch apart and look at each stem. Discard any stems that are brown or wilted. Rinse well and drain. Trim the hard bottom portions of the stems and use the rest as instructed in the recipes.

Storing: Store garlic chives in the refrigerator for 1–2 days, wrapped in paper towels or sealed in plastic bags or in airtight containers to prevent their strong garlic aroma from impregnating other foods.

Substitutes: Green onions or Western chives can be substituted for garlic chives but they will not give the same distinctive garlicky aroma and flavor.

Ginger flower ~ *bunga kantan*

This edible flower bud is an amazingly perfumed herb—statuesque, beautifully colored and well-proportioned, with exquisite aromas of floral ginger and lemony rose and a musk-and-strawberry sweetness. With its startling pink, red-edged leaves reaching up to a sharp point with yellow flame-like streaks, it is not only one of the most attractive of Asian herbs but the most aromatic as well, with a perfume that remains even when it is chopped into salads or ground into a curry paste.

The ginger flower has a stem as thick as a man's thumb with leaves pointing to the sky like a pair of folded, praying hands. And the aroma? Think of ginger ale, lemony rosewater from the sharbat drinks of Persia, and a whiff of jasmine as you breathe in deeper. This spectacular flower is very uncommon in countries outside the tropics, although it has been growing sucessfully in sub-tropical Darwin and Queensland (Australia) for several years. It flowers along with the other gingers used in Queensland for desserts and pickling, although this particular ginger is not used in Western food. The Thais, Malaysians and Laotians use it quite a lot—ground up into curries and chopped up in salads—where the aroma is unmistakable in its fresh form. It seems almost a desecration to chop up something so beautiful, if the ginger flower arrives fully-formed in the kitchen, although by the time they have arrived at the markets of Asia, you will find some of the petals marked, damaged and blackened through rough handling. Sometimes soaking them in a solution of sugar water helps restore the shape and the quality of the flower. However, for eating, it does not matter if the flower reaches you slighty damaged, as it is either going to be chopped up or processed.

The torch ginger plant is one of the many varieties of ginger flowering plants. It produces the pink flower in the midst of long, thin sheaths. The entire plant can grow up to 16 feet (5 meters) in height, so expect to find large ginger flowers up to about 8–12 in (20–30 cm) long and 3 in (8 cm) thick. You may find smaller ginger flowers in the market, but treat them all in the same way. Scratch the surface of the flower and sniff it—if you get a strong, perfumed gingery aroma, you are on the right track.

Purchasing: Look for this flower in Asian markets. I was surprised to find it in that Ali Baba's cave of shopping, the Ka De Wa in Berlin, sitting alongside fresh lemongrass stems, galangal roots and a durian, of all things. Choose fresh-looking buds without too much wilting or browning at the edges.
Culinary uses: This flower is an essential ingredient for many Malaysian and Nonya salads, curries, *rojak* and *laksa*, and also for the Thai *nam prik* mixture (a spicy dip) and many Vietnamese dishes. It is best to add chopped ginger flower at the end of cooking, so its flavor and aroma are retained.

Preparation: Wash the buds and in between each of the stems that make up the central core, then halve and slice each bud finely, discarding the stems.
Storing: The ginger flower has a shelf life of about a week. Wrap it in several layers of paper towels and store in the vegetable compartment of the refrigerator. You can freeze the flower, but bring it to room temperature naturally, not in a microwave. However, freezing destroys some of the flavor and aroma.
Substitutes: A mixture of lemongrass and young ginger slices.

Kaffir lime and lime leaves ∽

Words of wisdom from Amah (nanny) hinged around the fact that the sweetest and tastiest things in life are always thorny. And we learned that lesson early in our lives with the thorny durians—the thorniest fruits invariably produced the sweetest flesh. It was therefore easy to infer that the thorniest kaffir lime leaves were the most flavorful. My kaffir lime tree has survived three transplants and is still producing the glossiest and most perfect hourglass-shaped leaves with as many thorns as leaves.

Kaffir lime leaves are prized for their distinctive incense-like aroma and sharp citrus oils. When the leaves are pressed together between the fingers, sweetish lower notes of orange and clove underpin the immediate top notes of citrus and lime, giving way to a wonderful blend of aromas that translate into flavors when they are used as garnishes and in curries. They can also be crushed or ground to release the oils for use in sambals and sauces, especially Thai green curries and Malaysian laksas, adding top notes to the coriander and pepper garnishes used.

Kaffir lime leaves are versatile in their uses, adapting to Western as well as Eastern recipes. You can use them as fine garnishes in seafood salads and pastas; their strong citrus flavor will give a perfect balance in any recipe where lemon or lime are required.

Purchasing: Kaffir lime leaves are easily spotted for their distinct female hourglass figure. Look for plastic packets of fresh, green and glossy kaffir lime leaves in Asian stores. Don't buy them on the stems as you will be paying for extra weight. Although dried or frozen leaves as well as essence and powder are available, try to use fresh leaves for their superior aroma and flavor.

Culinary uses: Kaffir limes are small limes with a very rough and intensely fragrant skin, but virtually no juice. The rind or skin is often grated and added to dishes as a seasoning. The fragrant leaves are added whole to soups and curries, or finely shredded and added to salads or deep-fried fish cakes, giving a wonderfully tangy taste to these dishes.

Preparation: When cutting fine strips as a garnish, first remove and discard the central veins of the leaves. Roll several of them into a tight cylinder and slice them very thinly using a very sharp knife. These fine strips are attractive when used as a garnish on salads, seafood dishes and even on lime ice cream or a **Lime and Mint Granita Sorbet** (page 77). I use kaffir lime shreds to garnish onion and garlic omelets and laksa. When flavoring curries, use whole leaves and add them during the last minute of cooking. Mincing or finely chopping the leaves may overpower the other delicate flavors in the dish.

Storing: Freeze fresh leaves in a plastic bag. Even though they will lose their dark-green color and turn a muddy brown when frozen, the flavors are retained and are just as effective for daily use. Kaffir lime tree can be potted successfully in both tropical and temperate climates, but grow better in the ground. The leaves may wilt or turn yellow and drop in winter, but they grow back green and glossy in spring.

Substitutes: Dried kaffir lime leaves are a poor substitute. Young lemon, lime or even grapefruit leaves may be used as a last resort.

COOKING WITH AROMATIC ASIAN HERBS

Lemongrass ⌁

Dig into a thick lemongrass stem and the sweet and effervescent aroma of citrus-lime obliterates everything else. It is a comforting and lingering perfume reminiscent of the kitchens and gardens of tropical Asia. Although it can be used in many combinations, care should be taken not to overpower this scent with too much shrimp paste or other invasive aromas.

The lemongrass I was familiar with at home was the one we grew in our backyard in Malaysia. As a child, I helped to prepare the pastes used to make curries, long before I set off for school. A favorite chore of mine was to cut one or two plump stalks from the clump, remove the outer skins and then grind them in a mortar. The strong scent of this herb would fill my nostrils and cover my hands, leaving the citrusy oils on my palms for the rest of the day. What a wonderful difference from the sharp aromas of garlic and ginger that I normally had to work with! I often wore the perfumes from my garden to school. Lemongrass was naturally my favorite scent.

When I moved to Australia, my mother couldn't bring in fresh lemongrass. She used to brine the stalks and bring them in as salted pickles so that we could make curry pastes from these brined herbs. This was never satisfactory but we managed as best we could. Imagine my delight and surprise when I whiffed the delicious citrusy scent of lemongrass as I walked past the school ground—one of my Vietnamese students in Canley Vale was savoring a bowl of noodles with the aroma of fresh lemongrass. It used to surprise me when I found out that people in Perth drank lemongrass tea.

Lemongrass has been in Asia for centuries, growing wild on the fringes of the tropical forests. Locals must have discovered their scented lemon aroma, perhaps by brushing against the leaves of the main clump that would have grown like tropical elephant grass. Today, this citrus-scented, lemony herb is used all over the world wherever Thai and other Southeast Asian foods are cooked.

The fragrant grass grows in clumps to a height of 20 in (50 cm). The lemony aroma comes from the tightly-packed, creamy-colored lower part of the stem and up to 4 in (10 cm) of the stalk; these have the most flavor and aroma. Lemongrass should be used when fresh and juicy; once the stems dry out they lose their aroma and flavor and appear woody. The thinner top leaves may be used for tea or for a soup stock (as I found out a long time ago). If lemongrass is your favorite herb, you can grow it in pots and use it throughout the year.

Purchasing: Choose firm stems that end in fat bulbs with no signs of wilting.

Culinary uses: Lemongrass is ground with garlic, galangal, onion and chili pepper into a paste used to make curries and soups. Its distinctive aroma is best complemented with the use of coconut milk. Very finely-sliced lemongrass is often used raw in salads and bruised lengths of the stem are also added to some soups and curries for flavoring. The entire stem, trimmed to a point, can also be used as an aromatic skewer for grilling meats and seafood. In Thai, Cambodian and Laotian temples, lemongrass tea has been served for years as a calmative. Dried lemongrass stems are also used in cupboards and meat safes as an insect repellent. Replace after two months.

Preparation: Use only the inner part of the thick bulb of the stem (the bottom one-third of the stem). Peel off and discard the tough outer leaves to get to the portion, then bruise, slice, chop or grind as directed in the recipe.

Storing: Stand the stems in a glass with their ends in water and keep in a warm place, or wrap stalks of them in paper towels and refrigerate. Lemongrass keeps for 2 weeks in this manner. Do not freeze them.

Substitutes: Sliced lime leaves or sliced lime or lemon rind can be substituted.

Mint ⁓

A breath freshener and a touch of spring—all in a mint leaf. As one of the most favored herbs—I have found mint invaluable when cooking Indian food—it is not only used in pharmaceutical products such as toothpaste and mouth-fresheners, lotions and bath soaps, but has even invaded the massage tables of spas. It is impossible to imagine that mint has taken on such importance from being a humble aromatic herb that grows wild near taps and garden hoses. Unchecked mint plants can become invasive in temperate gardens. For a long time, mint has always been a very useful and prized herb in Asia, used not only in cooking but also as an insect repellent and potpourri in the cupboards of Nonyas (Straits Chinese) in Malacca.

There are many varieties of mint; peppermint and spearmint are the most common. Peppermint has a strong, true mint flavor and is used mainly in pharmaceuticals and candy. Asians prefer the type of mint which has dark-green, crinkly round leaves, sometimes called Moroccan mint. Asians also use spearmint—the Vietnamese add them to bowls of *pho* noodles while Thais use them for stuffing fish or cooking shrimp. In this book, spearmint is used in the recipe for Grilled Beef Parcels with Thai Herbs (page 34).

Purchasing: Look for fresh leaves on green stems, with strong aromas of mint.

Culinary uses: Mint often forms a part of Asian table salads and is used as a garnish for laksa and curries, especially those made with fish. It is also an ingredient in Vietnamese spring rolls. **Mint Pesto** (page 30) can be made with mint as the main ingredient instead of curry leaves. You may have to use a dash of lime juice to keep the refreshing flavors intact. Mint is also a well-known calmative and a cure for nausea. A little mint infused in hot water for 2 minutes is an ideal drink to have when you're stressed.

Preparation: Pull the leaves from the stems just before using and always garnish with whole leaves unless otherwise stated in the recipe.

Storing: Mint leaves keep well when left on the stem. Wrap the mint leaves in paper towels enclosed in a plastic bag and refrigerate as you would other herbs.

Substitute: Use 1 tablespoon dried mint leaves in place of $^1/_4$ cup (10 g) fresh leaves.

Pandanus leaves ~ *daun pandan*

Pandanus leaves, described as the "vanilla of the East," have been used for generations because their subtle grassy fragrance combine with the freshness of mint and rich coconut. Though a member of the pandanus palm family, this plant is a far cry from the stiff and thorny cactus-like spikes of the pandanus. The glossy green domestic pandanus leaves are narrow, spear-like and pliant, with a firm central vein. Their distinctive and subtle grassy aroma is only released when the leaves are bruised, twisted or ground into a paste.

Pandanus leaves grow in small clumps in domestic gardens in Southeast Asia, where they are used in a variety of dishes—from drinks, jellies, meat and fish dishes to rice dishes and desserts—and also in many domestic applications. Asians are fond of green colored foods and drinks dyed with pandanus juice pressed from the ground pandanus leaves. As a child, I used to be intrigued by my mother's Nonya friends and their pandanus-perfumed face powder. The powder was made from rice flour ground in an intricate process until it was so fine it could pass through the finest muslin. The pandanus juice was then added and the strained drops piped onto sheets of greaseproof paper where they would be dried in the sun. To use it, they mixed a little bit of water with a drop of the rice powder and spread it on the face. You could always tell a true Nonya lady from the subtle perfume of the pandanus rice powder that she wore. In my memory, this is the aroma of hospitality, of New Year cakes and good cooking.

The Fragrant Pandanus Coconut Rice (*nasi lemak*—see page 103) served with various sambals in Malaysia, Indonesia and the rest of Southeast Asia is often perfumed with the addition of pandanus leaf, which is added to the rice as it cooks.

Purchasing: Pandanus leaves are usually sold in a bundle in Asian markets. But they are either sold frozen or in powdered form in other parts of the world. When buying, always look for firm glossy-green, juicy leaves.

Culinary uses: In Southeast Asia, pandanus leaves are mainly used for their fragrance in desserts and meat and rice dishes, while the green juice is also used to provide a bright green color to foods. Whole pandanus leaves are also used as wrappers or containers for food. They are folded into elaborate origami-like containers to hold coconut custard cakes which are steamed to create a delightful perfumed dessert. In many exotic street markets, it is possible to find streets stalls which offer grilled seafood snacks wrapped in pandanus leaves. You don't have to look for these snacks, the aromas will lead you to them!

Preparation: For maximum effect, always rake the leaves by holding them flat on a work surface and running a fork down their length so the juice is released, then tie each leaf into a knot before adding it to a dish. To prepare pandanus juice, slice several leaves and grind them in a mortar or food processor until fine, then strain, squeezing out the juice.

Storing: The leaves keep for a week in the refrigerator, wrapped in paper towels and sealed in a plastic bag. You may freeze them to keep for a longer period.

Substitutes: Use fresh pandanus leaves whenever possible; commercial pandanus essence does not give a true pandanus aroma or flavor. If they are unavailable, the closest substitute would be lemongrass.

Perilla or shiso leaves ~

My first encounter with perilla or *shiso* was on a visit to Japan where I studied the art of sashimi cutting. I watched a sushi master chef nonchalantly wrap a piece of tuna with an almost perfectly heart-shaped green leaf and place it on a wooden tray. I was curious what the leaf was, so I asked for one and tentatively bit in. Wow! The flavor was a mixture of mint with beefy aniseed aromas. The combination with the piece of tuna and a lashing of wasabi lit up my palate and the aroma sent up from my mouth to my nose was unmatched. Later I found out that the leaf is called the "beefsteak" herb in Japanese. As I could not bring the seeds home, I continued to look for this plant in Japanese restaurants. I finally found it in Cabramatta, where red perilla is used as a garnish for Vietnamese *pho* soups.

Perilla is native to China and Burma. There are two varieties, red and green, and both are heart-shaped with serrated edges. They have a refreshing minty and slightly beefy and aniseed-like aroma—one of the reasons why the name "beefsteak" herb has often been used. Red perilla is doubled colored, with dark green on one side and reddish-purple on the other, and the green is bright and flat. This variety of perilla is used in Japan for making *ume boshi*, a kind of pickled plum paste. The green variety is used in soups. The Japanese use these leaves extensively in cooking. The leaves, the small stems of the flowering seed pods (*hana hojiso*), and the sprouts of the plant (*mejiso*) are all used as an edible garnishes for sushi and sashimi—the leaves are used as sushi wraps and sometimes deep-fried as tempura. The Vietnamese and Japanese also value this plant for its antibiotic properties. Perilla has been used by Asian herbalists to relieve the effects of fish poisoning and to treat influenza and coughs.

Purchasing: Look for packets of perilla leaves in Japanese stores. Soft, floppy leaves can easily be refreshed by soaking their stems in water.

Culinary uses: Perilla leaves are an integral part of Japanese and Vietnamese cuisine. The larger leaves are finely sliced and used in salads or as a wrapper for barbecued meats. I have used red perilla for cooking beef stir-fries with great success. Chopped red perilla should be added just before the cooking ends.

Preparation: Wash, dry and use the leaves as instructed.

Storing: Wrap in damp paper towels and keep in the refrigerator for 2–3 days. Perilla should not be kept for too long or the aromas will be lost.

Substitutes: Vietnamese mint or basil.

COOKING WITH AROMATIC ASIAN HERBS

Vietnamese mint ~ laksa leaf or polygonum

Accidentally trample on a bed of Vietnamese mint and you will receive a burst of herbaceous aromas: minty, peppery, lemony and aniseed with a hint of bitter basil in the back notes. Crunch a leaf and you will get the tart, sharp-tasting bitterness that lends a distinctive quality to this versatile herb, which is not only used in Vietnam but in the rest of Asia in countless ways. This leaf is not really a mint but a closer relative to basil than to coriander or mint. The dark-green, almond-shaped leaves are long and tapering with a bright green color and a distinctive dark red or green "arrow" shape in the center.

As a child, I always had a bush of Vietnamese mint or *daun kesom* in my backyard, growing among the pandanus and lemongrass beds. The chickens scratched among these herb beds and they were often trampled upon when we looked for wayward shuttlecocks from the badminton court near-by, but the mint plant never died. This was the mint we used for a special sour tamarind-broth laksa that came from the north of Malaya, which bore a striking similarity to the hot and sour *tom yum* soup from across the border in Thailand.

Whenever we used this mint in any of our laksas or a soup dish from Indonesia called *soto*, the kitchen was filled with aromas that gave everyone an appetite in eager anticipation of dinner. This is a mint that I choose when I want to impress my guests in a salad or spring roll. It is an unusual little herb that can go undetected until it is crushed and scattered over a salad or soup, when it can light up the palate and create wonderful combinations of aromas and tastes.

Fish for instance, when cooked with Vietnamese mint, can suddenly taste minty or peppery. Squid stuffed with Vietnamese mint and a very finely ground pork mixture changes the flavor of the squid. My laksa sauces are renowned for their flavor, and I believe the secret lies in their combination of onion, garlic and a bit of lemongrass with this quiet little herb. It is a plant that grows easily so anyone can have fresh Vietnamese mint on hand and it could be used in any culinary situation where mint is called for.

Purchasing: Look for dark green leaves in firm bunches with a fresh aroma. They should look plump and fresh, without any signs of bruising.
Culinary uses: Vietnamese mint is used in Vietnamese and Laotian table salads and in laksas, especially Penang Laksa. You should try some leaves in a ham or chicken sandwich or with boiled eggs mashed with a dash of home-made mayonnaise.
Preparation: Strip the leaves and tender stalks from the central stem before using.
Storing: Wrap in a damp paper towel and keep refrigerated in a plastic container. Place the stems in a glass of water and they will root easily, after which they can be planted in pots. A wilted bunch may be revived by soaking them in iced water.
Substitutes: Equal parts of mint and coriander leaves or Asian pennywort.

8 oz (250 g) fresh tuna or salmon fillets,
   poached and flaked with a fork
2 medium potatoes (8 oz/250 g), peeled,
   boiled and mashed
1 onion, finely diced
1 green onion, chopped
2 tablespoons minced curry leaves
1 teaspoon amchoor mango powder
1 teaspoon bottled sweet chili sauce
$\frac{1}{2}$ teaspoon ground turmeric
1 teaspoon ground cumin
1 teaspoon salt
$\frac{1}{2}$ teaspoon ground white pepper

3 eggs, lightly beaten
$\frac{1}{2}$ cup (125 ml) oil, for frying
1 egg white, beaten
$\frac{1}{2}$ cup (30 g) breadcrumbs

CURRY LEAF PESTO
1 cup (40 g) curry leaves
2 Asian shallots
2 cloves garlic
3 tablespoons dried unsweetened grated
   (desiccated) coconut
1 green finger-length chili, deseeded
Salt, to taste
$\frac{1}{4}$ cup (60 ml) fresh lime juice, mixed with
   $\frac{1}{4}$ cup (60 ml) water
$\frac{1}{4}$ cup (60 ml) oil

Salmon fish cakes with curry leaf pesto

The delicate flavor of salmon added to the tantalizing and assertive fragrance of cumin and *amchoor* green mango powder provide a rich and sensuous aroma. This is a refreshing new take on the ubiquitous crab cakes served around the world today. Serve them as an appetizer, a party food or as part of a meal. If you cannot get curry leaves for the Pesto, use coriander leaves or mint leaves instead—both are equally wonderful!

Prepare the Curry Leaf Pesto by processing all the ingredients to a smooth paste in a blender, adding the lime juice a little at a time, and adjusting the seasonings to your taste. Transfer to a serving bowl and set aside.

Combine the flaked fish and mashed potato in a mixing bowl. Add all the other ingredients except the eggs, oil and breadcrumbs, and mix well. Add the lightly-beaten eggs and mix until well blended.

To make the fish cakes, grease your hands with a little oil. Scoop 2 heaping tablespoons of the fish mixture and roll it into a ball, then flatten it slightly into a patty. Continue to make the fish cakes in the same manner until all the remaining fish mixture is used up.

Heat the oil in a wok over medium heat. Working in batches, dip the patties in the egg white then roll them in the breadcrumbs until well coated. When the oil is hot enough, fry the coated patties in the hot oil for 3–4 minutes, turning from time to time, until golden and crispy on both sides. Remove from the heat and drain on paper towels.

Arrange the fish cakes on a serving platter and serve hot with the Curry Leaf Pesto on the side.

MAKES: *20 cakes*   **PREPARATION TIME:** *30 mins*   **COOKING TIME:** *15 mins*

8 fresh medium shrimp (7 oz/200 g)
8 dried rice paper wrappers, each 10 in
  (25 cm) across
8 lettuce leaves
7 oz (200 g) cooked roast beef, pork or
  chicken, thinly sliced
2 handfuls (4 oz/100 g) dried rice
  vermicelli, soaked in hot water until soft
8 (or more) garlic chives

CHILI LIME DIP
3 tablespoons hoisin sauce
1 tablespoon bottled sweet chili sauce
2 teaspoons fish sauce or soy sauce
3 tablespoons fresh lime juice
1 teaspoon chopped red finger-length chili
  pepper (optional)

Vietnamese rice paper rolls with chili lime dip

There are many versions of this popular Vietnamese dish. The simple rolls with lettuce leaf, roasted meat and shrimp inside is best made and served as soon as they are prepared. Use the freshest fillings and the best dried rice paper wrappers that you can find—available in Asian food stores in plastic packets of 10 sheets. It is well worth the effort.

Half-fill a saucepan with water and bring to a boil, then poach the shrimp for 1–2 minutes until pink or just cooked. Remove from the heat and drain, then peel and halve each shrimp. Divide the rice vermicelli into 8 equal portions.

To make the Rice Paper Rolls, briefly dip a rice paper wrapper in a bowl of water until soft, then place it on a dry work surface, smoothing it with your fingers. Place a lettuce leaf on the bottom third of the wrapper, top with several slices of roast meat and a portion of the rice vermicelli. Fold the bottom end of the rice paper over the filling, then fold in the sides and roll up tightly halfway. Place 2 shrimp halves, end to end, in the fold and continue rolling up firmly. Before reaching the end, place a garlic chive (or more if preferred) along the fold with one end protruding and then continue rolling up until the edges seal. Make all the rolls in the same manner with the remaining ingredients.

Combine the Chili Lime Dip ingredients in a serving bowl and mix well, adjusting the seasonings as desired. Arrange the Rice Paper Rolls on a serving platter and serve with the dip on the side.

MAKES: *8 rolls*   **PREPARATION TIME:** *30 mins*   **COOKING TIME:** *5 mins*

3 sheets frozen puff pastry (9$^{1}/_{2}$ in/24 cm), thawed
1 egg, beaten

SWEET POTATO FILLING
1 tablespoon oil
2 cloves garlic, minced
$^{1}/_{2}$ tablespoon minced fresh ginger
1 small onion, minced
2 sweet potatoes (10 oz/300 g) peeled and diced to yield 2 cups, then blanched until soft
1 cup (100 g) finely sliced green beans or fresh or frozen green peas
1 tablespoon chopped Vietnamese mint
1$^{1}/_{2}$ tablespoons curry powder
1 cup (250 ml) water
$^{1}/_{2}$ teaspoon ground red pepper (optional)
1 teaspoon sugar
1$^{1}/_{2}$ teaspoons salt

Sweet potato curry puffs with vietnamese mint

A twist on the familiar vegetarian curry puffs, this great party dish is a pure vegetarian version with rich mint and onion aromas that are released with each bite into a savory parcel. Serve the puffs with Mint Pachidi Chutney (page 243) if you like.

Prepare the Sweet Potato Filling first by heating the oil in a wok and stir-frying the garlic and ginger over medium heat until fragrant, about 1 minute. Add the onion and stir-fry until transparent. Stir in the cooked sweet potato, green beans or peas, mint and curry powder, and add 1 cup (250 ml) of water. Cook the ingredients for about 2 minutes, season with the red pepper, sugar and salt. Remove from the heat and allow to cool.

Preheat the oven to 360°F (180°C). On the lightly floured work surface, cut each puff pastry sheet into 9 equal squares. To make the puffs, brush two opposite sides of a pastry square with the beaten egg. Place 1$^{1}/_{2}$ tablespoons of the Sweet Potato Filling in the center of the pastry square and fold the pastry diagonally over the filling, forming a triangle, and then crimp the edges to seal. Place the puff on a baking pan and brush the top with the beaten egg. Continue to make the puffs in the same manner with the remaining ingredients.

Bake the puffs for about 20 minutes until golden and serve immediately.

MAKES: *27 puffs* **PREPARATION TIME:** *20 mins* **COOKING TIME:** *40 mins*

8 fresh witlof or betel (*chaplu*) leaves, or any
other leafy lettuce leaves, rinsed and dried,
to wrap the parcels
1 small jicama or baby cucumber (about
8 oz/250 g), peeled and cut into
matchsticks about the length of the witlof
leaves
1 onion, sliced into rings
1 stalk lemongrass, thick part only, outer
layers discarded, inner part chopped
Sprigs of coriander leaves (cilantro)
Thinly-sliced red Asian chili peppers
(optional), to garnish

FILLING
8 oz (250 g) grilled beef sirloin (medium rare)
or chicken breast, sliced into long strips the
length of the witlof leaves
1 tablespoon sugar
2 tablespoons fresh lime juice
5 cloves garlic, minced
1 tablespoon fish sauce, or to taste
1 teaspoon freshly ground black pepper, or to
taste
$^1/_4$ cup (10 g) chopped fresh spearmint or
mint leaves

Grilled beef parcels with thai herbs

A David Thompson-inspired morsel, the slightly bitter witlof or betel leaf beautifully wrapped around tender beef strips impresses the palate, while the fresh lime and lemongrass aromas engage the senses. By contrast, the jicama provides a sweetness and crunch in this ideal party food. Grilled chicken breast works equally well, and any leafy lettuce leaves can be used to wrap the parcels.

Prepare the Beef Filling first by combining the beef strips, sugar and lemon juice in a bowl and mix until the sugar is dissolved. Add all the other ingredients except the mint leaves and mix until well blended, adjusting the taste. Set aside for 10 minutes to marinate, then stir in the chopped mint leaves.

To assemble, divide the Beef Filling into 8 equal portions. Place 1 portion of the Beef Filling with 1 (or more, if desired) jicama stick and onion ring on each betel leaf. Sprinkle with chopped lemongrass and garnish with coriander sprigs and sliced chili (if using). Arrange the assembled wraps on a serving platter and serve immediately.

MAKES: *8*   **PREPARATION TIME:** *30 mins*

COOKING WITH AROMATIC ASIAN HERBS

FILLING

1 tablespoon oil
4 cloves garlic, minced
$1/2$ cup (4 oz/100 g) ground pork
$1/2$ cup (4 oz/100 g) ground chicken
5 fresh or canned water chestnuts, chopped
1 carrot, peeled and coarsely grated
2 tablespoons oyster sauce
2 tablespoons plum sauce
10 green beans, very thinly sliced
2 tablespoons chopped Vietnamese mint
1 handful (50 g) dried rice vermicelli,
    blanched in hot water until soft, drained
$1/2$ teaspoon salt, or to taste
Pinch of ground white pepper

14 square Chinese spring roll wrappers
1 egg, lightly beaten
Oil for deep-frying

ORANGE CHILI SAUCE

1 tablespoon Sambal Oelek Chili Paste
    (page 240) or other sweet chili paste
$1/2$ cup (125 ml) fresh orange juice

Spring rolls with orange chili sauce

A classic spring roll recipe that has all the flavors and aromas of Asia rolled into one bite. Crispy chopped garlic and water chestnuts provide a pleasing crunch and a peppery burst of Vietnamese mint reminds you of Asia.

Prepare the Sambal Oelek Chili Paste by following the recipe on page 240.

Prepare the Filling first. Heat the oil in a wok and stir-fry the garlic over medium heat until fragrant, about 1 minute. Add the ground pork and chicken and stir-fry until they change color, breaking the meat up as you stir. Stir in the water chestnut, carrot, oyster sauce and plum sauce, and simmer covered for 5–7 minutes until tender. If the mixture appears dry, add some water. Add the green bean slices, mint and rice vermicelli, and stir-fry for another 1 minute. Season with the salt and pepper to taste, and remove from the heat. Set aside to cool.

To make a Spring Roll, spoon 2 heaping tablespoons of the Filling onto the center of a spring roll wrapper. Fold a corner of the wrapper diagonally over the Filling, then fold in both sides and roll up tightly. Before reaching the end, brush the edge of the wrapper with the beaten egg, then continue to roll up tightly, pressing the end down to seal. Make all the spring rolls in this manner with the remaining ingredients.

Heat the oil in a wok until very hot, then deep-fry the spring rolls in batches over high heat for about 3 minutes, turning often, until crispy and golden on all sides. Reduce the heat to medium, continue to deep-fry for 1 more minute and remove the rolls from the hot oil. Drain on paper towels.

Make the Orange Chili Sauce by mixing all the ingredients in a serving bowl. Arrange the spring rolls whole or halved on serving platters, garnish with Begonia flowers (if using) and serve with the Orange Chili Sauce on the side.

Note: The spring rolls may be prepared earlier and refrigerated until you are ready to deep-fry and serve them. To reheat, bake in an oven at 320°F (160°C) for 10 minutes. If you like, the same amount of ground shrimp can be substituted for the pork.

MAKES: *14 rolls*　　**PREPARATION TIME:** *45 mins*　　**COOKING TIME:** *20 mins*

COOKING WITH AROMATIC ASIAN HERBS

1 cup (200 g) dried channa dal (split peas), soaked overnight to soften, then boiled for 2 hours and drained, or 2 cups (400 g) canned garbanzo beans, drained and mashed
1 teaspoon cumin seeds, dry-roasted and ground, or $1/_2$ teaspoon ground cumin
1 egg, beaten
Oil, for deep-frying

SWEET CHILI DIP
2 tablespoons Sambal Oelek Chili Paste (page 240) or other sweet chili paste with shrimp paste in it
1 tablespoon balsamic or Chinese vinegar
1 tablespoon fresh lime juice
2 kaffir lime leaves, minced

1 tablespoon oil
2 cloves garlic, chopped
1 tablespoon finely chopped onion
$2/_3$ cup (100 g) all-purpose flour
$3/_4$ cup (100 g) rice flour
Pinch of baking powder
Pinch of salt
Pinch of ground white pepper
$1^1/_2$ cups (375 ml) water
1 small green chili pepper, deseeded and chopped finely

Vegetarian fritters with sweet chili dip

Shallow-fried crispy onions and inviting garlic tease out the flavors in this recipe. You may include anything else your imagination devises, for instance roasted dried shrimp, so travel that path for a fragrant result. These simple fritters may be served on their own with a dipping sauce or chopped and add to a summer salad for crisp texture.

Prepare the Sambal Oelek Chili Paste by following the recipe on page 240.

Prepare the Sweet Chili Dip first by combining all the ingredients in a bowl and mixing well. Set aside.

Heat the oil in a wok or skillet and sauté the garlic over medium heat until golden brown and fragrant, about 1 minute. Remove from the heat and drain on paper towels. In the same pan, sauté the onion for 1–2 minutes in the same manner.

Sift both types of flour into a mixing bowl. Add the baking powder, salt, pepper and water, and whisk the mixture until smooth. Add the sautéed garlic and onion, and all the other ingredients to the flour mixture and mix well, then leave the batter to stand for 15 minutes.

Heat the oil in a wok or saucepan until very hot. Spoon 1 tablespoon of the batter mixture, roughly shape it into a patty with your fingers and then lower it into the hot oil. Deep-fry the patty for 3–4 minutes, adjusting the heat and constantly turning it, until the fritter is golden brown on all sides. Remove from the oil and drain on paper towels. Continue to deep-fry the rest of the Fritters in the same manner. Serve them hot with a bowl of Sweet Chili Dip on the side.

Note: Instead of using channa dal or garbanzo beans, substitute 1 cup (100 g) soaked green beans mixed with 1 cup (200 g) mashed potato. You can also add 1 cup (7 oz/200 g) of fresh shrimp or dry-roasted dried shrimp in place of the dal for a non-vegetarian version.

SERVES: *4–6*   PREPARATION TIME: *30 mins*   COOKING TIME: *20 mins*

COOKING WITH AROMATIC ASIAN HERBS

1 cup (200 g) canned or cooked garbanzo
    beans, rinsed and drained
1 cup (200 g) canned or cooked red kidney
    beans, rinsed and drained
8 baby potatoes (about 10 oz/300 g total),
    boiled and quartered
1/2 cup (75 g) raw almonds, dry-roasted
    then roughly chopped or ground
2 green apples, skin on, sliced into eighths
    and rubbed with 1/2 teaspoon salt
1 cup (30 g) watercress or mint leaves
1/2 cup (20 g) chopped coriander leaves
    (cilantro)
2 ripe tomatoes, sliced into wedges

1 onion, halved and thinly sliced
1–2 small green chili peppers, deseeded
    and chopped
1/4 teaspoon ground red pepper or dried
    chili flakes
Sprigs of coriander leaves (cilantro) or
    basil, to garnish

TAMARIND HONEY DRESSING
1/2 cup (125 ml) vinegar
1/4 cup (60 ml) tamarind juice (prepared
    by mixing 2 tablespoons tamarind pulp
    with 1/3 cup (100 ml) hot water, mashing
    and straining to obtain the juice)
2 tablespoons fresh lime juice
2 tablespoons honey
2 teaspoons sugar
1 teaspoon salt, or to taste
Pinch of ground white pepper

Mixed bean and potato salad with herbs

Colorful, healthy and minty, the main strength of this dish lies in its simplicity. The aromatic punch of herbs like coriander, mint and basil sprinkled over the salad speaks for itself. Garbanzo and kidney beans, sliced potatoes and tomatoes are the staples of a salad often served in tiny puffed breads called *chaat puri* or *bhel puri* by Mumbai street stalls. Indians have managed to stay healthy as vegetarians because they understand the importance of maintaining a balanced diet of lentils and vegetables.

Prepare the Tamarind Honey Dressing first by combining all the ingredients in a bowl and mixing well. If preferred, bring the Dressing to a boil and simmer uncovered for 1 minute in a saucepan and then cool.

    Assemble all the ingredients (except the beans, red pepper and garnish) in a large salad bowl and add the beans. Drizzle the Dressing over and toss well to combine. Sprinkle the salad with red pepper or chili flakes, garnish with coriander or basil sprigs and serve immediately.

Note: This salad is often eaten as is or used as a filling in tortilla, wraps or bread. Canned beans are much quicker and just as tasty.

SERVES: *4–6*   **PREPARATION TIME:** *30 mins*

24 young asparagus spears
24 wonton wrappers
12 slices square gruyère or cheddar cheese,
    cut in half
1½ tablespoons Sambal Oelek Chili Paste
    (page 240) or other sweet chili paste
    with shrimp paste
Fresh basil leaves
4 tablespoons water mixed with
    4 teaspoons cornstarch to form a paste
2 cups (500 ml) oil for shallow-frying

DIPPING SAUCE
¼ cup (60 ml) mayonnaise
2 tablespoons bottled sweet chili sauce
1 tablespoon chopped mint
2 tablespoons capers, drained and
    chopped

Asparagus spears in crispy wonton skins

The wonton "apron" wrapped around the asparagus is stuffed with cheese and exotic basil that releases a heady aniseed aroma contrasting with crunchy vegetable. For maximum effect, flash cook and serve at once.

Prepare the Sambal Oelek Chili Paste by following the recipe on page 240.

Cut off the bottom one-third of each asparagus spear and discard. If using large asparagus, bring 2 cups (500 ml) of water to a boil in a saucepan and blanch the asparagus for 1–2 minutes. Remove from the heat and drain well.

Place a wonton wrapper on a flat work surface. Dab a half of a cheese slice with Sambal Oelek and place it on the wrapper with a basil leaf along the side nearest you. Place an asparagus spear on top of the cheese, parallel to the edge of the wrapper. Fold the edge of the wrapper over the asparagus and roll up firmly around the asparagus, sealing the inside of the far edge with a dab of the cornstarch paste. Continue to wrap the remaining ingredients in the same manner.

Heat the oil in a skillet until hot and pan-fry the wrapped asparagus spears over medium heat until golden and crispy on all sides, about 1 minute each. Remove from the heat and drain on paper towels.

Combine the Dipping Sauce ingredients in a serving bowl and mix well. Arrange the fried asparagus on a serving platter and serve hot with the bowl of the Dipping Sauce on the side.

MAKES: *24 asparagus rolls*   **PREPARATION TIME:** *30 mins*   **COOKING TIME:** *5–10 mins*

1 tablespoon olive oil
1 leek, trimmed and coarsely chopped to make 1 cup
$\frac{1}{2}$ onion or 3 Asian shallots, chopped
2 cloves garlic, minced
2 medium potatoes (preferably Pontiac), peeled and thinly sliced
1 bay leaf
1 stalk lemongrass, thick part only, outer layers discarded, inner part bruised
2 cups (500 ml) Chicken Stock (page 245), or water
1 teaspoon salt, or to taste
$\frac{1}{2}$ teaspoon ground white pepper
$\frac{1}{4}$ cup (60 ml) sour cream
$\frac{1}{4}$ cup (60 ml) yogurt, plus extra to serve
Dried chili flakes (optional)
Chopped chives, to garnish

Leek and potato vichyssoise with lemongrass

This summer soup, served by my good friend Martin Morrison, whose years in Malaysia have influenced the flavors, has a romantically light aroma. The potato and leek become infused with the fresh, citrusy aroma of lemongrass—producing a lemony perfume that makes this interesting soup unusual and addictive. A must-have for summer entertaining!

Prepare the Chicken Stock by following the recipe on page 245.

Heat the olive oil in a wok and stir-fry the leek and onion over medium heat until the onion becomes transparent, 2–3 minutes. Add the garlic and stir-fry for 30 seconds. Stir in the potato slices, bay leaf and lemongrass and pour in the Chicken Stock, then bring to a boil. Simmer uncovered for about 30 minutes until the potato and leek are very tender. Season with the salt and pepper, then remove from the heat and cool.

Remove and discard the bay leaf and lemongrass, then process the soup to a purée in a food processor, adding the sour cream and yogurt gradually. Chill the soup before serving. Ladle into 4 individual serving bowls, sprinkle with chili flakes (if using), garnish with chopped chives and serve with a bowl of extra yogurt on the side.

Note: This is a very flexible recipe. Celery or other vegetables can be added in place of or in addition to the potato, then cook and process as instructed. You can vary the proportions of the various ingredients to suit your taste.

SERVES: *4*   PREPARATION TIME: *30 mins*   COOKING TIME: *40 mins*

1 banana flower or 1 1/2 cups (200 g) sliced cabbage
Salted lime juice water (prepared by combining 1 tablespoon salt, 1/2 cup [125 ml] fresh lime juice and 8 cups [2 liters] water)
1/4 cup (25 g) freshly grated coconut or dried unsweetened (dessicated) coconut
1/2 ginger flower (about 4 oz/100 g) or 2 stalks lemongrass, finely chopped
1/2 tablespoon freshly grated galangal root

7 oz (200 g) roast or barbecued pork, cut into strips, or 5 thick slices of prosciutto fried until brown and then sliced into strips
1/2 finger-length chili pepper, deseeded and cut into thin strips
Crushed pork cracklings or crisp bacon bits, to garnish
Mint leaves, to garnish

DRESSING
1 tablespoon Sambal Oelek Chili Paste (page 240) or other sweet chili paste
2 tablespoons water
2 tablespoons fresh lime juice
1 tablespoon sugar
1 teaspoon salt, or to taste
2 tablespoons crème de menthe (optional)

Tropical salad with barbecued pork

A palette of perfumes you can really eat. A bowl of this Balinese *babi guling* salad is brimming with the floral scents of banana flower, coconut and lime. Added to this are the refreshing rose-like fragrance of ginger flower and shavings of galangal with a spike of mint on top.

Prepare the Sambal Oelek Chili Paste by following the recipe on page 240.

Prepare the banana flower by pulling off the outer petals and the long narrow yellow blossoms until the pinkish white inner heart is revealed. Halve the heart lengthwise with an oiled knife to avoid the sticky sap clinging to it and soak the halves in a pot of salted lime juice water for 1 hour. Remove and drain. Squeeze the soaking liquid from the heart and slice finely into thin shreds.

In a skillet, dry-fry the grated coconut over low heat until fragrant and golden, 10–15 minutes. Alternatively, microwave on medium for a total of 5 minutes, removing and stirring every 2 minutes.

Just before serving, combine the banana flower (or cabbage), ginger flower or lemongrass, galangal, pork, bacon, chili strips and grated coconut in a large salad bowl. In a small bowl, combine the Dressing ingredients and mix until the sugar is dissolved. Drizzle the Dressing over the salad and toss thoroughly until well combined. Spread the pork cracklings or bacon bits on top of the salad and serve with steamed rice, garnished with mint leaves.

Note: This salad, like *rojak*, has herbs instead of vegetables with the pork as the hero. A few teaspoons of my Sambal Oelek (page 240) could be the spike that adds aroma and a chili hit.

SERVES: *4*   PREPARATION: *20 mins + 1 hour to soak the banana flower*   COOKING: *15 mins*

1/4 cup (60 ml) oil, for frying
12 wonton skins, cut into thin strips
1 lb (500 g) beef tenderloin
1/2 cup (20 g) mint leaves, torn
1/4 cup (10 g) coriander leaves (cilantro), torn
1 stalk lemongrass, thick bottom part only,
    outer layers discarded, inner part minced
1/2 cup (125 g) grated green papaya
1 onion, halved and sliced into thin strips
1 mandarin orange, peeled and segmented
Lettuce leaves, washed and torn
1 sheet nori, thinly sliced into strips

TANGY THAI DRESSING
5 cloves garlic, peeled
1–2 green finger-length chili peppers, halved
    lengthwise and deseeded
1 tablespoon fish sauce
3 tablespoons Chinese black rice vinegar
4 tablespoons shaved palm sugar or dark
    brown sugar

Beef salad with thai herbs and mandarin orange

The wild aromas of Thai mint, lemongrass and coriander leaves join forces to form a herbal mélange in this recipe. This is the first Thai salad I ever made, under the tutelage of Charlie Amatyakul of the Bangkok Oriental Cooking School, and it has been my favorite since. Here I have added more texture with crispy wonton skins and nori strips for a swirling festive dish, great for New Year's parties with fireworks as a backdrop.

Heat the oil in a wok and fry the wonton strips over medium heat until they curl up and become crispy, about 1 minute. Remove from the heat and drain on paper towels. Drain off most of the oil, reheat the wok until very hot and sear the beef for 1 minute on each side. Remove from the heat and cool, then slice into thin strips across the grain.

Prepare the Tangy Thai Dressing by grinding the garlic and chili peppers in a mortar or process in a food processor until fine. Transfer to a bowl, add all the other ingredients and mix well.

Place all the ingredients except the orange, lettuce leaves, nori and wonton strips in a salad bowl. Drizzle the Dressing over them and toss well to combine. Arrange the lettuce leaves on a serving platter and spoon the beef salad on top. Garnish with the orange segments, wonton strips and nori strips and serve chilled.

SERVES: *6*　　**PREPARATION TIME:** *45 mins*　　**COOKING TIME:** *5 mins*

1 lb (500 g) fresh jumbo shrimp
1/2 teaspoon salt, or to taste
1 teaspoon melted butter
1 small onion, halved and thinly sliced
1 carrot, cut into matchsticks
1 green tomato, halved and thinly sliced
2 tablespoons dried channa dal, soaked
 overnight, drained and dry-roasted
1/2 cup (40 g) besan or chickpea flour, dry-
 roasted in the microwave for 1–2 minutes
 on high

5 kaffir lime leaves, sliced into thin shreds
Sprigs of coriander leaves (cilantro), to
 garnish

CRISPY FRIED GARLIC
2 tablespoons oil
3–4 cloves garlic, minced

PLUM DRESSING
1 tablespoon Garlic Oil (page 56)
1 tablespoon fish sauce
1 tablespoon bottled Chinese plum sauce
1 teaspoon dried chili flakes

Fragrant shrimp salad with plum dressing

Burma, now known as Myanmar, lies at the confluence of two major cuisines—those of India and China. This dish combines Indian and Chinese influences—with the aroma of young kaffir lime leaves and the richness of buttery shrimp. Crayfish or lobster may be substituted for the shrimp, if you prefer.

Prepare the Garlic Oil by following the recipe on page 56.

 Prepare the Crispy Fried Garlic first by heating the oil in a skillet and sautéing the garlic over medium heat until golden and crispy, about 1 minute. Remove from the oil and drain on paper towels. Alternatively, cover the garlic with 1 tablespoon of oil in a heatproof dish and microwave for 1 minute on high, then stir and microwave for another minute.

 Combine the shrimp, salt and butter in a large bowl and mix well. Set aside to marinate for 5 minutes, then grill the shrimp on a preheated pan grill or under an oven broiler until pink and just cooked, 1–2 minutes on each side. Remove from the heat and cool. Peel the shrimp, leaving the tails on.

 Place the shrimp in a large salad bowl with the onion, carrot, tomato, roasted channa dal, besan flour and kaffir lime leaf shreds. Combine the Plum Dressing ingredients in a small bowl and mix well, then pour it over the salad and toss until well blended, adjusting the seasonings as desired. Sprinkle with the Crispy Fried Garlic and serve immediately, garnished with coriander sprigs.

SERVES: *4*   **PREPARATION TIME:** *30 mins + overnight soaking*   **COOKING TIME:** *20 mins*

PICKLED TEA LEAVES
$\frac{1}{4}$ cup (10 g) dried green Chinese tea
   leaves
1 teaspoon salt
2 cups (500 ml) boiled and cooled water

CHILI OIL
4 dried red finger-length chili peppers,
   stems removed, broken into small pieces
$\frac{1}{4}$ cup (60 ml) oil

DRESSING
Fresh juice of 2 limes
2–3 tablespoons Chili Oil (see above)
2 tablespoons white vinegar
$\frac{1}{2}$ cup (125 ml) fresh pineapple juice
$\frac{1}{2}$ cup (125 ml) coconut juice
1 teaspoon sugar, or to taste
$\frac{1}{2}$ teaspoon salt, or to taste

$\frac{1}{2}$ cup (100 g) dried chickpeas (split peas)
$\frac{1}{2}$ cup (100 g) dried urad dal
4 cloves garlic, sliced
1 jicama (1 lb/500 g), peeled and sliced
   into thick strips
2 small green mangoes (7 oz/200 g total),
   peeled and pitted, flesh thinly sliced
10 cherry tomatoes, halved
$\frac{1}{2}$ onion, sliced
1 tablespoon roasted peanuts
1 tablespoon roasted cashew nuts
1 tablespoon roasted sesame seeds
4 fresh shiso or perilla leaves, chopped
2–3 bird's eye red chili peppers, sliced
   (optional)

Tea leaf salad with green mango and cashews

The serving of this pickled tea leaf salad, known as *laphet thoke* in Myanmar, is a social custom—a peace offering and a palate cleanser. Old folks chew pickled tea leaves to keep their teeth strong. Young Burmese usually serve it in a lacquer tray with the individual compartments containing the ingredients that make up the salad. The dressing is served on the side. Guests are then invited to toss their own tiny portions of scented and crisp salad with garlic, onion and perfumed green mango together with pickled green tea leaves and dressing to suit their personal taste. This is a recipe sent to me by my friend, Daul Mien Sin Sin.

Make the Pickled Tea Leaves first by combining all the ingredients in a jar, then cover tightly and shake the jar until the ingredients are mixed well. Allow the tea leaves to soak for at least 2 days, a week is better. Before using, drain the tea leaves and squeeze out the liquid.

Make the Chili Oil by dry-roasting the dried chili pepper in a skillet over low heat until fragrant and light brown, about 2 minutes. Remove from the heat and grind finely in a mortar then add to the oil. Alternatively break the dry-roasted chili peppers into small pieces and return them to the pan, then pour in the oil and leave to marinate for 30 minutes, then simmer over medium heat for 1 minute. Remove from the heat and cool. Store the unused Chili Oil in a bottle.

To prepare the salad, soak the dried chickpeas and urad dal, separately, in water for several hours until soft, then drain and dry-roast them in a skillet over medium heat for 3–4 minutes. Remove from the pan and set aside. In the same skillet, sauté the garlic in 3 tablespoons of oil over medium heat for 1–2 minutes until crispy. Combine all the salad ingredients with the Pickled Tea Leaves in a mixing bowl and toss well.

Combine the Dressing ingredients in a small bowl, then drizzle it over the salad and toss thoroughly until the salad is coated well. Transfer the salad to a serving platter and serve immediately. Alternatively serve the salad with a bowl of Dressing on the side.

SERVES: *4–6*   PREPARATION TIME: *30 mins + time to prepare the Pickled Tea Leaves*   COOKING TIME: *30 mins*

COOKING WITH AROMATIC ASIAN HERBS

2 tablespoons oil
3 cloves garlic, minced
$\frac{1}{2}$ cup (50 g) diced tempeh
2 dried sweet Chinese sausages (*lap cheong*)
   or other sweet sausages, thinly sliced
   (optional)
3 cups (150 g) sliced bok choy or other
   Chinese greens
2 packets instant noodles
Sprigs of basil leaves, to garnish

DRESSING
1 tablespoon soy sauce
$\frac{1}{2}$ tablespoon fish sauce
1 tablespoon oyster sauce
1 teaspoon bottled sweet chili sauce
$1\frac{1}{2}$ teaspoons sugar
$\frac{1}{4}$ ground white pepper
$\frac{1}{2}$ tablespoon oil

Quick tossed asian noodles

Tossed, not stirred! Build the ingredients, flavors and aromas as you create your own masterpiece. Great cooking is all about control. Work with a hot pan, the freshest ingredients available, and keep the food moving. This recipe works well as a vegetarian noodle dish but sweet sausage slices can be added if you like. You can also use a fried omelet—rolled up and shredded—as a garnish, together with some crispy fried garlic and onions.

Heat the oil in a wok and stir-fry the garlic over medium heat until golden and fragrant, about 1 minute. Remove from the heat and set aside. In the same oil, stir-fry the tempeh until golden brown and crispy, 2–3 minutes. Remove from the heat and drain on paper towels, then stir-fry the Chinese sausage slices until crisp.

Combine the Dressing ingredients in a large bowl and mix well. Set aside.

Half-fill a saucepan with water and bring to a boil. Blanch the sliced greens until tender, about 1 minute. Remove from the heat and drain the blanched greens. Set aside.

In the same saucepan of water, cook the noodles following the instructions on the packet until soft. Do not use the flavoring sachet. Remove the noodles from the pan and drain well. Transfer the noodles to the bowl of Dressing, add the blanched greens and toss well to combine. Divide the noodles equally in 2 serving platters and top with the stir-fried garlic, tempeh and Chinese sausage. Garnish with the basil leaves and serve immediately.

SERVES: *2*   **PREPARATION TIME:** *20 mins*   **COOKING TIME:** *10 mins*

4 cups (400 g) cooked rice

3-4 betel leaves, soaked in water (enough to cover) mixed with 1 tablespoon sugar for 2 hours, then drained and cut into thin shreds

1 onion, finely sliced and stir-fried until golden in 1 tablespoon oil

1 cup (50 g) dried shrimp, rinsed and dry roasted until crisp

$\frac{1}{2}$ turmeric leaf, rolled and thinly sliced

2 sprigs curry leaves, chopped

3 sprigs Vietnamese mint, chopped

1 cup (40 g) Thai basil leaves, chopped

1 cup (40 g) mint leaves, chopped

2 kaffir lime leaves, cut into fine threads

1 small sprig fresh thyme, chopped

$\frac{1}{2}$ tablespoon grated fresh galangal root

1 cup (250 g) grated green papaya

10 peppercorns, roasted and crushed

2 tablespoons tamarind pulp, mashed with 4 tablespoons boiling water and strained to obtain the juice

Salt, to taste

PICKLED CUCUMBER

4 baby or Lebanese cucumbers

$\frac{1}{2}$ teaspoon salt

1 cup (250 ml) vinegar

2 tablespoons sugar

$1\frac{1}{2}$ cups (225 g) sliced cucumber

Rice salad perfumed with herbs ~ *Nasi ulam*

This rice dish originates from the east coast of Malaysia where it is served cold during the fasting month by the Muslims. The fast is broken with a sweet rosewater drink to slake the thirst, followed by this aromatic herbal rice, searingly hot and tart with fresh lime juice, with a spicy sweet sambal on the side. Herbal rice is said to aid digestion, cleanse and refresh the body. It is served in many parts of Asia, including Myanmar and Indonesia. The Indians serve a similar Ayurvedic-influenced tamarind rice salad believed to "cool" the body.

Prepare the Pickled Cucumber first by thinly slicing the cucumbers with a mandolin as shown. In a large bowl, mix the cucumber slices with a little salt and set aside for 5 minutes. Squeeze the liquid from the cucumber slices, then rinse quickly, drain and dry on paper towels. Combine the vinegar and sugar in a bowl and mix until the sugar is dissolved. Add the sliced cucumber and mix until well coated. Allow to marinate for 2 hours, then drain and set aside.

In a large bowl, combined the cooked rice with all the other ingredients except the tamarind juice and salt. Gently toss the mixture until well blended, adding the tamarind juice a little at a time. Do not use all the tamarind juice; add just enough to separate the rice grains. Season with salt to taste, transfer to a serving platter and serve immediately with the Pickled Cucumber on the side. This dish goes well with pickled limes too.

SERVES: *4-6*   **PREPARATION TIME:** *45 mins + 2 hours to marinate*   **COOKING TIME:** *5 mins*

1 lb (500 g) fresh rice stick noodles,
   or 8 oz (250 g) dried rice stick noodles
4 dried sweet Chinese sausages (*lap cheong*),
   finely sliced
8–10 fresh medium shrimp (5 oz/150 g),
   peeled and deveined, or freshly shucked
   cockles or oysters
4 cloves garlic, finely chopped
1 tablespoon salted black beans, mashed
   with the back of a spoon
2 tablespoons Sambal Oelek Chili Paste
   (page 240) or other sweet chili paste
$^1/_2$ teaspoon dried shrimp paste, dry-roasted
   and crumbled
3 tablespoons thick sweet soy sauce
   (*kecap manis*)
1 tablespoon light soy sauce
$^1/_4$ cup (60 ml) water or as needed
1 bunch garlic chives (about 30), washed
   and cut into short lengths
3 cups (150 g) bean sprouts, trimmed
Fresh lime juice, to taste
Pinch of salt, to taste
Pinch of ground white pepper, to taste

CRISPY PORK CRACKLINGS
$^1/_4$ cup (50 g) diced pork fatback
1 tablespoon water

Bean sauce noodles with shrimp and sausage

Char kway teow is a traditional dish that never fails to please with its hot and smoky aromas of spluttering pork fat deliciously browned in spicy black bean sauce. And when the rice noodles and emerald garlic chives are finally thrown in and tossed with the glistening dark sweet soy, the scents are complete in a dish with memorable aromas that linger long after the taste.

Prepare the Crispy Pork Cracklings first. Heat a skillet until hot and sauté the pork fatback for 2 minutes, then pour in the water and let it sizzle. As the water evaporates, the fat is rendered. Continue stirring until the pork fat becomes golden and crispy. Turn off the heat, transfer the Cracklings to a platter and reserve the oil for stir-frying the noodles.

If using dried rice stick noodles, half-fill a saucepan with water and bring to a boil, then cook the rice noodles for 2–3 minutes until soft. Remove from the heat and drain well.

Heat 2 tablespoons of the pork oil in a deep wok and stir-fry the sausages and shrimp over medium heat for 1 minute. Move the sausages and shrimp to the sides of the wok to make a well in the center, add the garlic and stir-fry for 30 seconds until fragrant, then add the black beans, chili paste and shrimp paste, and continue to stir-fry for 1 more minute. Combine all the ingredients in the wok and mix well. Add the noodles, a little at a time, and toss well. Drizzle in both soy sauces and toss until the noodles are coated evenly with the sauce—you may need to add a little water to mix the sauces evenly. Finally stir in the chives, bean sprouts, Crispy Pork Cracklings, lime juice, salt and pepper to taste and toss well. Remove from the heat, transfer to individual serving plates and serve immediately.

SERVES: *4-6*   **PREPARATION TIME:** *30 mins*   **COOKING TIME:** *10 mins*

8 oz (250 g) dried spaghetti
2 tablespoons Green Chili Coriander Butter (page 59)
2 tablespoons sliced sundried tomatoes
1 teaspoon Sambal Oelek Chili Paste (page 240) or other sweet chili paste
1 tablespoon olive oil
3-4 small ripe tomatoes, quartered
10 green beans, sliced and blanched
3 cloves garlic, thinly sliced
$1/_2$ teaspoon freshly ground black pepper
Salt, to taste
2 strips bacon, fried until crisp and crumbled
Mint or arugula leaves, to garnish

Vegetarian pasta with chili coriander butter

A simple recipe with surprising results when tossed with the herbed butter and slightly pepper arugula leaves.

Prepare the Green Chili Coriander Butter and Sambal Oelek Chili Paste by following the recipes on pages 59 and 240.

Bring a saucepan of lightly salted water to a boil and cook the pasta according to the instructions on the packet, until just tender or *al dente*. Remove from the heat and drain well. Transfer to a mixing bowl.

Add all the other ingredients, except the bacon and garnish, to the pasta and toss well. Sprinkle the bacon bits on top, garnish with the mint or arugula leaves, and serve hot.

SERVES: *4-6*   PREPARATION TIME: *15 mins + time to prepare the Coriander Butter*   COOKING TIME: *10 mins*

6 large quails (each 8 oz/250 g) or 3
    Cornish game hens (each 1 lb/500 g)
Vietnamese mint (laksa) leaves and
    coriander leaves (cilantro), to garnish

GARLIC OIL
3 cloves garlic, minced
2 tablespoons fresh ginger juice (from
    grated fresh ginger)
1 tablespoon olive oil

MARINADE
2 tablespoons oil
1 stalk lemongrass, thick part only, outer
    layers discarded, inner part minced
3 cloves garlic, minced
4 green onions, finely sliced
$^{1}/_{2}$ teaspoon ground red pepper
1 tablespoon fish sauce
$^{1}/_{3}$ teaspoon salt
$^{1}/_{2}$ teaspoon Chinese five spice powder
1$^{1}/_{2}$ teaspoons soy sauce
$^{1}/_{2}$ teaspoon sugar

DIPPING SAUCE
4 tablespoons hoisin sauce
2 tablespoons soy sauce
2 tablespoons Chinese black vinegar

Grilled quail with lemongrass and ginger

Like a potpourri, the combination of fragrant lemongrass, green onions and garlic provides a sensual kaleidoscope that works well for grilling or barbecuing meats, especially tender quails. This dish is a must-try even for beginners. Quails have been sadly ignored and are underused as most think they have very little meat. I use them for their succulent flesh and they make a beautiful grilling party dish, serving one to each guest. This recipe also works well with Cornish game hens.

Prepare the Garlic Oil first by combining the ingredients in a bowl and mixing them well. Set aside to infuse for 30 minutes before using.

On a chopping board, spatchcock each bird by placing it on its back and cutting downward through the breastbone with a sharp knife to split it open. Then turn the bird over and press to flatten it out.

To prepare the Marinade, heat the oil in a skillet and sauté the lemongrass, garlic, green onion and ground red pepper over medium heat until fragrant, 1–2 minutes. Remove from the heat. Add all the other ingredients and mix until the sugar is dissolved.

Arrange the prepared birds in a shallow dish large enough to hold them all in a single layer. Pour the Marinade over the birds and allow them to marinate for 1 hour, turning often to steep well.

Thread the marinated quails on metal skewers and reserve the Marinade. Brush the quails with the Garlic Oil and grill, skin-side down, on a preheated pan grill or under a preheated broiler for 3–4 minutes, basting with the Marinade as they cook. Then turn over and grill on the other side until cooked, another 3–4 minutes. Do not overcook or the birds will dry out. Alternately, bake in a preheated oven at 375°F (190°C) for about 20 minutes, basting with the Marinade and covering them with a thin layer of sliced onions to prevent drying out. If using cornish hens, bake in the same way for 30–45 minutes until cooked.

Combine the Dipping Sauce ingredients in a bowl and mix well.

Arrange the birds on a serving platter or on a banana leaf (as shown in the photo), garnish with the mint and coriander leaves, and serve hot with the Dipping Sauce on the side.

SERVES: *4-6*   **PREPARATION TIME:** *30 mins*   **COOKING TIME:** *20 mins*

COOKING WITH AROMATIC ASIAN HERBS

2 lbs (1 kg) lamb chops, fat trimmed
1 tablespoon oil
1 in (3 cm) fresh ginger, cut into strips
1 onion, diced
$\frac{1}{2}$ cup (125 ml) water
$\frac{1}{2}$ teaspoon salt, or to taste
1 teaspoon freshly ground black pepper
Coriander leaves (cilantro), to garnish

MASHED PARSNIPS
1 lb (500 g) parsnips, peeled and chopped
2 tablespoons butter

PLUM GINGER MARINADE
2 tablespoons bottled Chinese plum sauce
1 tablespoon thick mushroom sauce
1 teaspoon fresh ginger juice (from grated
    fresh ginger)
2 green finger-length chili peppers,
    deseeded and ground

GREEN CHILI CORIANDER BUTTER
$\frac{1}{4}$ cup (60 g) butter
$\frac{1}{2}$ cup (20 g) coriander leaves (cilantro)
$\frac{1}{2}$ green finger-length chili pepper,
    deseeded
1 tablespoon fresh lime juice
$\frac{1}{4}$ teaspoon salt, or to taste

Lamb chops with sweet plum ginger marinade

The rich aromas of onion and ginger with tangy sweet plum sauce create a special lingering fragrance that enlivens the tastebuds—a sure way to attract hungry diners to the kitchen!

In a large bowl, combine the Plum Ginger Marinade ingredients and mix well. Place the lamb in the marinade and mix until well coated. Cover and marinate for 3–4 hours in the refrigerator. Drain the Plum Ginger Marinade from the lamb chops and reserve.

To prepare the Mashed Parsnips, bring a saucepan of water to a boil and cook the parsnips uncovered over medium heat until soft, about 10 minutes. Remove from the heat and drain. Transfer to a large bowl and mash with a fork or a potato masher, then stir in the butter and mix until well blended. Keep warm until ready to serve.

Meanwhile, process the Green Chili Coriander Butter ingredients in a blender or food processor until smooth. Transfer to a small bowl and refrigerate until ready to serve.

In a heatproof casserole, heat the oil and fry each lamb chop over high heat for about 30 minutes, turning them as they brown. Move the lamb chops to the sides of the casserole dish.

Reduce the heat to medium, place the ginger and onion in the center of the casserole and stir-fry until golden and fragrant, about 2 minutes. Pour in the reserved marinade, mix well to combine with the lamb chops and cook for 1 more minute.

Stir in the water, reduce the heat to low and simmer covered until the lamb chops are cooked, 20–30 minutes. Remove the lamb chops from the pan, increase the heat to high and continue to simmer the sauce until it reduces to half, about 2 minutes. Season with the salt and pepper, and remove from the heat.

Place a spoonful of the Mashed Parsnips on each serving platter and top with the lamb chops. Add a dollop of the Green Chili Coriander Butter, garnish with coriander sprigs and serve immediately.

SERVES: *6*   PREPARATION TIME: *45 mins + 4 hours to marinate*   COOKING TIME: *45 mins*

1 tub (10 oz/300 g) soft tofu, mashed with the
   back of a spoon
$^1/_2$ cup (20 g) chopped yellow chives or green
   onions
$^1/_4$ cup (50 g) ground pork
$^1/_2$ cup (100 g) peeled and minced fresh
   shrimp
1 tablespoon soy sauce
$^1/_2$ teaspoon salt, or to taste
Pinch of ground white pepper
1 egg white
Sesame oil, to drizzle and for brushing

Silken tofu with pork and shrimp

Subtle and simple, this dish will appeal to the health conscious. Steamed shrimp and pork add their own aromas as a marinade of soy sauce and fresh chives or green onions breathes life into the dish. It can be served on its own or as a lunch starter.

In a large bowl, combine the mashed tofu, chopped chives or green onions, pork, shrimp, soy sauce, salt and pepper, and mix well. Beat the egg white in a small bowl until stiff, then stir into the tofu mixture. Pour the mixture into a greased bowl or individual bowls and sprinkle with sesame oil.

Half-fill a wok with water and bring to a rapid bowl. Place the bowls of tofu mixture into a bamboo steamer, then place the steamer over the boiling water and steam for 10 minutes until cooked. Remove from the heat. Brush the top of the steamed tofu with more sesame oil if desired and serve immediately.

Note: For a variation, halve several fried tofu puffs and stuff each half with the steamed tofu mixture after draining off the liquid, then thread onto short bamboo skewers and very briefly fry in hot oil.

SERVES: *Serves 4-6*   **PREPARATION TIME:** *20 mins*   **COOKING TIME:** *10 mins*

2 lbs (1 kg) white fish fillets, sliced into 2-in (5-cm) chunks
½ teaspoon ground turmeric
Twelve 8-in (20-cm) banana leaf squares, blanched in boiling water to soften
½ cup (125 ml) fresh lime juice
Toothpicks, to fasten
1 tablespoon ghee or melted butter mixed with 1 tablespoon oil
Chopped red chili peppers, to garnish
Mint leaves, to garnish

COCONUT AND GREEN MANGO PASTE
2 cups (250 g) freshly grated coconut or 1½ cups (150 g) dried unsweetened grated (dessicated) coconut
3–4 green finger-length chili peppers, halved and deseeded
1 cup (40 g) coriander leaves (cilantro)
8 cloves garlic, peeled
2 teaspoons ground cumin, dry-roasted
½ teaspoon sugar, or to taste
1 teaspoon salt, or to taste
1 green mango (about 5 oz/150 g), peeled and pitted, flesh cut into thin strips
1 tablespoon ghee or melted butter mixed with 1 tablespoon oil

Coconut and green mango fish parcels

This recipe is one of my favorites for it shows off fish in an aromatic and beautiful way. I first tasted it in Mumbai at a food writer's home and I can never forget the experience. Whiting is a good fish to use in this recipe if you do not mind the bones, as it cooks fast and has the most tender and sweet flesh. Bream, mackerel or any other firm white fish works just as well.

Wash the fish fillets and pat dry with paper towels. Place in a large bowl with the ground turmeric and mix until well coated. Set aside.

Prepare the Coconut and Green Mango Paste by processing the grated coconut in a food processor until fine. Add the chili, coriander leaves and garlic, and process to a smooth paste. Transfer to a bowl and stir in the cumin, sugar, salt and mango strips. Heat the ghee and oil in a nonstick skillet and sauté the ground mixture over medium heat until fragrant, 2–3 minutes. Remove from the heat and set aside.

Divide the fish into 12 equal portions. Place a portion of the fish in the center of a banana leaf square, coat it with the Coconut and Green Mango Paste on all sides and sprinkle lime juice on top. Fold the banana leaf up into a parcel and secure the open side with a toothpick. Continue to make the other fish parcels in the same manner with the remaining ingredients.

Heat the ghee and oil in a large skillet over medium heat. Handling 2 parcels at a time, fry the parcels over medium heat for about 3 minutes on each side, until the fish is cooked. Alternatively, bake the parcels in a preheated oven at 340°F (170°C) for 25 minutes in a fan forced oven. Remove from the heat, unwrap the parcels and serve hot with saffron or coconut rice, garnished with chopped chili pepper and mint leaves.

MAKES: *12 parcels*   **PREPARATION:** *45 mins*   **COOKING:** *25 mins*

2–3 fresh crabs (total of 4 lbs/2 kg)
1 tablespoon oil
1 teaspoon dried shrimp paste, dry-roasted
  and crumbled
1 tablespoons brown bean paste (*taucheo*),
  rinsed to remove excess salt, mashed
8 cloves garlic, smashed with a cleaver
1 tablespoon finely grated fresh ginger
2 tablespoons Sambal Oelek Chili Paste
  (page 240) or other sweet chili paste
  containing shrimp paste
2 tablespoons Chinese sweet vinegar
2 tablespoons tomato ketchup
2 teaspoons sugar
1 tablespoon cornstarch mixed with $1/2$ cup
  (125 ml) water
$1/2$ teaspoon salt, or to taste
5–8 garlic chives, cut into lengths

Chili crabs with ginger and garlic chives

Singapore Chili Crab is perhaps intimidating to anyone not used to strong flavors. But the combination of bean paste, shrimp paste and chili adds a tantalizing aroma to this dish. And diners are beguiled into enjoyment as they taste this extraordinary dish. Chili crab is best cooked and eaten at home where everyone can relax and enjoy the fun of prying the crabshells with a fork or fingers to get at that final tasty morsel inside.

Prepare the Sambal Oelek Chili Paste by following the recipe on page 240.

  Scrub the crabs thoroughly and rinse well. Detach the claws from each crab and lift off the shell. Scrape out and discard the gills. Quarter each crab with a cleaver and crack the claws with a mallet or nut cracker.

  Heat the oil in a wok and stir-fry the shrimp paste and bean paste over medium heat until fragrant, about 30 seconds, taking care not to burn the mixture. Add the garlic, ginger and chili paste and stir-fry for 1 minute. Stir in the crab pieces and toss well, then add $1/2$ cup (125 ml) of boiling water, mixing to coat the crab well with the sauce. Cover and simmer for 3–5 minutes. Season with the vinegar, tomato sauce and sugar, and simmer for 2 more minutes. Pour in the cornstarch mixture and toss until the sauce thickens and the crab pieces are cooked. Season with the salt and remove from the heat. Sprinkle with the garlic chives and serve immediately.

SERVES: *6*   **PREPARATION TIME:** *30 mins*   **COOKING TIME:** *15 mins*

2 tablespoons oil
2 cloves garlic, minced
1/2 tablespoon finely grated fresh ginger
1 lb (500 g) fresh shrimp, peeled, with tails
   left on
1 tablespoon vinegar
1 tablespoon soy sauce
1 teaspoon sugar
1/4 cup (60 ml) water
1 teaspoon salt, or to taste

GINGER FLOWER SAMBAL
5–8 red finger-length chili peppers, halved
   lengthwise and deseeded
3 in (8 cm) fresh turmeric root, peeled
   and sliced
4 in (10 cm) fresh galangal root, peeled
   and sliced
5 stalks lemongrass, thick bottom part only,
   outer leaves discarded, inner part sliced
1/2 turmeric leaf
1 ginger flower, sliced
1/4 cup (10 g) Vietnamese mint
1 pandanus leaf
2 teaspoons dried shrimp paste, dry-roasted

Amah's fragrant sambal shrimp

The ginger flower—with its rose-like pungency of turmeric, spike of ginger and freshness of galangal and lemongrass all rolled into one—is irresistible; something that leaves diners intrigued and returning for more. It is the most beautiful of all herbs, ranging from light to startling bright pink, with petals that appear to fold themselves into a prayerful pose. A sambal or salsa made with this mix of ingredients will create its very own perfume that is unmatched by any other combination of herbs in the Nonya repertoire.

Prepare the Ginger Flower Sambal first by grinding the chili peppers in a food processor until smooth. Add all the other ingredients and continue grinding to a smooth paste. Set aside.

   Heat the oil in a wok and stir-fry the garlic and ginger over medium heat until golden, 1–2 minutes. Add the Ginger Flower Sambal and stir-fry until fragrant, about 3 minutes. Stir in the shrimp and toss for 1–2 minutes until pink and coated well with the ground paste. Add the vinegar, soy sauce, sugar and water, mix well and simmer uncovered for 1 minute. Season with the salt and remove from the heat. Transfer to a serving platter and serve with steamed rice or a noodle dish.

SERVES: *4–6*   **PREPARATION TIME:** *40 mins*   **COOKING TIME:** *10 mins*

COOKING WITH AROMATIC ASIAN HERBS

1 lb (500 g) fresh jumbo shrimp
Bamboo skewers (1 for each shrimp), soaked
    in water for 1 hour before using
Fresh juice of 1 lime mixed with $\frac{1}{2}$ teaspoon
    ground turmeric
Coconut cream and bottled chili sauce, for
    brushing on the shrimp (optional)
Lettuce leaves, to garnish
Lemon wedges, to serve

SPICE PASTE
$\frac{1}{2}$ cup (125 ml) Lemongrass Paste (page 242)
1 teaspoon Sambal Oelek Chili Paste (page
    240) or other sweet chili paste (optional)
$\frac{3}{4}$ cup (200 ml) coconut cream
1 tablespoon fish sauce
1 tablespoon shaved palm sugar or dark
    brown sugar
1 tablespoon oil

Grilled shrimp with lemongrass and coconut

This recipe uses my favorite ingredient—lemongrass—which becomes lightly aromatic when ground and softened by the "coconutty" aroma of palm sugar on beautifully grilled shrimp. What better gift for a lover or friend than to prepare these fragrant skewers?

Prepare the Sambal Oelek Chili Paste and Lemongrass Paste by following the recipes on pages 240 and 242.

Clean and trim the shrimp and cut the shells open along their underside. Then thread each one onto a bamboo skewer lengthwise. Place in a large grilling tray and drizzle with the lime and turmeric mixture. Set aside.

Prepare the Spice Paste by combining all the ingredients, except the oil, in a bowl and mixing well. Heat the oil in a skillet and sauté the Spice Paste over medium heat for 3–5 minutes until fragrant. Remove from the heat. Spread the Spice Paste over the skewered shrimp and into the underside cavities. Brush with a little coconut cream and chili sauce if desired. Grill the shrimp on a preheated pan grill or under a broiler for about 3 minutes or until cooked, turning often and making sure they do not burn. Arrange the grilled shrimp on serving platters lined with lettuce leaves and serve immediately.

SERVES: *4-6*   **PREPARATION TIME:** *20 mins*   **COOKING TIME:** *20 mins*

3 tablespoons oil
1 cup (100 g) diced tempeh
2 tablespoons Lemongrass Paste (page 242)
2 medium onions, finely chopped
3 cloves garlic, finely chopped
1 tablespoon Sambal Oelek Chili Paste
   (page 240) or other sweet chili paste
12 oz (350 g) green beans, trimmed ad
   sliced diagonally to make 3 cups
1 teaspoon brown sugar, or to taste
$^{1}/_{2}$-1 (125 ml–250 ml) cup thick coconut
   milk
2 bay leaves
1 teaspoon salt, or to taste
1 tablespoon fresh lemon juice

Tempeh and green beans in lemongrass paste

A fragrant crunchy vegetarian dish that may be enjoyed with rice or tossed with noodles.

Prepare the Sambal Oelek Chili Paste and Lemongrass Paste by following the recipes on pages 240 and 242.

Heat 2 tablespoons of the oil in a wok and fry the tempeh cubes over medium heat until crisp, about 2 minutes. Remove from the heat and drain on paper towels.

Wipe the wok clean and heat the remaining oil, then stir-fry the Lemongrass Paste, onion, garlic and Sambal Oelek over high heat until aromatic, 1–2 minutes. Add the beans and fried tempeh and stir-fry for 2–3 minutes until the vegetable is tender. Add the brown sugar and toss well. Add the bay leaves and the coconut milk, reduce the heat to low and simmer uncovered until the sauce thickens, 3–5 minutes. Season with the salt and removed from the heat, then stir in the lime juice. Serve hot as part of a rice meal.

Note: Always remove the pan from the heat before adding the lime juice to the coconut milk, or it will separate and curdle.

SERVES: *4-6*   PREPARATION TIME: *20 mins + time to prepare Lemongrass Paste*   COOKING TIME: *10 mins*

3 tablespoons oil
2 cups (200 g) diced tempeh
$^1/_2$ onion, thinly sliced
1 clove garlic, minced
1 stalk lemongrass, thick bottom part only,
    outer leaves discarded, inner part sliced
    and ground in a mortar
$^1/_2$ teaspoon ground red pepper
$^1/_2$ teaspoon dried shrimp paste, dry-roasted
$1^1/_2$ tablespoons shaved palm sugar or
    brown sugar
$^1/_4$ cup (60 ml) water
Fresh juice of $^1/_2$ lemon
Salt and ground white pepper, to taste
1 cup (100 g) snowpeas, trimmed and
    blanched for 2 minutes (optional)
3 kaffir lime leaves, cut into thin shreds

Tempeh sambal with snowpeas

A form of cultured soybeans similar to tofu, the smoky-tasting tempeh has more protein and textural flavor than normal tofu. With a blend of lemongrass, dried shrimp paste and sugar that reminds you of the sweet aromas of laksa, this delicious sambal provides both taste and health.

Heat 2 tablespoons of the oil in a wok and fry the tempeh cubes over medium heat until crisp, about 2 minutes. Remove from the heat and drain on paper towels.

Wipe the wok clean, then heat the remaining oil and stir-fry the onion and garlic over high heat until golden and tender, about 1 minute. Add the lemongrass, red pepper, shrimp paste, sugar and 3 tablespoons of the water and stir-fry for 2 minutes. Reduce the heat to medium and continue to stir-fry the ingredients until they caramelize.

Return the fried tempeh to the wok and toss until well coated with the caramelized spices, adding more water as necessary. Season with the lemon juice and salt and pepper to taste and remove from the heat. Arrange the snowpeas (if using) on a serving platter and place the cooked tempeh on top. Sprinkle with the kaffir lime leaf shreds and serve hot.

SERVES: *4*   PREPARATION TIME: *30 mins*   COOKING TIME: *10 mins*

1 tablespoon oil
1 teaspoon whole black mustard seeds
2 cloves garlic, chopped
1 large onion, halved and finely sliced
4 cups (500 g) thinly sliced cabbage
Pinch of ground turmeric
2 eggs, beaten
1 teaspoon salt, or to taste
$\frac{1}{2}$ teapoon ground white pepper
6–8 curry leaves, chopped

Cabbage sautéed with black mustard seeds

This is an ideal recipe to dress up plain tasting cabbage. Nose-spiking mustard seeds combine with the aromas of onion, garlic and curry leaves to spice up the dish. Sri Lankan in origin, this cabbage dish has been cooked in our home for as long as I can remember, and is as surprising as it is tasty. This dish goes well with any of the fish curries in this book.

Heat the oil in a wok and fry the mustard seeds over high heat until they pop. Add the garlic and onion and stir-fry until golden and tender, about 2 minutes. Stir in the cabbage and turmeric, and toss well. Reduce the heat to a simmer, cover and cook for 3–5 minutes, stirring occasionally.

Remove the cover, push the cabbage to the sides of the wok to make a well in the center and pour in the beaten egg. Cook the eggs until set, then scramble gently and toss with the cabbage until well blended. Season with the salt and pepper, adjusting the taste. Stir in the curry leaves and remove from the heat. Serve immediately with steamed rice.

SERVES: *4–6*   PREPARATION TIME: *20 mins*   COOKING TIME: *10 mins*

1/4 cup (60 ml) oil
1/2 cup (50 g) diced dried salted fish
  (preferably threadfin or Thai mergui)
7 cups (350 g) fresh bean sprouts,
  trimmed
2 cloves garlic, chopped
2–3 dried finger-length chili peppers,
  deseeded and broken into pieces, or
  1 teaspoon dried chili flakes
2 teaspoons soy sauce
Vietnamese mint sprigs, to garnish

Bean sprouts with dried fish and chili

Don't be fooled by the simplicity of this dish. Crispy-fried salt fish adds an appealing salty taste and aroma to the otherwise plain bean sprouts, and has made this dish a favorite among the Malaysians and Thais. It is a home-cooked dish, to be shared around the table with bowls of steaming hot rice. I remember we used to tuck in with chopsticks or forks, ladling some of the bean sprouts and that precious gravy, and searching for the last morsels of fish among the remains...which when found, how sublime! An aroma and taste I would climb Mount Fuji for!

Heat the oil in a wok until hot and fry the salted fish over medium heat for 2–3 minutes until crisp. Remove from the heat and drain on paper towels.

Pour off all but 1 tablespoon of the oil in the wok. Reheat the oil and stir-fry the garlic and red chili peppers over high heat until golden and fragrant, about 30 seconds. Add the bean sprouts and toss well, about 1 minute. Stir in the fried fish and remove from the heat, then season with the soy sauce. Transfer to a serving platter, garnish with mint sprigs and serve hot with steamed rice.

SERVES: 4   PREPARATION TIME: *30 mins*   COOKING TIME: *5 mins*

1²/₃ cups (400 ml) coconut milk
1²/₃ cups (400 ml) fresh cream
¹/₂ stick cinnamon, broken
1 star anise pod, to infuse into the custard
³/₄ cup (150 g) sugar
1 teaspoon grated lime rind
2 teaspoons ginger juice (pressed from grated
    fresh ginger)
2 stalks lemongrass, thick part only, outer
    layers discarded, inner part bruised
3 whole eggs
5 egg yolks

CARAMEL SYRUP
1¹/₂ cups (300 g) sugar
¹/₂ teaspoon fresh ginger juice (pressed from
    grated fresh ginger)
³/₄ cup (200 ml) water

Lemongrass and coconut crème caramel

This Asian crème caramel, colonial in origin, takes different forms in different parts of Asia.
I grew up with the Malaysian version, perfumed with pandanus, while the Sri Lankans and Indians
incorporate cardamom and cinnamon in their egg custards. This particular crème caramel is
reminiscent of the French influence in colonial Indochina with its characteristic citrusy aromas.
It is served in the best restaurants as well as on the streets all over Vietnam and Cambodia.

To make the custard, combine all the main ingredients except the eggs in a saucepan and heat them gently over
medium-low heat until the mixture is just about to boil, 1–2 minutes. Do not allow the mixture to boil. Remove
from the heat and set aside to cool, allowing the flavors to infuse. Strain and discard the solids. Break the whole eggs
into a bowl. Add the egg yolks and beat gently with a fork (too much beating will result in bubbles in custard). Add
them to the custard mixture and stir slowly to combine.

In a clean saucepan, bring the Caramel Syrup ingredients to a slow simmer over low heat, stirring until the sugar
is dissolved and the mixture caramelizes. If the mixture gets too hot, cool down the saucepan by placing it in a basin
of cold water for a few seconds. When the mixture begins to bubble and turn golden brown, quickly remove it from
the heat (or it will harden). Pour the Caramel Syrup equally into the prepared custard molds or souffle cups, swirling
the molds or cups so the syrup spreads and forms a thin layer across the bottom, then fill up the molds or cups with
the custard mixture.

Preheat the oven to 285°F (140°C). Place the molds or cups in a large baking dish filled with hot water up to
¹/₃ the height of the cups. Cover with aluminum foil and bake in the oven for about 1 hour until set. Remove from
the heat and cool in a water bath until firm. Run a knife around the edges of each custard to loosen and then turn
them onto serving dishes.

Note: If you prefer a milder version, use the same amount of milk in place of the cream.

MAKES: *9*   **PREPARATION TIME:** *15 mins*   **COOKING TIME:** *1 hour 10 mins*

Black rice pudding with ginger coconut cream

Black sticky rice is unusually dark purple in color. I am often asked if it has been colored. It is indeed natural, coming with its own pandanus-like grassy fresh perfume with a hint of coconut in the top notes that is reinforced by adding coconut cream as a final swirl in this dessert. Black sticky rice has a ready following whenever it is served as it engages the instincts with its contrasting colors, textures and subtle scents.

$1/2$ cup (100 g) uncooked black sticky (glutinous) rice, washed
4 cups (1 liter) water
1 fresh pandanus leaf, cut into long strips and then tied into knots, or 2–3 drops pandanus essence
$1/2$ in (2 cm) fresh ginger, thinly sliced
$3/4$ cup (150 g) sugar
Salt, to taste
Coconut cream, to serve

In a saucepan, bring the rice, water, pandanus leaf or essence and ginger to a boil. Reduce the heat to a simmer and cook the mixture uncovered for about 30 minutes until the grains are soft, adding more water as necessary.

Add the sugar and stir until it is dissolved. Season with salt to taste and remove from the heat. Ladle into serving bowls and serve hot or chilled with a drizzle of coconut cream on top.

SERVES: *4*   PREPARATION TIME: *5 mins*   COOKING TIME: *30 mins*

Lime and mint granita sorbet

This is a contest of melon and mint—the aromas and fruity textures of a simple "granita" of grainy ice crystals jostling their way to impress and recharge the tired palate. Choose spectacular glasses to flaunt the granita after a hot Thai salad or a chili curry.

3 young kaffir lime leaves, roughly chopped
1 cup (40 g) mint leaves, roughly chopped
$1/2$ teaspoon (3 g) gelatin or agar-agar powder
2 cups (500 ml) boiling water
$1/2$ cup (125 ml) fresh lime juice
$1/4$ cup (50 g) sugar
1 tablespoon Midori liqueur
Kaffir lime or mint leaves, to garnish

SERVES: *4*

PREPARATION TIME: *20 mins +*
   freezing time

Coarsely process the kaffir lime and mint leaves with 2 tablespoons of water in a mortar or blender. Transfer to a muslin bag and squeeze the juice into a bowl. Set aside.

Combine the gelatin or agar-agar and boiling water in a saucepan and heat over medium heat until it melts completely, 2–3 minutes. Remove from the heat and strain.

Add the mint and kaffir lime leaf juice, lime juice and sugar to the melted gelatin while it is still warm. Stir until the sugar is dissolved, then transfer the mixture to a stainless steel container and freeze for at least 2 hours. Remove the frozen gelatin mixture from the freezer, transfer to an electric mixer and beat well at high speed for about 1 minute. Pour the gelatin mixture back to the same container and return to freeze until solidified. Remove from the freezer and defrost at room temperature, then use a fork to break it up. Add the Midori to the gelatin mixture, mix well and return to freeze for a short while until grainy, then serve.

To serve as a granita, scrape into individual cocktail glasses, drizzle with extra Midori if desired and garnish with kaffir lime or mint leaves.

½ cup (125 ml) coconut cream
1 cup (230 g) butter
¾ cup (175 g) superfine (caster) sugar
¼ cup (50 g) shaved palm sugar or dark
   brown sugar
5 eggs
Pinch of salt
2 cups (250 g) self-raising flour, sifted three
   times with a pinch of salt.
½ cup (50 g) grated fresh coconut,
   dry-roasted over low heat for 10 minutes

PANDANUS JUICE
5 pandanus leaves, rinsed and sliced
1 tablespoon water

PALM SUGAR SYRUP
1 cup (200 g) shaved palm sugar
1⅓ cups (300 ml) water

Pandanus coconut cake with palm sugar syrup

This is essentially a buttercake recipe with fresh pandanus juice substituted for vanilla, enriched with coconut cream and grated coconut. You will enjoy this enticingly moist cake with its delicate grassy and floral aromas reminiscent of waving palms and sandy beaches.

Make the Pandanus Juice first by grinding the sliced pandanus leaves in a mortar or blender until fine, adding the water gradually. Wrap the mixture in a muslin cloth and squeeze out the juice, or use a very fine sieve. Add the juice to the coconut cream and mix well.

Preheat the oven to 340°F (170°C). Cream the butter and sugars with an electric mixer until smooth. With the motor running, add the eggs, one at a time, and mix well after each addition. Fold in the flour and coconut cream alternately with a spatula or wooden spoon, and mix until well blended, then fold in the grated coconut. Spoon the mixture into a greased round cake pan, smooth the top and bake in the oven, on the middle shelf, for 40 minutes. The cake is ready when it pulls away from the sides of the cake pan. Remove from the oven and set aside to cool, then turn out onto a serving plate.

While the cake is baking, prepare the Palm Sugar Syrup by combining the palm sugar and water in a heatproof dish. Microwave the mixture for 1 minute on high, then remove and stir. Repeat to cook for 2 more minutes in the same manner until all the sugar is dissolved.

To serve, drizzle the Palm Sugar Syrup over the cake or over each portion.

MAKES: *1*   PREPARATION TIME: *30 mins*   COOKING TIME: *40 mins*

COOKING WITH AROMATIC ASIAN HERBS

Mint vodka collins with watermelon fingers

Watermelon fingers served with an iced mint vodka collins is a refreshing summer fruit combination courtesy of my friend Lyndey Milan, food director of the Australian Women's Weekly. We had a good time cooking before a crowd of holidaymakers at Club Med, Lindeman Island. I made a hot Laksa and Lyndey showed off her refreshing Vodka Collins drink. This is a good palate cleanser, especially after a spicy curry dish.

½ cup (125 ml) chilled vodka
¼ cup (60 ml) fresh lime juice
1 tablespoon grated lime rind
6 shot glasses
6 sprigs of mint leaves
½ medium watermelon, sliced into wedges

Combine the vodka, lime juice and lime rind in a pitcher and stir until well combined. Pour into 6 chilled glasses. Garnish each glass with a sprig of mint leaves and serve with the watermelon wedges.

SERVES: 6   PREPARATION TIME: *10 mins*

Honeydew sorbet with passionfruit

An appealing golden dessert with wonderful fragrances of honeydew and passionfruit, this is a fruity celebration. My guests feel truly special whenever I serve them this sorbet in red wine glasses with parfait dessert spoons.

1 honeydew melon (about 2 lbs/1 kg),
    peeled, deseeded and sliced
Pulp of 4 fresh passionfruits or ¾ cup
    (200 g) canned passionfruit pulp
2 teaspoons fresh lemon juice
Grated lemon rind, to garnish

PANDANUS SYRUP
3 cups (750 ml) water
1½ cups (300 g) sugar
1 pandanus leaf, tied into a knot,
    or 2–3 drops pandanus essence

SERVES: 6

PREPARATION TIME: *20 mins +
    overnight freezing*

COOKING TIME: *5 mins*

Prepare the Pandanus Syrup first by heating all the ingredients in a saucepan over medium heat and stirring until the sugar is dissolved. Bring to a boil, then simmer uncovered for about 30 seconds and remove from the heat. Discard the pandanus leaf and set the syrup aside to cool.

Process the honeydew to a purée in a food processor and combine it with the passionfruit pulp and Pandanus Syrup in a mixing bowl. Add the lemon juice to taste and mix until well blended. Pour into an ice cream maker and process to a sorbet according to manufacturer's instructions.

If you do not have an ice cream maker, pour the mixture into a large shallow cake pan, cover with aluminum foil and freeze overnight. Remove from the freezer, break the frozen mixture into pieces and then process to a smooth sorbet again in a food processor. Return to the freezer until ready to serve.

Remove the sorbet from the freezer 30 minutes before serving. Make balls of sorbet using a warmed ice cream scoop. Top each sorbet ball with grated lemon rind and serve immediately.

Note: If you cannot find pandanus leaf or essence use vanilla essence instead. Other fruits such as mango, canteloupe, watermelon or starfruit can be substituted for the honeydew.

'The main fruits are all used in Asian cooking and reflect the very essence of the cuisines. One of the most iconic is the coconut ...'

Cooking with
aromatic asian fruits

The aromas of Asian fruits are unashamedly self-assertive. Not for the Asian kitchen is the soft, honeyed sweetness of peaches, or the tart bite of fresh strawberries; rather a brazen assault of strident, festive aromas and perfumes characterizes its tropical cornucopia of fruits. There are many perfumed fruits in Asia—ranging from the distinctive floral scent of a ripe mango to the buttery smoothness of a banana, the giddy sweet-sharp sensory bite of a ripe pineapple to the tart notes of the lime and the pungent cologne-like fragrance of the starfruit.

The main fruits are all used in Asian cooking and reflect the very essence of the cuisines. One of the most iconic is the coconut, which runs like a mighty undercurrent through many Southeast Asian dishes with its perfumed, sweetish milk-like liquid—a ubiquitous ingredient that is one of the pivots of Asian cuisine and an ingredient that has, until now, been only tentatively experimented with in Western kitchens. Another major fruit is the mighty chili pepper (inadvertently introduced to Asia by the Arab Traders or the Portuguese after Columbus brought it to Europe from the Americas). Asian food is synonymous with the fragrance and pungency of the chili pepper. And to balance the creamy sweetness of coconut and the heat of chili pepper, there has always been the sour tartness of the lime. Coconuts, chili peppers and limes are three basic fruits around which the recipes in this book revolve.

Fruits in Asia are always present in domestic gardens and are sold peeled and sliced at street stalls along the roadsides. They are commonly enjoyed as table fruits, and are also used in religious ceremonies. During the Hindu New Year, fresh mango leaves are stripped from the stem, knitted into long strings and hung above doorways in Hindu homes to decorate and serve as a reminder of the Earth's renewal each spring. Coconuts are split open at the sacred altar at weddings, to symbolize God's presence by the purity of its white flesh, which blesses the marriage. Ornamental golden kumquats, mandarin oranges and small orange trees grace Chinese homes at Chinese New Year as these are considered lucky—their golden hues being the color of prosperity.

Pomelos are used as special altar offerings to Lady Kuan Yin, the goddess of mercy. In Malay homes, fresh green mango flowers or paper imitations are used to decorate the bridal dais where the bride and groom are seated during the wedding. Boiled eggs in elaborate egg cups or cases are presented to guests, decorated with crêpe paper mango flowers as symbols of fecundity for the marriage.

But symbolism aside, these same fruits are above all enjoyed for their unmatched flavors and aromas.

Experience the unique flavor of the ripe jackfruit, golden in color and crisp in texture, emanating an intense aroma of pineapple, mango and peach. These can be sliced into salads or made into ice cream or custard. Fruits are also used in refreshing perfumed salads. A famous tropical fruit salad called *rojak*—always available in food stalls in Malaysia and Singapore—is made up of pineapple, pomelo, starfruit and tart shards of green mango drizzled with a black, pungent treacle-like sauce and garnished with chopped peanuts. You are bound to sniff the captivating aroma of a *rojak* salad a mile away if you are a fan! Other Southeast Asian countries have different versions of this aromatic and spicy fruit salad, sometimes scattered with chili peppers, deseeded for flavor not bite, and finished off with liberal splashes of lime. Sometimes cucumber and carrot slices are added to the salad and a whole array of tangy minty herbs completes the visual and sensory experience.

As well as being enjoyed raw, fruits are often cooked into curries and soups. Look for the tartness of pineapple added to a fish curry, and the earthiness of an unripe banana added to a potato curry. Raw jackfruit is treated like a starchy vegetable and is a staple ingredient in curries in vegetarian homes across South India. The tiny *belimbing* or baby starfruit is used by the Nonya people (who cook a traditional cuisine that is Chinese-Malay in origin) as a souring agent in their sambals and laksas. The ripe persimmon-like aroma of the tamarind fruit is another souring ingredient that is used in place of lime or lemon juice, and is added to soups for tartness and to thicken curries and dressings. The feathery leaves are also prepared as a green vegetable in some parts of Asia and the raw green tamarind fruit is an essential ingredient in Filipino soups.

Asian fruits are seldom cooked into desserts as in the west, but there are a few exceptions. Pineapples make a delicious jam when cooked with sugar—and during the Chinese New Year, buttery pineapple tarts will be invariably served in Nonya homes. The flesh of the stinky, custardy durian is made into jams, cakes and ice creams while the mango is made into countless jams, custards and jellies. The Thais serve durian flesh and ripe mangoes with sweet sticky rice in a dessert which is then drenched generously with coconut cream. This may not be to everyone's taste, but desserts made this way taste close to heaven to an aficionado—myself included.

Due to the popularity of Asian cuisines across the globe now, many of these so-called "exotic" fruits are now readily available in many supermarkets ... so let your imagination run free and enjoy the passionate aromas of Asian fruit in your cooking and on your table.

Asian limes ~ kalamansi and other limes

Press an Asian lime between your palms and you will receive an intense and vibrant whiff of citrus that stimulates the senses and promises great flavor. Grate some of the rind and you will be presented with the unmistakable tropical notes of fragrant orange and lemon. If any one aroma has the ability to conjure up Southeast Asian cuisine, it is the green kalamansi lime that reminds the diner of a sharp, sour-sweet perfumed lemon with a cleansing freshness.

Limes are used extensively in Thai, Malaysian and Indian cooking as a flavor enhancer and to balance other pungent, sweet and spicy flavors. They also cleanse the palate in oily meat dishes and enhance the flavor of seafood.

Various types of limes are available in Asian markets. The most common is the persian or tahitian lime which is dark green, elliptical, as big as a lemon and usually seedless. It has a fresh taste that is sharper and more tart than a lemon, and is best juiced for salad dressings, curries and refreshing drinks. It also lends itself well to pickling or zesting.

Kalamansi limes are the most "typical" of Asian limes and are small and green, the size of a kumquat, with a taste that is a cross between a lemon and a mandarin orange. These very juicy limes are widely used in Philippines and all over Southeast Asia. They are normally halved and served with laksa and other noodle soups, as a flavoring, and also as a garnish to an Asian meal.

Kaffir limes and lime leaves have already been described in the previous chapter on Asian herbs, since they have very little juice and are normally used as a herb for their incomparable fragrance (see page 24).

Purchasing: Always look for brightly colored, smooth-skinned fruits that are heavy and firm to the feel. These will have more juice. Avoid those with blemishes or spots. The thick skinned limes tend to be dry, although they make good zest.
Culinary uses: In Asia, lime leaves are commonly used as a seasoning in fragrant curries and the flesh and juice in accompaniments such as sambals.

Preparation: To get more juice from a lime, roll it around your palms or on a hard surface to soften before juicing. When I was a kid, I used to bounce them on the kitchen floor until they were soft. Be sure to wash the lime thoroughly if using the rind.
Storing: Fresh whole limes can be refrigerated up to 10 days wrapped in plastic bags. They will keep much longer but the flavor will greatly diminished the longer they are stored.

COOKING WITH AROMATIC ASIAN FRUITS

Coconut, coconut milk and coconut juice ～

The term "coconut" refers to the fruit of the coconut palm. Coconuts grow in bunches on tall palm trees that grow up to a height of 100 feet (30 m) in some varieties. They hang from the top of the tree just under the leaves. The brown, hard-shelled coconuts sold in supermarkets look nothing like the original; they are obtained after removing the smooth green outer covering and the thick husk of brown coarse fibers.

The coconut is the most versatile of tropical fruits, providing a wide range of useful by-products and cooking ingredients. Coconut milk, which is pressed from the grated flesh of the coconut, is one of the most valuable commodities in Southeast Asia.

The hollow center of this fruit is full of a highly nutritious, clear sweet liquid, known as the coconut water or juice, which makes a delicious thirst quencher. Unripe or young coconuts, green or yellow in color depending on the variety, are often harvested for this juice. Their delicious jelly-like young flesh is also eaten together with the juice. Rows of these coconuts, their tops trimmed to make them easier to open, are a common sight throughout tropical Asia. The vendor will slash the fruit open once it is purchased, adding a few ice cubes on the spot, and a spoon is then provided to scoop out the flesh. In some well-stocked supermarkets, it is possible to buy fresh young coconuts with the husks and tops sliced off, leaving a hexagonal-shaped white fruit that is easier to pack and ship. To drink the juice, simply knock a hole in the top with the corner of a large cleaver, and insert a straw. I have used coconut water to make a delicious cocktail drink in Vodka Sour with Young Coconut Juice (page 133).

When a mature nut is cut open, a thick creamy white flesh can be found clinging to its inner walls. The flesh of a mature nut is not eaten as a fruit but is usually grated and pressed to produce coconut cream or milk. The grated flesh is also used to make a variety of Asian cakes and desserts.

A staple ingredient in curries, sauces, soups and desserts throughout Southeast Asia, creamy white coconut milk has a sweet and floral jasmine aroma with a slightly sour backnote, which is not obvious in the unprocessed coconut flesh. The aroma of coconut milk is most of the time masked by spices and herbs when added to curries, but it is best highlighted with a salty lime-like fragrance when used in desserts and rice dishes.

Purchasing: Fresh coconuts can be found in Asian markets. Select coconuts that are heavy for their size, and slosh with liquid when shaken. Avoid ones with damp or leaky eyes which have a sour aroma. Nowadays canned, bottled or packet coconut milk or cream are readily available in the Asian food sections of most supermarkets and provide the best alternative to fresh coconuts. These vary widely in consistency and flavor, depending on the brand, and you will need to try them out and adjust the consistency by adding water as needed. In general, you should add 1 cup (250 ml) of water to 1 cup (250 ml) of coconut cream to obtain coconut milk. Packets of dried or fresh grated coconut, sweetened or unsweetened, are also available in the baking sections of supermarkets.

Culinary uses: Coconut milk is a common ingredient used in most tropical Asian cuisines, notably as a base for curries. Coconut cream is the creamy liquid extracted from the first pressing of the grated coconut flesh. It is mainly used to make desserts and rich curries. Coconut milk is obtained from the second and third pressings. In Asia, it is possible to buy fresh coconut milk, but when fresh milk is not available, canned or packet coconut milk can be used instead. Coconut juice is a popular drink in Southeast Asia, available fresh as well as in cans. You can easily turn it into a cocktail by adding a dash of rum, fresh lime juice and some fresh mint leaves. Coconut juice is also used to make desserts, and is processed and solidified to make a transparent "jelly" called *nata de coco*, an ingredient in the famous Filipino *halo halo*.

Preparation: If you are using a fresh coconut, you will first need to open it by tapping firmly on the center with the blunt end of a cleaver until a crack appears. Drain the coconut water into a bowl and continue tapping until the coconut cracks into two. Separate the flesh from the coconut shell with a knife or spoon. Do not bake the coconut to separate the flesh as suggested by some books as you will not get much coconut milk from cooked flesh. Use a vegetable peeler to remove the outer brown skin, then grate the flesh using a blender or food processor. Add $\frac{1}{2}$ cup (125 ml) of water to the grated coconut flesh, knead a few times then strain with a cheesecloth or a fine sieve to obtain the thick, white cream. This first pressing of the coconut flesh is known as coconut cream. Thick coconut milk is obtained by the same method but by doubling the amount of water to 1 cup (250 ml). The grated flesh when pressed again for the second time with 1 cup (250 ml) of water gives a lighter coconut milk known as thin coconut milk.

Storing: Fresh coconuts are best stored unopened; they can be kept for a month or two in a dry, cool room. Once opened, they must be pressed into coconut milk, which can be stored frozen in a sealed container or plastic bag. Defrost frozen coconut milk to room temperature before using. Fresh coconut milk must be refrigerated if not used immediately.

Substitutes: If coconut milk is not available, use powdered coconut milk or fresh milk or cream.

Mandarin orange ~

Peel a mandarin orange and a burst of citrus oils—a perfumed mixture of cloves, ginger and orange blossom—tempt you before you can reach the juicy segments inside. Each segment has a mellow fruitiness reminiscent of sunny slopes and Mediterranean skies. With hidden notes of star anise and saffron as well, it is difficult to imagine how all these are contained in a mandarin orange. One will notice that an essential ingredient in Chinese sauces is the dried mandarin orange peel which imparts a wonderful citrusy flavor with its perfumed oils.

The mandarin orange is native to China. This fruit, with aromatic top notes of orange blossom and jasmine, is an important symbol in Chinese culture and tradition. The red-gold color of mandarin oranges that are piled high on family altars during Chinese New Year is synonymous with wealth and prosperity, appearing next in importance to red, the auspicious color of good luck and success. A symbol of good fortune, mandarin oranges are exchanged as offerings of goodwill during this festive season. Marking the end of the Chinese New Year celebration, the Chap Goh Meh (literally the fifteenth day of the lunar New Year) Festival traditionally serves as a day for matchmaking. Mandarin oranges are thrown by girls into the rivers to honor the full moon in the hopes of gaining a husband. The streets are jam-packed with young men attempting to catch a glimpse of the young damsels, who would normally not be allowed out-of-doors in the old days.

A popular table fruit, mandarin oranges are also used in salads and drinks throughout Asia. A favorite drink called *oleng* in the markets of Asia is the mandarin orange flavored fizzy drink that is served at restaurants and various festivals.

Mandarin oranges are variously marketed as tangerines, ponkan, clementines and dansy oranges. Most canned mandarins are *satsuma* oranges, the Japanese mandarins that are almost seedless. Mandarin oranges should not be mistaken for kumquats, a much smaller citrus fruit that is often made into marmalade and jelly.

Purchasing: Look for mandarin oranges when they are in season (December to January) as they are at their juiciest. Pick heavy fruits with smooth skins.

Culinary uses: Segments of this fruit are used in fruit salads, desserts, cakes and drinks. In this book, I have included mandarin segments in Beef Salad with Thai Herbs and Mandarin Orange (page 44) as they are colorful and juicy, and combine well with the Tangy Thai Dressing. The dried peel of this fruit is often used as an aromatic in Chinese cooking, especially for duck and pork dishes, adding the lower notes of cloves and citrus oils that perfume the dish and removing the oily taste. Dried mandarin peel is available in Chinese herbal and food shops, but it is easy to make at home: just save the peel after eating the fruit and remove the membranes from the inside, then dry it in the sun or in the oven on very low heat until it curls and darkens. Store in a cool place sealed in a container and use as needed.

Preparation: Wash thoroughly under running water if you plan to use the peel, otherwise simply peel the skin, separate the segments, and use as instructed.

Storing: Store mandarin oranges in a cool dry place for up to 2 weeks. Refrigerate only when they are too ripe.

Mango ～

The peach-like scent of mango flowers tempts the senses; the perfumed night is cool and dark, filling the air with the subtle fragrance of cinnamon and ripe grapes, and the cream-colored flowers are strung across the main stem, a bract of subtle aroma. Breathe deeply and there is a whiff of coconut, some jackfruit and a hint of ripe raisins. The aroma of mango is a delicate mixture of all these, and the taste is a combination of all their flavors. Chinese poets romantically liken the aroma of mangoes to the velvety grace of musty wood in spring.

The ubiquitous sweet golden mango has been featured for centuries in Indian art, culture and religion. Mango leaves are strung over Hindu homes each year during *Pongal*, the Hindu New Year, in a renewal of spring. The mango design is a recurring theme on sari textiles and Indian temple carvings and was the inspiration for the famous English paisley designs used on bedspreads and quilts. However, there is also a green mango variety that is popularly used in Asian salads with very little aroma but a great tart flavor. This mango does not sweeten but retain its tartness even when it is ripe. It has a pale green skin like a green apple, and is crisp as a choko flesh but has a wonderful sour taste with a hint of sweetness that goes well with salads and Asian curries cooked with tamarind and kokum.

The choko (*Sechium edule*) is a vegetable that grows on a vine and looks similar to a mango with a slight tart flavor and it is crisp when slices are vinegared and served in thin slices in a salad. Kokum is a sour fruit almost like Assam Gelugor and it is used to sour Indian curries especially in Kerala where it is used for fish.

Purchasing: You can smell a ripe mango miles away. Its aroma is a good indication of its sweetness. Select unblemished fruits that are not overripe. Always include some semi-ripe mangoes so that you can have a continuous supply as they ripen. Green mangoes should be firm and without any black spots.

Culinary uses: Mango is prepared in many different ways in Asian cuisines. The ripe fruit is often eaten raw as a table fruit and is used in desserts or blended with yogurt and sugar to make mango lassis. A Thai meal always ends with a delicious dessert of mango slices and sweet sticky rice drizzled with coconut cream.

Green mango slices are used in Thai and Malaysian salads or eaten fresh as a snack dipped in a hot and spicy sauce of soy, chili pepper and salt. In Asia it is quite common to see children on their way to school eating this snack from a banana leaf cone. The Indian *chaat papri* salad sometimes has slivers of green mango added to balance the tangy taste and is a street snack found along the streets of Mumbai. The green fruit is also pickled in jars in beautiful yellow semi-circular slices. Although pick-led mango has an unusual flavor and is an acquired taste, it is a popular snack with Asian children. It is also used in Nonya Pickled Vegetables with Dried Shrimp (page 218) and stir-fries, and is served as a condiment with duck dishes. Amchoor is a dry powder made from tart green mangoes that is used to add a bite to many sour-spicy southern Indian curries.

Preparation: Peel the mango first, then slice the flesh away from the seed. Discard the seed and slice the flesh as directed by the recipe.

Storing: Green mangoes keep up to 2 weeks refrigerated in a vegetable drawer. Once ripe, they keep up to 8 days.

Substitute: Mango is such a distinctive fruit that a substitute would be hard to find. The closest would be a firm almost ripening yellow peach with similar floral aromas as raisins, ripe grapes and cinnamon. If green mangos cannot be found for the Asian salads in this book, perhaps you could use an unripe paw paw or crisp green apples instead.

Pineapple ~

The tantalizing aroma of a ripe pineapple is the aroma of islands and the tropics—a mixture of jackfruit, mango flower, tropical lily and mangosteen flower. When I was a kid, we lived near a pineapple farm where the fruits grew in raised beds in militant rows. They were very attractive, gradually turning orange and filling the fields and surrounding area with a mellow honey perfume that attracted bees and tempted humans. Once they were collected, they would arrive at the market where they would be ridge-cut to remove the "eyes," and to my eyes they looked like many golden sultans' turbans awaiting a sweet feast—because there were so many recipes that we can could use them in. Pineapple provides a tart contrast when added to salads, is wonderful when cooked into curries especially with fish and shrimp, is jammy and sticky when made into preserves and jams, and adds just the right touch when added to upside-down cakes and pies—balancing its sweet citrus acidity against the sweetness of iced cakes. Such versatility is not found in any other fruit.

It is truly an amazing and a gratifying sight to see such an elegant perfume reminiscent of warm nights and tart salad days emanating from such a strange-looking object. The aroma of ripe pineapple conjures up memories of Asian salads, especially *rojak* and *gado-gado*—the Indonesian vegetable and chopped chili salad—or a simple pineapple and cucumber mix used in many households with soy sauce and chopped chili.

There are many varieties of pineapple, ranging from the large green Hawaiian variety to the dimunitive yellow–orange Asian one. The large green pineapple is the one commercially grown in the West, but the smaller and redder ones are much sweeter, especially if they are kept until just ripe. The flesh contains the enzyme bromeline which aids protein digestion but prevents gelatin from setting if the fruit is included in a jelly. It is acid-slippery and can be sharp to the tongue. Asians salt semi-ripe pineapples to reduce the acid content and remove its tartness, making it sweeter and pleasant to eat both fresh or when added to salads or curries. The Mauritian variety which Australians call "roughies" are my favorite and best used for juice or desserts. But in general, the tart semi-ripe pineapples are better in salads as long as the acidity is removed with a smear of salt; when dipped in a mixture of chili salt, the taste of these pineapples is amazing.

The pineapple is native to South America, but is so much a part of Asia that I grew up believing it was "our" fruit. If you look at it carefully, those little "flowers" on the sides are in fact made up of seedless fruits, which are the regular segments on the outside. The "eyes" or small round holes arranged in spiralling rows with short brown hairs around them are the remnants of flowers that we take out when we peel and segment the pineapple.

Pineapple curries are very familiar to Malaysians, Indonesians and Thais who cook it in fish and shrimp dishes. The laksas of Penang, tomyum soups of Thailand and Cambodian larb salads almost always contain a hint of pineapple.

Purchasing: When purchasing pineapples, always be guided by their scent and give a tug at the small outer leaves at the top. If these leaves detach easily, the pineapple is ripe. You can easily recognize an overripe pineapple from its aroma. Never keep a pineapple that is overripe.

Culinary uses: Ripe pineapple is a favorite table fruit and its juice can be strained and added to cocktails. It is the semi-ripe pineapple that is often used in cooking—half-ripened pineapple is ideal for making Thai, Malaysian or Vietnamese salads; just-ripened pineapple can be cooked with fish or shrimp to make a refreshing curry, which is uniquely Southeast Asian.

A speciality of the Nonyas in Malacca, pineapple jam is made into lovely thick tarts lightly spiced with cloves and brown sugar. These jam tarts made with rich butter pastry are a Portuguese or Dutch contribution to the cuisine. Frilled around the edges with a knob of jam in their centers, like a sunflower, they are served at weddings and during Chinese New Year.

Preparation: Some pineapples sold in Asian supermarkets have been ridge-cut in a decorative spiral that removes the "eyes." To do this yourself: lightly skin the pineapple, then working from top to bottom, cut V-shaped ridges diagonally down one row of "eyes." As you work, you will find yourself creating a spiral. The eyes are set in a diagonal pattern. Continue to cut a ridge to remove all the eyes. Repeat until the remaining rows are done and you will have a pineapple the shape of a sultan's turban. After peeling, slice the fruit along its length, cut the core out and discard. The rest can be sliced and served fresh or sliced into small wedges for salads.

Storing: Whole fruits do not need refrigeration when they are ripening. Store cut fruit dusted with a dash of salt in a closed plastic container in the vegetable crisper of the refrigerator.

Substitute: Use canned pineapple if fresh pineapple is not available, although the tartness and aroma will be missing.

Pomelo ～

The pomelo is a close relative of the grapefruit. Cultivated by the Chinese for many thousands of years, the fruit is now widely grown throughout Southeast Asia. It is the largest of all citrus fruits although much of its bulk is a thick spongy skin and the fruit inside is about the same size as a large grapefruit.

A subtle perfume of lime and roses mingled with orange blossom is revealed as the pomelo is peeled and the segments are separated. The pomelo is eaten alone as a table fruit or added to Thai and other Southeast Asian salads for its refreshing aroma and attractive pink or white pulp. Many varieties have been cultivated for their sweetness and color as the pomelo has long been prized as an offering to the gods in temples and domestic altars in Chinese homes. During Chinese New Year, the fruit is dressed in red collars inscribed with Chinese characters, and is one of the many offerings made to the gods.

The pomelo is nothing like the common yellow grapefruit in taste, but more like a sweeter ruby red grapefruit available in markets these days.

When I was a kid in Malaya, we would carefully peel the pomelo by slicing open the sides and one end then peeling the rind from the fruit in whole pieces that were all connected at one end. We would then wear the rind as a cap for a lovely citrus halo that lingered as a pleasant reminder of the fruit for the rest of the day. Dried pomelo rind was also added to hot or boiling water to perfume baths and hair shampoos.

Purchasing: Select fruits that are heavy for their size with unblemished skins and a sweet fragrance. Heavier pomelos are more juicy but there is no way to ascertain if they are sweet unless you open them up.

Culinary uses: Chinese cooks use the pomelo mainly in desserts. In China, the rind is parboiled and used as a vegetable, or cooked with citron rind into a healthy tea. In Southeast Asia, the pomelo pulp is crumbled and served with chilies and shrimp.

Preparation: To peel a pomelo, cut the rind into seven equal sections by slicing through it vertically with a sharp knife, being careful not to cut into the inner segments. Starting from the top of the cut, carefully peel away the rind to expose the segments. You will now have a citrus-like pomelo fully exposed like a peeled grapefruit. Remove the citrus membrane and separate the segments. To make a salad, simply peel the segments and crumble the pulp and combine it with other fruits and vegetables, tossing with a finely balanced dressing (see Fresh Tuna with Citrus, Starfruit and Jicama—page 127).

Storing: Store unopened pomelos at room temperature for up to 1–2 weeks. Once peeled, the segments should be refrigerated sealed in a container or wrapped in plastic wrap.

Substitute: Ruby grapefruit pulp with added sugar.

Starfruit ~ carambola

Biting into a juicy and citrusy piece of starfruit is like sipping a very light lemonade. The fruit can be used to make amazing salads because of its crisp texture and is too often overlooked by people who otherwise treasure the flavors and aromas of Asia.

To discover this interesting fruit, look for the elongated yellow-green cylinders up to five inches (13 cm) in length with five prominent ridges along its length which yield a star-shaped cross-section when cut. The starfruit has a waxy green skin which turns yellow as it ripens. There are two main types of starfruit grown in Asia. The tiny variety called *belimbing* is about the thickness and length of a finger, and is very sour and commonly used to flavor fish and shrimp dishes. The larger variety shown in these photos is eaten as a table fruit or added to light salads, especially in Malaysia.

Starfruit does not have an overpowering flavor, but a subtle tart sweetness that works well in juices. It has a very light aroma of guava that is lost if it is mixed with ripening pineapple and lime or lemon. A native of Sri Lanka, starfruit has been cultivated in Southeast Asia for several centuries. Starfruit should be eaten while still firm for it quickly loses its flavors once it softens.

Purchasing: Look for unblemished firm and shiny, even-colored fruits with green edges along the ridges. Avoid fruits with brown, shriveled ribs.

Culinary uses: Starfruit is enjoyed as a dessert fruit, used to make juice or in salads, with star-shaped slices scattered beautifully among the other fruit and vegetable pieces. The star-shaped slices also make a decorative garnish. Starfruit juice is best served with a dash of fresh lime juice. Rich in vitamin C and A, it is believed to be a good cure for hangovers.

Preparation: Rinse the fruit well and shave off the tops and edges of the ridges, then use as instructed in the recipe.

Storing: Store unripe green starfruit at room temperature, turning often, until they ripen and the skins turn yellow. Ripe starfruit can be stored at room temperature for 2–3 days or refrigerated wrapped in a plastic bag for up to one week. Once cut, sprinkle with a little salt to prevent it from darkening.

Substitute: Firm kiwi fruit may be substituted.

Tamarind ～

The fruity aroma of this raisin-like fruit contains hints of dates, sour-sweet guava and apricots. Tamarind is used in sauces rather than as a table fruit. Lip-puckering green tamarind is used to sour soups, while the mature full-bodied ripe fruit lends a balance to curries, laksa and salads, and is irreplaceable with any other souring agent.

The name tamarind literally means "Indian dates" (*tamar Inde*) although there is no relation between the two fruits, other than the aroma. In Malaysia, tamarind is known simply as *asam*, which means acidic or sour. The tamarind fruit grows in pods. When unripe, the pods are green but as they mature, they became brittle and brown and contain a brown–golden flesh with large seeds and fibers. The pods grow on tall spreading trees with small feathery leaves that are commonly seen along country roads all over Southeast Asia and along the coast of northern Queensland, where they are much prized for the cool shade they provide.

There are two varieties of tamarind fruit; one is tart while the other is sour-sweet. In Thailand and the Philippines, pods of the tart variety are eaten fresh with salt and chili or a dip, or chopped and added to a tamarind chili sauce. They are also pickled and eaten as snacks. The pulp is often puréed and sold in a block, in jars or bottles. This is used as a souring agent for soups, curries, stews, salads, dressings and sauces. The tart tamarind purée is also used with salt as a cleaning agent to polish brass and copper. As a child, my favorite chore was to polish brass trays with this mixture. The end result was very satisfying—the pinkish sheen of the brass was restored when it dried.

The sweet tamarind is used to make desserts and a special candy, where the seeds and pulp are rolled in chili and sugar and then dried. In many Asian countries, tamarind is cooked with sugar to make cordials and sauces.

Purchasing: Tamarind is available in Mexican grocery stores and Asian markets as well as some health food stores. Choose dried tamarind blocks by their colors. Gold-colored blocks are best as they are softer and reconstitute more quickly, while darker blocks tend to be drier. Look for blocks that do not have seeds or skins as they are easier to work with. Tamarind purée comes in jars and is very convenient but may have been salted or sweetened and this will affect the taste of your dish. Always taste the tamarind before deciding how much to use. Nowadays, premixed, ready-to-use tamarind juice is also available in the market, but it is not as fresh as making your own.

Culinary uses: Usually a juice or purée is first obtained from the tart tamarind fruit and this is then used in cooking—as a souring agent for curries, chutneys, sauces and some desserts and drinks. Young feathery leaves and flowers can be eaten fresh in salads with chili dips. Toss them with garlic, coconut milk, a pinch of turmeric powder and shrimp for an interesting stir-fry, or add them to a curry with some green tamarind pods and chili and serve with a bowl of rice.

Preparation: To make tamarind juice, break off a chunk of the pulp from the dried tamarind block and mix it with some warm water (more water for a thin purée, less for something thicker). Mash the mixture with your fingers to break up the pulp until it is fully dissolved in the water to form a thick, reddish brown liquid or paste. Strain the mixture through a fine sieve to obtain the juice. Discard the fibrous husks and seeds. How much pulp and water to use depends on whether there are seeds and the amount of pulp and how sour it is, so taste it first before using. Always begin with about 1 tablespoon of pulp to $1/4$ cup (60 ml) of water and then add more water or pulp as needed.

Storing: Tamarind blocks do not need refrigeration. They will keep indefinitely wrapped in plastic wrap and stored in an airtight container in a cool place. Premixed tamarind juice must be refrigerated and keeps for only a couple of weeks.

Substitute: Substitute 2 dates puréed with 2 tablespoon fresh lime juice for 1 tablespoon of tamarind juice.

Two 6-oz (185-g) cans tuna in water
1 cup (250 ml) oil, for shallow-frying
1 cup (200 g) green mango or green apple
    shreds, mixed with 2 tablespoons fresh lime
    juice
1 cup (250 g) green papaya strips
$^1/_2$ onion, thinly sliced
$^1/_2$ ginger flower, finely chopped (optional)
$^1/_2$ cup (60 g) dry-roasted whole cashew nuts
$^1/_4$ cup (10 g) chopped coriander leaves
    (cilantro)
1 green onion, chopped

DRESSING
4 tablespoons sugar
$^1/_2$ cup (125 ml) vinegar
$^1/_2$ teaspoon fish sauce, or to taste
$^1/_2$ tablespoon dried chili flakes, to taste
Fresh juice of $^1/_2$ lemon
Salt, to taste

Tuna salad with green mango and papaya

I have adapted this Thai salad with the addition of the exotic rose and peach aromas of ginger flower—a very fragrant flower used for centuries in the native cuisines of the region. Nonya kitchens have always made a place for this magical flower, shredded into aromatic strips. Canned tuna mashed and crispy-fried is tossed with green mango, paw paw and cashews and infused with the refreshing aromas of ginger flower and lime juice to create this amazing salad.

Drain the tuna well and squeeze out all the liquid, then mash the tuna in a mortar or food processor until all the fibers are separated.

Heat the oil in a wok until smoking and drop the tuna in small batches of 3 tablespoons at a time, into the hot oil, breaking it up into pieces. Fry for about 1 minute until fluffy. Using a fine wire-meshed sieve, gather the tuna together to form clumps and remove them from the hot oil, then drain on paper towels. Set aside.

In a small bowl, combine the Dressing ingredients and mix until the sugar is dissolved. Place all the other ingredients in a large salad bowl, add the tuna floss, pour over the Dressing and toss thoroughly until well blended. Serve immediately.

SERVES: *4*   **PREPARATION TIME:** *30 mins*   **COOKING TIME:** *5 mins*

COOKING WITH AROMATIC ASIAN FRUITS

Arugula salad with tangy citrus dressing

This is a salad that can be easily adapted to your liking. Arugula, baby spinach and lettuce all go well with this tasty orange dressing. The salad can also be served with grilled shrimp or roast pork in place of the roast duck. For a pure vegetarian version, omit the meat.

2–3 cups (50–75 g) fresh arugula (rocket) leaves, rinsed and dried
1 bell pepper, cored, deseeded and diced
1 roast duck breast, deboned and sliced

TANGY CITRUS DRESSING
2 tablespoons olive oil
$1/2$ cup (125 ml) fresh orange juice
$1/4$ cup (60 ml) fresh lime juice
2 tablespoons balsamic vinegar
2 bay leaves
1 tablespoon hoisin sauce
1 teaspoon sugar, or to taste
$1/2$ teaspoon salt, or to taste
Pinch of freshly ground black pepper

Combine the Tangy Citrus Dressing ingredients in a bowl and beat well with a fork until blended, then allow to infuse for 3–4 hours. As the olive oil and orange juice will separate on standing, the dressing must be beaten again before using.

Combine all the other ingredients in a salad bowl, drizzle the Tangy Citrus Orange Dressing over them and toss thoroughly until well blended. Alternatively arrange the salad ingredients on individual serving plates, top with the roast duck pieces and serve (as shown in the photo) with a bowl of the Citrus Orange Dressing on the side.

SERVES: 2-4   PREPARATION TIME: *20 mins + time to infuse*

Tomato rasam

Rasam, a peppery and watery tamarind soup, has been eaten for centuries in Indian vegetarian homes as a digestive food, at the end of a rice and dry curry meal. It was later transformed into the colonial *mulligatawny* soup, a name deriving from a corruption of the Tamil words *mulahu* (pepper) and *thanni* (water). This dish was created by the British Raj as a substantial soup course served either as an appetizer or a main meal with chicken, stock and cream.

1 teaspoon cumin seeds, dry-roasted
10 white peppercorns
1 tablespoon coriander seeds, dry-roasted
3 cloves garlic, peeled
1 tablespoon oil
4 cups (1 liter) Vegetable Stock (page 245)
1 tablespoon tamarind pulp, mashed with $1/2$ cup (125 ml) Vegetable Stock or water and strained to obtain juice
2 ripe tomatoes, chopped
$1/2$ teaspoon ground turmeric
1 tablespoon oil
5 Asian shallots, diced
1 dried red finger-length chili pepper, stem discarded, halved
1 sprig fresh curry leaves
Salt, to taste

SERVES: 4   PREPARATION TIME: *15 mins*
COOKING TIME: *45 mins*

Prepare the Vegetable Stock by following the recipe on page 245.

Grind the cumin, peppercorns and coriander seeds to a powder in a mortar or spice grinder, then add the garlic and grind to a smooth paste. Heat the oil in a heavy skillet and sauté the ground spices over medium heat until fragrant, 1–2 minutes. Add the Vegetable Stock, tamarind juice and tomato and bring to a boil. Stir in the turmeric and simmer uncovered for about 20 minutes until the tomato is soft.

In another pan, heat the oil and sauté the sliced shallot, dried chili and curry leaves over medium heat for 1–2 minutes. Pour in the simmering stock mixture and bring to a boil. Season with salt to taste and remove from the heat. Process the soup in a food processor to a smooth purée. Transfer to a serving bowl and serve with steamed rice.

Note: If preferred, use chicken stock in place of the Vegetable Stock and add some chicken meat. If tamarind pulp is not available, substitute the fresh juice of 1 lime and add it just before serving.

2 cakes (each 5 oz/150 g) pressed firm
  tofu, cubed and deep-fried
2 Chinese fried bread sticks (yu tiao, see
  note), sliced or 1 cup (60 g) croutons
1 cucumber, halved lengthwise and thinly
  sliced
1 small jicama, peeled and sliced into thin
  wedges
1 ripe fresh pineapple, peeled, cored and
  sliced into chunks
1 unripe green mango, peeled, pitted and
  sliced
2 medium starfruits, sliced
1 tablespoon roasted sesame seeds
2 tablespoons crushed roasted peanuts or
  cashew nuts
Grated lime rind, to garnish (optional)

SPICY SWEET ROJAK DRESSING
1 1/2 tablespoons black sweet shrimp paste
  (hae koh)
2 tablespoons boiling water
2–3 tablespoons sugar
2 teaspoons Sambal Oelek Chili Paste
  (page 240) or other sweet chili paste
1 tablespoon oyster sauce
Fresh juice of 1 lime
1/4 teaspoon salt, or to taste

Crisp *rojak* salad with spicy sweet dressing

A ubiquitous classic, this tossed crisp salad known as *rojak* is a tumbled blend of bold aromas—the glistening black molasses-like shrimp dressing and roasted peanuts overpower everything else with their strong aromas. But take a bite and you will release the crisp scented flavors of green mango, ripe sweet pineapple and fresh jicama chunks that give texture to this salad, and a special sweet, tart and pungent taste that no other Asian salad provides. So prepare to be seduced by the most exciting salad imaginable as you crunch each mouthful, evoking memories of good food and colorful markets in Asia. This cold dish is eaten as a snack or appetizer in Malaysia and Singapore, and needs no accompaniments.

Prepare the Sambal Oelek Chili Paste by following the recipe on page 240.

Prepare the Dressing first by adding the boiling water to the black sweet shrimp paste in a bowl and mixing well. Add the sugar and stir until the sugar is dissolved, then stir in all the other ingredients, adjusting the taste.

Place all the salad ingredients in a large bowl, drizzle the Spicy Sweet Rojak Dressing over them and toss thoroughly until the salad is well coated with the sauce. Transfer to individual serving plates, sprinkle with the sesame seeds, ground peanuts or cashews, and serve immediately garnished with grated lime rind.

Note: Chinese fried bread sticks (*yu tiao*) are dough strips that are deep-fried into puffy, crisp sticks. The Chinese usually have them with coffee or congee for breakfast. They can be found fresh in Chinese food stores and well-stocked Asian supermarkets. If unavailable, substitute crisp bread croutons.

SERVES: *6*   **PREPARATION TIME:** *30 mins*

2 cups (400 g) diced fresh pineapple
$^1/_2$ cup (100 g) diced fresh dragon fruit or
   mango (optional)
$^1/_2$ cup (100 g) diced fresh firm kiwi fruit or
   starfruit (optional)
1–2 red finger-length chili peppers,
   deseeded and chopped
1 small onion, chopped
3 tablespoons chopped fresh mint
Grated rind of 1 lime
3 tablespoons fresh lime juice
2 teaspoons sweet bottled chili sauce or
   paste
Salt and sugar, to taste

Pineapple lime salsa with mint

This is a very piquant salsa that can be served on its own, or with fish, or as a topping for hamburgers.

Combine all the ingredients in a large bowl and mix well. Set aside for 30 minutes to allow the flavors to blend, then chill in the refrigerator until ready to serve.

SERVES: *4*   PREPARATION TIME: *15 mins + 30 mins to infuse*

2 semi-ripe mangoes, peeled and seed
removed, then sliced
1/2 teaspoon salt
6 ripe plums (not blood plums), peeled,
pitted and cubed
1 onion, halved and thinly sliced (optional)

PISTACHIO GINGER DRESSING
4 cloves garlic, chopped
2–4 red finger-length chili peppers,
deseeded and chopped
Juice of 2 limes
2 teaspoons ginger juice (pressed from
grated fresh ginger)
1 teaspoon sugar
1/2 teaspoon salt
1/2 teaspoon freshly ground black pepper
1/2 cup (60 g) chopped roasted pistachios

Mango plum salad with pistachio ginger dressing

The sweet and sour perfume from the plums and mangoes combined with the luring aroma of ginger makes a light and summery foil for many of the hot and spicy flavors that confront you in tropical Asian foods. This salad is best eaten with roast chicken or fried tofu, and it can also be chopped into a chutney or salsa and served with curries.

Place the mango slices in a bowl, sprinkle them with the salt and rub it into the mango slices to draw out some of the water. Drain the mango slices well and then pat dry with paper towels.

Combine the Pistachio Ginger Dressing ingredients in a bowl and mix until the sugar is dissolved, adjusting the seasonings. Mix the fruits and onion together in another bowl. Drizzle the Dressing over them and toss thoroughly. Serve chilled.

MAKES: *about 2 cups*   **PREPARATION TIME:** *15 mins*

Crunchy ikan bilis with aromatic sambal

Baby anchovies or ikan bilis fished along the coasts of Southeast Asia are dazzling silver flakes when dried on mats in the sun. They are used not only in sambals but also in cruncy nibbles. Here the assertive flavors of chili, lemongrass and tamarind in the dip create a seductive snack.

2 cups (4 oz/125 g) dried baby anchovies or whitebaits, heads and intestines removed, rinsed, then drained well
Oil, for frying

AROMATIC SAMBAL
3 tablespoons oil
4 tablespoons Chili Jam (page 244)
4 tablespoons Aromatic Nonya Spice Paste (page 241)
6 candlenuts or macadamia nuts, crushed or ground
4 teaspoons dried shrimp, dry-roasted and ground in a blender or mortar
1 tablespoon tamarind pulp, mashed with $^1/_2$ cup (125 ml) water and strained to obtain juice
2 teaspoons tomato ketchup
2 teaspoons fresh lime juice
2 teaspoons sugar, or to taste
$^1/_2$ teaspoon salt, or to taste
$^1/_2$ cup (125 ml) coconut cream

Prepare the Aromatic Nonya Spice Paste and Chili Jam by following the recipes on pages 241 and 244.

Remove and discard the heads and intestines from the anchovies, then rinse well and pat dry with paper towels. Heat the oil in a wok until hot and fry the anchovies or whitebaits over medium heat until golden brown and crispy, 2–3 minutes. Remove from the heat and drain on paper towels. Keep warm.

To make the Aromatic Sambal, heat the oil in a skillet and sauté the Chili Jam, Aromatic Nonya Spice Paste and crushed candlenut or macadamia nut over medium–low heat for 3–5 minutes until fragrant, making sure the mixture does not burn. Add the dried shrimp, tamarind juice and tomato ketchup and cook for about 5 minutes. Season with the lime juice, sugar and salt to taste and cook for 1 more minute. Stir in the coconut cream, mix well and remove from the heat. Transfer the Sambal to a serving bowl. Serve the fried anchovies or whitebaits with the bowl of Sambal on the side.

SERVES: *4*   PREPARATION TIME: *20 mins*   COOKING TIME: *15 mins*

Fragrant pandanus coconut rice ~ *Nasi lemak*

Creamy and subtle coconut is cooked into my favorite rice dish, *nasi lemak* in Malay, which means rich and creamy rice—which is exactly what it is! When fresh pandanus leaf is added, the special fragrance created is unmatched. Traditionally this rice is served with a hot and spicy shrimp or fish sambal and a side dish of cucumber in a banana leaf packet, offering the diner a perfumed surprise when the parcel is unpacked.

2 cups (400 g) uncooked jasmine rice
2 pandanus leaves, tied into a knot, or 2 drops of pandanus essence
3 cups (750 ml) thick coconut milk
1 cup (250 ml) water
1 onion, finely chopped
2 teaspoons salt, or to taste

Place the rice in a container and wash it in a couple of changes of water until the water runs clear, then transfer to a microwave-proof dish.

Add all the other ingredients to the rice and mix well, then cook uncovered in the microwave oven for 20 minutes on high. Alternatively combine all the ingredients in a rice cooker and cook as you would normal rice. Fluff the rice with a fork before serving.

MAKES: *4 cups (400 g)*   PREPARATION TIME: *15 mins*
COOKING TIME: *20 mins*

2 onions
1 cup (125 g) freshly grated coconut or dried
   unsweetened (desiccated) coconut mixed
   with 2 tablespoons coconut cream
1 tablespoon ground red pepper
1–2 tablespoons paprika
Fresh juice of 1 lime
2 teaspoons ground southern Thai dried fish,
   Maldive dried fish or dried shrimp
3 curry leaves or bay leaves, crushed
$1/2$ teaspoon salt, or to taste
$1/2$ teaspoon ground white pepper, or to taste
Curry leaf shreds, to garnish

Coconut sambal with dried fish and onion

A Sri Lankan sambal taught to me by Herbert Fernando has the scent of coconut, lime and pandanus. What a priceless transformation when lime juice, onions, chili and coconut are combined to produce a blended perfume of hot, sour and peppery chili flavors.

Peel the onions and plunge them into boiling water for 1 minute to take away the bitterness, then drain well and slice them into pieces.

Coarsely grind the onion pieces in a mortar or food processor, gradually adding the grated coconut along with the red pepper and paprika. Add the lime juice and ground fish or dried shrimp and continue processing. Do not process until too fine; the dish should have a rough texture.

Finally stir in the crushed curry leaves or bay leaves, and season with the salt and pepper to taste. Transfer to a serving bowl and serve immediately, garnished with curry leaf shreds. This sambal can be eaten as a sandwich bread filling or with hot steamed rice.

Store the leftover sambal in an airtight container in the refrigerator for up to 3–4 days. Stored sambal can be refreshed by adding more lime juice to it.

SERVES: *4*   PREPARATION TIME: *20 mins*

1 tablespoon oil
2 tablespoons Sambal Oelek Chili Paste
 (page 240), mixed with 1 tablespoon
 Lemongrass Paste (page 242)
1 teaspoon dried shrimp paste, dry-roasted
 and crumbled
2 cups (500 ml) Chicken Stock (page 245)
2 tablespoons tamarind pulp, mixed with
 1 cup (250 ml) hot water, then mashed
 and strained to obtain juice
2 cups (500 g) pumpkin or butternut
 squash cubes
1 carrot, peeled and cubed the same size
 as the pumpkin or squash
1 bell pepper, cored, deseeded and cubed
 the same size as the other ingredients
2 tablespoons fish sauce
1 teaspoon sugar, or to taste (optional)
Fresh juice of 2 limes
$1/3$ cup (100 ml) fresh orange juice
Salt and ground white pepper, to taste
Coriander leaves (cilantro), to garnish

Pumpkin soup with citrus and lemongrass

This colorful nutty vegetarian soup has fresh lemongrass and a spike of ginger and chili pepper to tickle your olfactory senses. It is a festive curry that is pleasing to the eye, especially when it is dressed up with edible greens.

Prepare the Sambal Oelek Chili Paste, Lemongrass Paste and Chicken Stock by following the recipes on pages 240, 242 and 245.

Heat the oil in a wok or large saucepan and stir-fry the Sambal Oelek mixture and shrimp paste over medium heat until fragrant, 1–2 minutes. Stir in the Chicken Stock and tamarind juice and simmer covered over medium–low heat for about 5 minutes.

Add the pumpkin and carrot cubes, and continue to simmer covered for 15 minutes until they are tender. Stir in the bell pepper and add the fish sauce, lime and orange juice and sugar (if using) to taste, then cover and simmer for 3 more minutes. Season with salt and pepper and remove from the heat. Ladle into individual serving bowls and serve hot, garnished with coriander sprigs.

Note: For a creamy version, cool and purée the cooked soup in a food processor, then strain and warm through over low heat, garnish and serve.

SERVES: *4–6*   PREPARATION TIME: *10 mins + time to prepare pastes and Chicken Stock*
COOKING TIME: *20 mins*

Pineapple fish soup with tamarind and tomatoes

This popular Cambodian soup is as fragrant as it is soursweet and flavorsome. In this version I add the layers of citrusy lemongrass and peppery galangal in my Lemongrass Paste. When the Lemongrass Paste is added to the pineapple and tomato, it rounds the flavors and breathes fruity aromas into the soup. It should be served immediately as cooked pineapple loses its flavor when it is left to stand.

1 tablespoon oil
2 cloves garlic, finely chopped
1 Asian shallot, finely chopped
1 tablespoon Lemongrass Paste (page 242)
1 lb (500 g) white fish fillets, sliced into chunks
1 teaspoon fish sauce
1 cup (100 g) sliced fresh pineapple
2 ripe tomatoes, quartered
1 cake (5 oz/150 g) pressed tofu, diced
1 cup (100 g) chopped waterlily or choy sum stems
2 red finger-length chili peppers, deseeded and finely sliced
1 tablespoon sugar
1 tablespoon soy sauce
2 tablespoons fish sauce
1 tablespoon chopped garlic, crispy fried (see note)
1 tablespoon chopped onion, crispy fried (see note)
$1/4$ cup (10 g) chopped fresh Vietnamese mint or sawtooth coriander, to garnish

SOUP
4 cups (1 liter) Fish Stock (page 245) or water
2 tablespoons tamarind pulp, mashed with 1 cup (250 ml) warm water and strained to obtain juice
3 stalks lemongrass, thick bottom part only, outer layers discarded, inner part bruised
1 green onion, white part chopped, green part sliced for garnish

Prepare the Lemongrass Paste and Fish Stock by following the recipes on pages 242 and 245.

Heat the oil in a wok and stir-fry the garlic, shallot and Lemongrass Paste over medium heat until fragrant, about 2 minutes. Add the fish and stir-fry for 1–2 minutes to firm it. Season with the fish sauce and remove from the heat. Set aside.

Bring the Soup ingredients to a gradual boil in a pot and simmer covered over medium heat for at least 10 minutes. Add the stir-fried fish, pineapple, tomatoes, tofu and waterlily or choy sum stems, and continue to simmer for 3–4 more minutes. Stir in the chili pepper and season with the sugar, soy sauce and fish sauce, adjusting the seasonings. Remove from the heat and keep warm. Ladle into individual serving bowls, sprinkle with crispy fried garlic and onion and serve immediately, garnished with Vietnamese mint or sawtooth coriander.

Note: To prepare crispy fried garlic or onion, place the chopped garlic or onion in a small dish, cover with oil and microwave on high for 1–2 minutes, checking after 1 minute to make sure it is not burning. Remove and drain on paper towels, then use as directed.

SERVES: *6*   **PREPARATION TIME:** *20 mins*   **COOKING TIME:** *20 mins*

3 cloves garlic, peeled
1 in (3 cm) fresh ginger, peeled and sliced
2 tablespoons oil
1 onion, finely chopped
1 stalk curry leaves, plucked and minced
2 lbs (1 kg) boneless chicken thigh fillets,
    sliced into bite-sized pieces
2 cups (500 ml) thick coconut milk
6–8 whole curry leaves
1 tablespoon sugar (optional)
1 teaspoon salt, or to taste
$\frac{1}{2}$ teaspoon ground white pepper
Fresh juice of 1 lime

FRIED ONION RINGS
2 tablespoons ghee or butter
2 small onions, thinly sliced into rings

AMAH'S CURRY POWDER
3 tablespoons coriander seeds, dry-roasted
    and ground
1 tablespoon cumin seeds, dry-roasted and
    ground
1 tablespoon ground red pepper
2 teaspoons ground turmeric
2 teaspoons ground white pepper
1 teaspoon ground cassia or cinnamon

Amah's chicken curry

My Amah or nanny had the uncanny ability to tease the most tantalizing aromas from a handful of garlic gently sautéed with golden caramelized onions. She would then brown the chicken in this, smoother it with perfumed herbs and freshly dry-roasted ground coriander and cumin to produce this unforgettable dish, which combines fragrances reminiscent of anise, parsley and lemon.

Prepare the Fried Onion Rings first by heating the ghee in a skillet and sautéing the onion rings over medium heat until golden and crisp, 2–3 minutes. Remove the onions and drain on paper towels.

Grind the garlic and ginger to a smooth paste in a mortar.

Heat the oil in a wok and stir-fry the ground paste and chopped onion until fragrant, 2–3 minutes. Add the minced curry leaf and stir-fry for 1 more minute. Increase the heat to high, add the chicken pieces and stir-fry for 2–3 minutes until the meat changes color. Add the Amah's Curry Powder ingredients and stir-fry until well combined. Pour in 1 cup of the coconut milk, cover and simmer for 3–5 minutes.

Stir in the remaining coconut milk, reduce the heat to low and simmer uncovered until the curry has thickened, 3–5 minutes. Add the whole curry leaves and season with the sugar (if using), salt and pepper, stirring well to combine. Taste and adjust the seasonings as desired and remove from the heat. Transfer to a serving bowl, top with the Fried Onion Rings and drizzle the lime juice over the top. Serve immediately with steamed rice.

SERVES: *6-8*   **PREPARATION TIME:** *30 mins*   **COOKING TIME:** *20 mins*

20 chicken wings, mid-portion only
1 cup (125 g) rice flour or crushed corn flakes
1 pandanus leaf, torn lengthwise into long
  strips (optional)

PLUM SAUCE MARINADE
2 tablespoons bottled sweet chili sauce
4 tablespoons chinese plum sauce
1 tablespoon black soy sauce
1 tablespoon honey
2 tablespoons fresh lime juice
1 teaspoon salt
$1/2$ teaspoon ground white pepper

TANGY LIME GINGER DIP
Fresh juice of 2 limes
2 teaspoons sugar
1 teaspoon Sambal Oelek Chili Paste
  (page 240) or other sweet chili paste
2 teaspoons ginger juice (pressed from grated
  fresh ginger)

Plum sauce chicken wings baked in a flash

This is an interactive recipe where you can have fun. If some of the sauces are unavailable, clean out your refrigerator and create your own sensual combination by adding a cocktail of sauces for fragrance and taste. The wings make a great finger food when served with a delicate dipping sauce. For a really fragrant alternative, tie strips of pandanus leaf around the chicken wings; the leaf will brown but the flavor remains.

Prepare the Sambal Oelek Chili Paste by following the recipe on page 240.

Combine the Marinade ingredients in a large bowl and mix well. Add the chicken wings and mix until well coated. Allow to marinate for at least 2 hours.

Preheat the oven to 350°F (170°C).

Roll the marinated wings in the rice flour or corn flakes to coat on all sides, shaking off the excess flour or flakes. Tie a pandanus leaf strip around each coated wing (if using). Place the chicken wings on a large greased baking pan and bake in the oven for 15 minutes, then turn over and bake for another 10 minutes until done. If preferred, grill the chicken wings on a preheated pan grill or under a broiler for 5–10 minutes on each side, checking often to make sure the chicken does not burn.

Combine the Tangy Lime Ginger Dip ingredients in a serving bowl and mix well. Arrange the baked chicken wings on a serving platter and serve with the dip on the side.

MAKES: *20*   **PREPARATION TIME:** *20 mins*   **COOKING TIME:** *25 mins*

1¹/₂ lbs (700 g) pork shoulder, fat trimmed,
   sliced into 2-in (5-cm) long strips
Lime wedges, to serve
1 portion Pineapple Lime Salsa with Mint
   (page 100), to serve

MARINADE
4 cloves garlic, crushed to a paste
¹/₂ teaspoon freshly ground black pepper
1 teaspoon ground cumin
1 in (2 cm) fresh galangal root, peeled and
   crushed to make 1 teaspoon paste
1 tablespoon golden syrup
1 tablespoon ground red pepper
1 tablespoon chopped fresh mint leaves
2 tablespoons olive oil
Salt and ground white pepper, to taste

Grilled pork strips with pineapple lime salsa

The unusual use of galangal's fresh clean aromas not only perfumes this dish but also tenderizes the pork strips. The strips can also be wrapped in aluminum before grilling them to keep the meat moist and tender.

Prepare the Pineapple Lime Salsa with Mint by following the recipe on page 100.

Combine the Marinade ingredients in a large bowl and mix well. Place the pork strips in the Marinade and mix well, rubbing the Marinade into the pork strips with your fingers. Cover and refrigerate for 4 hours, then drain and reserve the Marinade.

Grill the marinated pork strips on a preheated pan grill, under a broiler or over a charcoal fire, basting with the reserved Marinade, until cooked, 3–4 minutes. Arrange the grilled pork on a platter and serve with lime wedges and the Pineapple Lime Salsa with Mint on the side.

SERVES: *4*   **PREPARATION TIME:** *20 mins + 4 hours to marinate*   **COOKING TIME:** *20 mins*

COOKING WITH AROMATIC ASIAN FRUITS

1 lb (500 g) fresh squid
Fresh juice of 1 lime
3/4 cup (80 g) potato flour
1 tablespoon ground white pepper
1 tablespoon salt
1/2 teaspoon ground red pepper
Oil, for deep-frying
Extra salt and ground white pepper, to
    sprinkle on top
Lemon halves, to serve

LEMON MANGO SAUCE
1 1/2 cups (150 g) mashed fresh mango flesh
1 tablespoon fresh lemon juice
2 teaspoons sugar, or to taste
1 teaspoon chopped or grated lemon rind
Sliced lemongrass rings to garnish

Salt and pepper squid with lemon mango sauce

The sweetness of squid balanced with salt and pepper and layered with the aroma of a crisp flour coating on the seafood is of Portuguese origin, perfected over the centuries. The potato flour crisps the squid most attractively, imparting a buttery aroma. Enjoy the textural crunch and sizzling aromas!

Rinse the squids, pulling the heads and attached intestines from the tubelike bodies. Discard the heads but retain the tentacles, and remove the beak from the mouth. Clean the body tubes, removing and discarding the long, thin cartilage. Halve each tube lengthwise and rinse the inside well. Using a sharp knife, score the flesh by making diagonal criss-cross slits across the surface, then slice the tubes into bite-sized pieces. Combine the lime juice with water in a large bowl and wash the squid pieces in it, then dry them thoroughly with paper towels.

Combine the potato flour with the pepper, salt and ground red pepper in a plate or shallow bowl and mix well. Dredge the squid pieces with this mixture.

Heat the oil in a wok until hot—the oil is ready when a wooden chopstick dipped in it bubbles. In small batches of a few at a time, deep-fry the squid pieces until crisp, about 1 minute. Remove from the heat and drain on paper towels. Lightly sprinkle the hot squid pieces with salt and pepper, if desired.

Combine the Lemon Mango Sauce ingredients, except the lemongrass, in a serving bowl and mix well, then sprinkle the lemongrass slices and chopped or grated lime rind on top. Arrange the deep-fried squid pieces on a serving platter and serve immediately with lemon halves and the bowl of Lemon Mango Sauce on the side.

SERVES: *4*   PREPARATION TIME: *40 mins*   COOKING TIME: *10 mins*

1¹/₂ lbs (700 g) fresh jumbo shrimp, peeled
   and deveined
1 tablespoon rice flour, for dusting
Skewers
1 ripe pineapple, peeled, cored and sliced
1 tablespoon melted butter
Sprigs of fresh Thai basil leaves, to garnish

TAMARIND RICE WINE MARINADE
¹/₄ cup (60 ml) rice wine
¹/₄ cup (60 ml) tamarind juice (made from
   2 tablespoons tamarind pulp mashed with
   ¹/₂ cup [125 ml] hot water and strained to
   obtain juice)
1 tablespoon fish sauce
2 teaspoons Chinese black vinegar
1 teaspoon sugar

GARLIC OIL
3 cloves garlic, minced
1 tablespoon oil

Grilled tamarind shrimp with pineapple

The rich buttery shrimp and ripe pineapple on the barbecue—enhanced with the earthy tang of rice wine, Chinese vinegar and sweet tamarind—create an amazing symphony of aromas and flavors in this quick-cooked dish from Macau.

Combine the Tamarind Rice Wine Marinade ingredients in a large bowl and mix well. Add the shrimp and mix until well coated. Allow to marinate for at least 1 hour.

Prepare the Garlic Oil by following the method described on page 56.

Place the rice flour in a shallow bowl. Roll the marinated shrimp in the rice flour to lightly coat them, then dip them in the Marinade again to ensure the flavors penetrate. Thread 3 coated shrimp onto each skewer.

Grill the skewers on a preheated pan grill or under a broiler until just cooked, turning often and brushing with the Garlic Oil a couple of times to keep the shrimp moist. Do not grill the shrimp for more than 4 minutes in total. Remove from the heat.

Brush the pineapple slices with the melted butter and grill for about 1 minute on each side. Remove from the heat and arrange in individual serving bowls. Top the pineapple slices with the grilled shrimp, garnish with basil sprigs and serve immediately with Mint Pachidi Chutney (page 243) or Green Chili Coriander Butter (page 59) if desired.

SERVES: *4–6*   **PREPARATION TIME:** *20 mins*   **COOKING TIME:** *15 mins*

1 whole fresh fish (about 1⅓ lbs/600 g)—sea bream, perch or snapper
1 large sheet banana leaf, rinsed in boiling water to soften (or aluminum foil), for wrapping

GINGER SOY MARINADE
1 tablespoon fresh ginger juice (pressed from grated fresh ginger)
2 tablespoons soy sauce
1 teaspoon ground white pepper
1 teaspoon fresh lime juice

SWEET TAMARIND DIPPING SAUCE
1 tablespoon tamarind pulp, mashed with ¼ cup (60 ml) water and strained to obtain juice
½ teaspoon Chili Jam (page 244)
1 tablespoon fish sauce
1 tablespoon soy sauce
2 tablespoons shaved palm sugar or dark brown sugar
1 in (2 cm) fresh ginger, peeled and sliced into thin strips

Baked ginger soy fish with sweet tamarind dip

The tang of the sea on freshly caught fish cooked with the delicate fragrance of ginger and soy. Chili Jam, tamarind and palm sugar combine beautifully with fresh ginger to make an exotic dip that complements the fish.

Prepare the Chili Jam by following the recipe on page 244.

Scale, gut and clean the fish well, then make several shallow diagonal cuts on each side. Pat the fish dry with paper towels. Combine the Ginger Soy Marinade ingredients in a bowl and mix well. Brush the entire fish, inside and outside, with the Marinade, and allow to marinate for at least 1 hour.

Place the marinated fish in the center of the banana leaf sheet, then pour the Marinade over the fish and wrap it by folding the sides and ends of the leaf to the center, overlapping them and enclosing the fish. Then fasten with toothpicks, forming a neat package. Use aluminum foil if a banana leaf is not available. Place the wrapped fish in a baking dish.

Preheat the oven to 350°F (170°C) and bake the fish for 10 minutes until cooked.

Combine the Sweet Tamarind Dipping Sauce ingredients in a bowl and mix until the sugar is dissolved. Place the package of fish on a serving platter, unwrap and serve hot with the Sweet Tamarind Dipping Sauce on the side. Invite your guests to drizzle the sauce over the fish before eating it.

SERVES: *4-6*   **PREPARATION TIME:** *30 mins*   **COOKING TIME:** *20 mins*

COOKING WITH AROMATIC ASIAN FRUITS

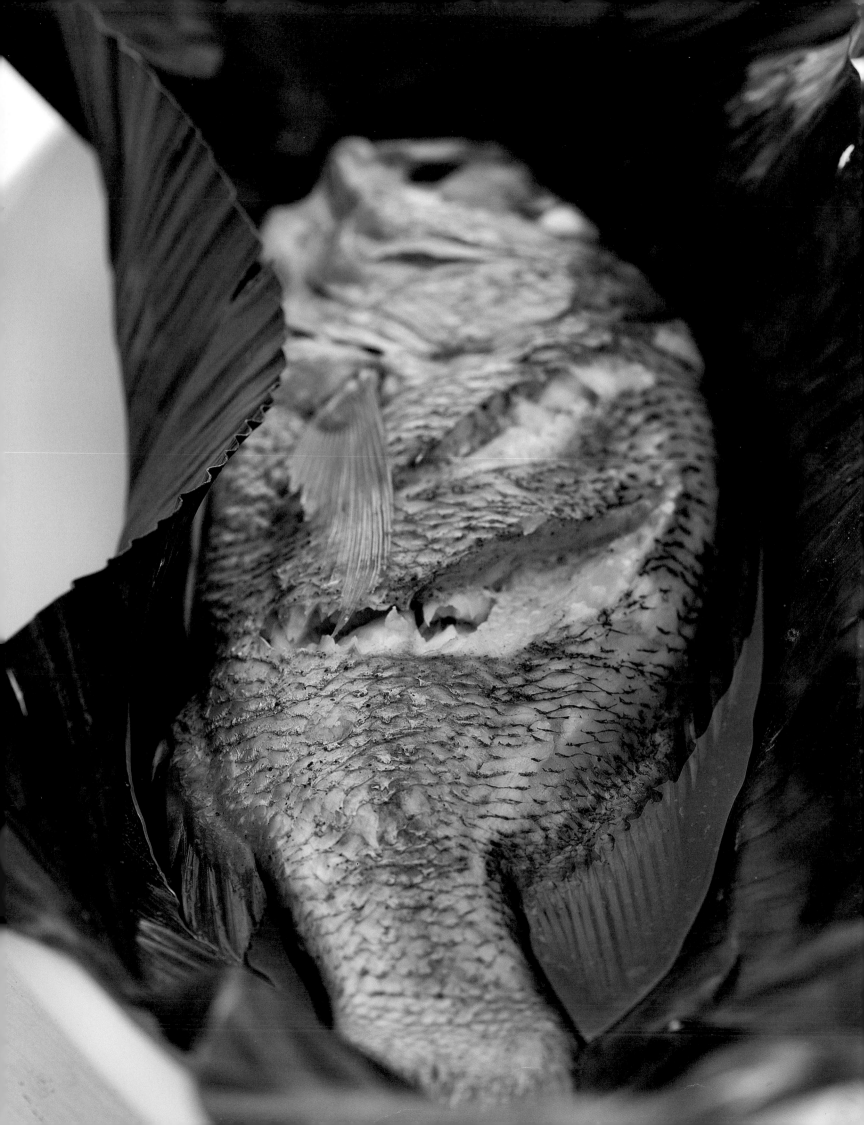

1 cup (125 g) grated fresh coconut or
  ½ cup (50 g) dried unsweetened grated
  (desiccated) coconut
1 lb (500 g) white fish fillets (preferably
  snapper or whiting), sliced
1 lb (500 g) fresh shrimp, peeled and deveined
1½ cups (375 ml) water
2 tablespoons oil
5 Asian shallots, sliced
2 tablespoons Fish Curry Powder (page 242)
1 teaspoon ground turmeric (optional)
1½ cups (375 ml) Fish Stock (page 245) or
  shrimp stock
3 cups (750 ml) thin coconut milk
1½ tablespoon tamarind pulp, mashed
  with 1½ cups (375 ml) of water and
  strained to obtain juice
1 teaspoon fish sauce
2 teaspoons salt
½ teaspoon ground white pepper
1 cup (250 ml) coconut cream
10 oz (300 g) dried rice stick noodles or
  rice vermicelli, blanched until soft

SPICE PASTE
7-10 red finger-length chili peppers, halved
  and deseeded
3 cloves garlic, peeled
3 stalks lemongrass, thick bottom part
  only, outer layers discarded, inner part
  sliced
½ in (2 cm) fresh ginger, peeled and sliced
½ in (2 cm) fresh galangal root, peeled
  and sliced
½ teaspoon dried shrimp paste, dry-
  roasted

GARNISHES
Cucumber shreds
Blanched bean sprouts
Vietnamese mint sliced into shreds
Sliced red finger-length chili peppers
Fresh juice of 1 lime

Shrimp with tropical coconut laksa gravy

This elegantly perfumed laksa is rich and flavorsome, befitting the royal kitchens in which it was created. It is a grand laksa, cooked lovingly with the fragrance of lime and ginger, sweet shrimp and spiky-hot Vietnamese mint that is finally graced with golden roasted coconut flakes which add a caramel-like depth that stops time. The soup should finally coat the spoon, dressing it in a swathe of lemony perfumed spices. The freshness of lime juice is added at the very end before the very first mouthful.

Prepare the Fish Curry Powder and Fish Stock by following the recipes on pages 242 and 245.

Prepare the Spice Paste first by processing the fresh ingredients in a food processor until smooth, then add the dried shrimp paste, mix well and set aside. Dry-roast the grated coconut following the method on page 43.

Place the sliced fish and half of the shrimp (the remaining half to be cooked whole at the end) in a saucepan and add the water to cover. Bring to a boil and then simmer uncovered over medium heat until cooked, 5–10 minutes. Remove from the heat and debone the fish. Process the fish, shrimp and stock into a thick paste in a food processor.

To make the laksa broth, heat the oil in a wok and stir-fry the shallot slices over medium heat until light brown, about 1 minute. Add the Spice Paste and stir-fry until fragrant, 3–5 minutes. Add the processed fish and shrimp and stir over low heat until the mixture sticks to the wok. Add the curry powder and turmeric powder (if using) and continue stirring for 1 more minute. Pour in the Fish Stock, thin coconut milk and tamarind juice, add the tamarind skins and simmer uncovered for 15–20 minutes until the broth is reduced slightly. Add the remaining shrimp and cook for about 2 minutes, seasoning with the fish sauce, salt and pepper. Stir in the roasted grated coconut and thick coconut milk, simmer for 1 minute and remove from the heat.

Divide the noodles equally into serving bowls and ladle the laksa broth over them. Top with the prawns, Garnishes and serve hot with a splash of lime juice.

SERVES: 6   PREPARATION TIME: *1 hour*   COOKING TIME: *45 mins*

3 tablespoons oil

1 onion, sliced

2 tablespoons Lemongrass Paste (page 242)

1–2 tablespoons Sambal Oelek Chili Paste (page 240), or other sweet chili paste added with shrimp paste

1 teaspoon dried shrimp paste, crumbled and dry-roasted

2 tablespoons tamarind pulp, mashed with 1 cup (250 ml) water and strained to obtain juice

2 tablespoons fresh pineapple juice

2 cups (500 ml) fish stock

$1^1/_2$ cups (200 g) fresh ripe pineapple chunks

1 tablespoon sugar

$^1/_2$ teaspoon salt, or to taste

$1^1/_3$ lbs (600 g) swordfish or mackerel fillets, sliced into bite-sized chunks

3 kaffir lime leaves, slice into fine strips, to garnish

Fish in sweet and sour pineapple broth

This traditional Malaysian sweet, sour and spicy fish dish (Ikan asam pedas) combines the breezy tropics with simple sour and sweet fruity tastes and is best served in summer when the flavors lend themselves to light dinners. Serve it with a light refreshing beer with a slightly bitter aftertaste and lots of fluffy white rice.

Prepare the Sambal Oelek Chili Paste and Lemongrass Paste by following the recipes on page 240 and 242.

Heat the oil in a wok and stir-fry the onion, Lemongrass Paste, Sambal Oelek or chili paste and shrimp paste over medium heat until fragrant, 2–3 minutes, making sure the mixture doesn't burn. Stir in the tamarind juice, pineapple juice and fish stock and bring to a boil, then simmer uncovered for 1 minute. Add the pineapple chunks and continue to simmer over low heat for 10–12 minutes for the flavors to penetrate, then season with the sugar and salt. The soup should be light, not too tart or sweet.

Gently lower the fish pieces into the simmering broth and simmer over medium heat for 3–5 minutes until just cooked, adjusting the seasonings as needed. Remove from the heat, transfer to a serving bowl and garnish with kaffir lime strips on top. Serve immediately with steamed rice or a simple fresh salad.

SERVES: *4-6*   PREPARATION TIME: *20 mins*   COOKING TIME: *15 mins*

1 fresh snapper head (about 1 lb/500 g)
2 tablespoons oil
2 tablespoons Aromatic Nonya Spice Paste
  (page 241)
1 tablespoon Sambal Oelek Chili Paste (page
  240) or other sweet chili paste
1 tablespoon Fish Curry Powder (page 242)
1 sprig curry leaves (about 15 leaves)
$^1/_2$ tablespoon tamarind pulp, mashed with
  $^1/_4$ cup (60 ml) hot water and strained to
  obtain juice
$1^1/_2$ cups (375 ml) water or Fish Stock
  (see note)
Salt and ground white pepper, to taste

Fish head curry with tamarind and lemongrass

Heaven to true gastronomes, this blend of perfumed Nonya herbs and spices—including citrusy lemongrass, refreshing galangal and mint—adds amazing scents and flavors to the sauce. Fish head curry is prized in Asia for the meat around the cheeks and eyes, but just hold a bowl of this curry in your hands and breathe in deeply to experience the brilliance of the tropics.

Prepare the Sambal Oelek Chili Paste, Aromatic Nonya Spice Paste and Fish Curry Powder by following the recipes on pages 240, 241 and 242.

Scale and clean the fish head thoroughly, cutting off the gills with a pair of kitchen scissors. Cut the head into half lengthwise so that the 2 halves can sit flat in the pan, rinse well, then pat dry with paper towels.

Heat the oil in a wok and stir-fry the Aromatic Nonya Spice Paste, Sambal Oelek, Fish Curry Powder and curry leaves over medium heat until fragrant, about 3 minutes. Stir in the tamarind juice and water or Fish Stock and bring to a boil. Reduce the heat to low, cover and simmer for about 3 minutes or until the curry is slightly thickened.

Add the fish head to the curry, increase the heat to high and bring to a boil, turning the fish a few times to coat it well with the curry. Lower the heat and simmer uncovered for about 3 minutes until the fish is cooked and the curry is thick. Season with salt and pepper to taste, adjusting with more tamarind juice if desired. Remove from the heat and transfer to a large serving bowl. Serve hot with steamed rice, Okra Stuffed with Dried Shrimp and Coconut (page 188) and a yogurt raita.

Note: To prepare Fish Stock, combine 10 oz (300 g) of fish bones, fish head or shrimp shells, 1 green onion, 2 teaspoons dried amchoor powder and $2^1/_2$ cups (625 ml) of water in a pot and bring to a boil. Reduce heat to low, then simmer covered for 20–30 minutes. Remove from the heat and strain, discarding the solids. This yields 2 cups (500 ml) of Fish Stock.

SERVES: *4-6*   PREPARATION TIME: *45 mins*   COOKING TIME: *10 mins*

2 tablespoons oil

$^1/_4$ teaspoon fenugreek seeds

5 cloves garlic, chopped

1 onion, chopped

1 stalk curry leaves plucked and chopped

1 green and 1 red finger-length chili pepper, halved and deseeded

3 ripe tomatoes, quartered

2 tablespoons tamarind pulp, mashed with 1 cup (250 ml) hot water and strained to obtain juice

3 tablespoons Fish Curry Powder (page 242)

Salt, to taste

One 16-oz (450-g) can sardines in tomato sauce

Tomato and tamarind sardine curry

Surprise your guests with the delicious aroma of fried garlic and onion combined with the sweet lemon-peppery fragrance of curry leaves as you build up this quick and easy curry using canned sardines. Malaysians often keep a can of sardines on standby in case their guests drop in unexpectedly.

Prepare the Fish Curry Powder by following the recipe on page 242.

Heat the oil in a saucepan and sauté the fenugreek for a few seconds. Add the garlic, onion, curry leaves and chili pepper and sauté until golden and fragrant, about 2 minutes. Stir in the tomato and sauté for 1–2 more minutes.

Pour in the tamarind juice and add the Fish Curry Powder, then cover and bring to a boil. Reduce the heat to low and simmer for 10 minutes. Stir in the sardines and continue to simmer uncovered for 3 more minutes. Season with salt to taste and remove from the heat. Serve immediately with steamed rice.

SERVES: *4*   PREPARATION TIME: *20 mins*   COOKING TIME: *20 mins*

8 oz (250 g) sashimi grade tuna fillets,
   thickly sliced across the grain
$^1/_2$ pomelo, peeled, removed, segmented
   and pulp separated
1 cup (100 g) jicama strips
1 starfruit, sliced
1 cucumber, halved lengthwise and sliced
Freshly ground black pepper, to taste

MARINADE
2 tablespoons mirin (or good sake mixed
   with 1 teaspoon sugar)
Fresh juice of 1 lime

DRESSING
2 tablespoons extra virgin olive oil
$^1/_4$ cup (60 ml) ponzu sauce (bottled)
Grated rind of $^1/_2$ orange
1–2 tablespoons balsamic vinegar, to taste
1 teaspoon sugar
$^1/_2$ teaspoon salt, or to taste

Fresh tuna with citrus, starfruit and jicama

This recipe relies on fresh fish, good quality mirin and freshly-squeezed lime and orange juice. The subtle fragrance of pomelo that is almost rose-like when it is fully ripe hits the top notes, creating an unusual and colorful appetizer.

Combine the Marinade ingredients in a large bowl and mix well. Add the tuna slices and mix until well coated, then refrigerate for 1 hour.

Combine the Dressing ingredients in a small bowl and mix well. Set aside.

To serve, arrange the starfruit and cucumber slices, pomelo pulp and jicama strips in individual serving bowls and top with the tuna slices. Spoon 2 tablespoons of the Dressing over each serving. Sprinkle with black pepper and serve immediately.

SERVES: *4–6*   **PREPARATION TIME:** *30 mins + 1 hour to marinate*

2 cups (500 ml) coconut cream
3 cups (750 ml) water
1¹/₂ cups (250 g) plain flour, sifted
4 eggs, lightly beaten
1¹/₂ teaspoons salt
3 tablespoons oil
1 *roti jala* cup, or empty can with very fine
holes punched in at the base

Lacy malay coconut pancakes ~ *Roti jala*

These lacy pancakes (the name literally means "fish net bread") are made by pouring a coconut pancake mixture through a can with very fine holes at the base to create whirls of thin batter. A little scent of the coconut remains to intrigue when these interesting net-like pancakes are cooked. It is simple enough for a child to do, as my grandson Isaac has demonstrated.

Dilute the coconut cream with the water in a large bowl and mix well. Place the flour separately in a mixing bowl and gradually pour in the diluted coconut cream, mixing well to form a smooth batter. Strain the batter through a sieve, discarding the solids, then add the beaten egg and salt and strain again.

Grease a non-stick griddle and heat over medium heat. Holding the cup or can over the griddle, pour ¹/₂ cup (125 ml) of the batter into it. As the streams of batter flow onto the griddle, move the cup or can in a circular motion to create a lacy pattern. Cook the pancake on one side for about 2 minutes, then turn it over to cook the other side for 1 minute. Remove from the heat. Continue to make the lacy pancakes in the same manner with the remaining batter. Serve the pancakes with Amah's Chicken Curry (page 108). They are just as delicious with maple syrup or honey for breakfast, or as a dessert.

SERVES: *6*   PREPARATION TIME: *10 mins*   COOKING TIME: *15 mins*

1 Pierce fine holes in the bottom of the can.

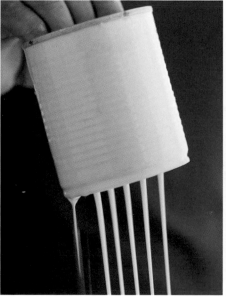

2 Drip streams of batter onto the griddle using the can.

3 Cook the lacy pancake on both sides.

Coconut custard with cardamom and ginger

Another coconut custard, this time Sri Lankan in origin, with spicy cardamom and the sweet aroma of pandanus or vanilla and ginger. It is interesting to note how a few spices can change the whole flavor of a humble custard.

$^1/_3$ cup (60 g) shaved palm sugar

2 cardamom pods, lightly smash, seeds removed and ground in a mortar to a powder or $^1/_2$ teaspoon ground cardamom

2 tablespoons water

7 egg yolks

1 cup (250 ml) thick coconut milk

2 pandanus leaves, each tied into a knot, or 1 vanilla bean, split

$1^1/_2$ cups (375 ml) coconut cream

4 tablespoons candied ginger, thinly sliced

Grated rind of 1 lime

1 tablespoon fresh lime juice

2 teaspoons rum plus 2 tablespoons rum for syrup

6 oven-proof bowls (each holding about 1 cup/250 ml)

Pandanus Syrup (page 81) or maple syrup, with 2 extra tablespoons rum added, to serve

SERVES: *6*

PREPARATION TIME: *10-15 mins*

COOKING TIME: *45 mins*

Prepare the Pandanus Syrup by following the recipe on page 81.

Preheat the oven to 350°F (170°C).

In a small saucepan, heat the sugar, cardamom and water over medium heat, stirring until the sugar is dissolved. Remove from the heat and set aside to cool. Transfer to a bowl, add the egg yolks and coconut milk, and beat until light and fluffy. Add 1 pandanus leaf or the split vanilla bean to the mixture.

Place the coconut cream, the other pandanus leaf and the ginger in the top of a double boiler and heat gently over medium heat. Gradually pour in the egg mixture but do not allow the mixture to boil. Cook over low heat for about 5 minutes then remove from the heat when the coconut mixture begins to simmer. Discard the pandanus leaves or vanilla bean, stir in $^1/_2$ of the grated lime rind, the lime juice and rum, and mix well.

Pour the mixture into 6 oven-proof bowls and arrange in a baking dish. Half-fill the dish with boiling water and bake in the oven for about 40 minutes or until the custard is firm and the top has browned. Remove from the heat and top the custard with the remaining grated lime rind. Serve warm or chilled, drizzled with 1 tablespoon Pandanus Syrup or warmed maple syrup.

Note: If you prefer to caramelize the top of the custard, omit the lime rind garnish. Sprinkle $^1/_2$ teaspoon of powdered sugar over the top of the custard and place the custard under a hot broiler grill until golden and crisp. Watch carefully as the sugar burns quickly.

Almond cake with mandarin apricot sauce

This recipe was specifically created to tease aromas into the cake while retaining its Asian character using spicy cinnamon, pungent cloves and ginger. It is a rich cake that could be served for afternoon tea or as a dessert after a main meaty meal like Basmati Rice with Spiced Chicken and Yogurt (page 160) which reflects similar spices.

2 normal or Valencia oranges, skin on, pitted and cut into small pieces
1 slice dried mandarin orange peel (see note)
6 eggs
1 cup (250 g) superfine (caster) sugar
2 cups (250 g) ground almond (raw) meal
1 teaspoon baking powder
1 teaspoon ground cinnamon
$1/2$ teaspoon ground ginger

MANDARIN APRICOT SAUCE
1 cup (250 g) apricot jam
1 cup (250 ml) water
2 slices dried mandarin orange peel
Chopped candied Chinese melon (*tang kuey*) or other candied fruit, to garnish

SERVES: *6–8*

PREPARATION TIME: *20 mins*

COOKING TIME: *1 hour 15 mins*

Preheat the oven to 360°F (180°C). Line a 12-in (30-cm) spring form or normal baking pan with aluminum foil or non-stick baking paper and set aside.

Place the orange pieces and mandarin orange peel in a saucepan and pour in enough water to just cover. Cook the mixture over low heat until soft, 5–10 minutes, then remove from the heat and cool, then process to a purée in a food processor.

In a mixing bowl, beat the eggs and sugar with a wooden spoon until light and fluffy, then fold in the almond, baking powder and spices, and stir in the orange mixture. Spoon the cake mixture into the prepared baking pan and bake in the oven for about 1 hour until golden brown and firm.

Prepare the Mandarin Apricot Sauce by combining the apricot jam, water and mandarin peel in a saucepan and warming the mixture over low heat for about 5 minutes until the mandarin flavor infuses into the sauce. Remove from the heat and strain.

To serve, drizzle the Mandarin Apricot Sauce over the cake and garnish with chopped candied melon or bits of candied fruit. Serve the cake warm with a bowl of the remaining Sauce on the side.

Note: Dried mandarin peel can easily be made at home by laying fresh mandarin skins on a metal tray and drying them in the hot sun for 3–4 days until they shrivel up and brown. Make sure that the mandarin peels are completely dry before storing them. Dried mandarin peel can be stored in an airtight container for months. Store-bought dried mandarin peel can be purchased in Asian supermarkets.

Vodka sour with young coconut juice

This refreshing cocktail began its life when I was residing in a tiny village in Papua New Guinea. We were surrounded by coconut palms which our houseboy would climb. The green young coconut has a light floral aroma and delicately sweet taste that I used to advantage each time our friends came to visit from the town. Limes were aplenty and the stalwart vodka bottle added punch to this cocktail. To the surprise of my guests, I would break the coconut open and spoon slivers of the soft pearly white flesh into each drink, which is the typical Asian way of eating young coconuts. For a change you can use rum or gin instead. Canned coconut juice with young coconut flesh is readily available in most supermarkets.

2 cups (500 ml) fresh or canned coconut water
1 cup (125 g) fresh or canned young coconut flesh (*buko*), sliced into strips (optional)
1 cup (250 ml) fresh lime juice
2 tablespoons Pandanus Sugar Syrup (page 135-optional) or regular sugar syrup
4 oz (125 ml) chilled vodka
2 kaffir lime leaves, sliced into fine strips, to garnish

Prepare the Pandanus Sugar Syrup by following the recipe on page 135.

Place all the ingredients (except the garnish) in a large pitcher and stir slowly to combine. Adjust the taste with more lime juice or sugar syrup as desired, making sure that the sweetness of the coconut water is not masked.

Pour the mixture into highball glasses filled with 2 ice cubes each, then garnish with the kaffir lime leaf and serve immediately.

Note: If left too long, this drink sours easily as it ferments. Vodka may be left out and replaced with a dash of grenadine for a non-alcoholic version.

MAKES: *4-6 glasses*   **PREPARATION TIME:** *10 mins*

Planter's punch

The agostura aromas of anise and cinnamon contrast with lime, a heady sugar-hit of rum and the rose-like grenadine give you an exotic, zesty and refreshing drink to enjoy at sundown with good company. This was served with lime slices in English social clubs throughout the colonial empire. Planters punch provides a more sophisticated tropical alternative to beer.

$1^1/_2$ oz (45 ml) dark rum
$1^1/_2$ oz (45 ml) fresh lime juice
Few drops angostura bitters
1 oz (30 ml) grenadine syrup
3 cups (750 ml) chilled soda water
4 swizzle sticks
Grated lime rind, to garnish
Crushed ice or ice cubes, to serve
4 chilled glasses

Pour the ingredients into a $1^1/_2$–2 liters pitcher, one on top of another, in the sequence as listed in the ingredient list. After the addition of chilled soda water at the end, stir the layers of ingredients with a swizzle stick. Pour into 4 chilled glasses and serve immediately garnished with grated lime and crushed ice.

SERVES: *4*   **PREPARATION TIME:** *20 mins*

Pineapple gin slings

The iconic gin sling, famous for its combination of fragrant aromas and flavors, has been enjoyed for over a century at the Raffles Hotel in Singapore. The sweet cherry brandy on top of zesty lime juice and aromatic pineapple, topped with the anise of angostura and cinnamon of Benedictine all contained in one drink—surely a piece of heaven in a glass!

8 oz (250 ml) gin
4 oz (125 ml) cherry brandy
2 oz (60 ml) fresh lime juice
4 cups (1 liter) unsweetened fresh or
   canned pineapple juice
3 oz (100 ml) grenadine syrup
3 dashes Benedictine Dom
Dash of triple sec
Few drops of angostura bitters
3 slices lime, halved, to garnish
Mint leaves, to garnish
6 swizzle sticks

Fill a large chilled pitcher a quarter full with ice cubes. Pour in all the ingredients, one by one, and stir the mixture twice. Strain the drink into 6 highball glasses filled with ice cubes. Garnish each glass with a half a slice of lime and serve with a mint leaf and swizzle stick.

MAKES: *6 glasses*   PREPARATION TIME: *45 mins*

Pineapple, starfruit and carrot cooler

This is a healthy and quick pick-me-up, especially if you have a juicer. The chili and ginger add a peppery aroma and bite to the ripe, floral notes of the pineapple. I would recommend this drink on a winter's morning or when you feel a cold coming on.

2 cups (350 g) fresh ripe pineapple slices
1 large starfruit or 2 green apples, sliced
1 carrot, peeled and sliced
1 tablespoon fresh lime juice
2 tablespoons honey
2 drops Tabasco sauce or $1/2$ teaspoon
   fresh ginger juice
4 thin slices of starfruit, to garnish

Chill the fruit and carrot, then juice separately in a juicer. Combine all the juices in a pitcher, add the lime juice and honey, and mix until well blended. Stir in the Tabasco sauce or ginger juice with a swizzle stick. Pour into individual glasses, garnish with the starfruit slices and serve at once.

SERVES: *4*   PREPARATION TIME: *15 mins*

COOKING WITH AROMATIC ASIAN FRUITS

Tamarind palm sugar cooler

A popular cooler for Indian summers, this fragrant tamarind juice drink with a distinctive aroma of burnt sugar and dates tastes sweet, sour, salty and tart all in one mouthful and glides smoothly down a parched throat. It refreshes almost instantaneously especially when mint leaves are added to boost the fragrance and soothe the body.

1 tablespoon tamarind pulp
3 cups (750 ml) water
2 tablespoons shaved palm sugar or dark
   brown sugar
Sprigs of mint leaves, to garnish

Mix the tamarind pulp and water in a large bowl. Mash the mixture well with your fingers, then strain to remove the seeds and fibers. Reserve the tamarind juice.

Warm the tamarind juice and sugar in a saucepan over low heat for 3–5 minutes, stirring until the sugar is dissolved. Remove from the heat and chill in the refrigerator until ready to serve.

Pour into individual serving glasses filled with some crushed ice, garnish with mint leaves and serve.

SERVES: *4*   PREPARATION TIME: *5 mins*   COOKING TIME: *5 mins*

Pandanus lemonade

Citrusy lemonade dressed up for the tropics with the grassy perfume of fresh pandanus—if you are adventurous, add a few slices of nose tingling ginger to the syrup. Serve this chilled on a hot summer evening. Pandanus and ginger lift the lemonade giving it a suggestion of a bite.

1 cup (250 ml) fresh lemon juice
1 cup (250 ml) fresh lime juice
8 cups (2 liters) iced water
Crushed ice
Grated lime rind, to garnish
Sprigs of mint leaves, to garnish

PANDANUS SUGAR SYRUP
2 pandanus leaves, tied into a knot
1 cup (200 g) sugar
$^{1}/_{2}$ cup (125 ml) water

Prepare the Pandanus Syrup by bringing the ingredients to a boil in a saucepan and stirring until the sugar is dissolved. Remove from the heat and cool.

Combine the cooled Syrup with the lemon juice, lime juice and iced water in a pitcher and stir well, then chill in the refrigerator until ready to serve.

To serve, pour into individual serving glasses filled with crushed ice, top with grated lime rind and garnish with mint leaves.

Note: A tablespoon of vodka or gin may be added to create a light cocktail.

MAKES: *6-8 glasses*   PREPARATION TIME: *15 mins*
COOKING TIME: *5 mins*

'In Asian cooking, spices with all their exotic nuances, cooked in partnership with fresh, green-scented herbs, are used freely across the entire spectrum of dishes—presenting a deliriously hedonistic rainbow of perfumed food flavors.'

Cooking with
aromatic asian spices

Spice is the life of Asia. For centuries spices have been prized above all other materials, including gold and precious stones. Throughout Asian history and lore one can find references, even eulogies, to their ethereal and almost heavenly properties. The use of spices has been well documented for thousands of years—famously mentioned during Cleopatra's reign and also in the anointing of Christ's body. In the last 500 years spices were brought out of Asia via the lucrative spice trade and were exclusive to the kings and queens of Europe and the very wealthy.

Because of its chequered history, the word "spice" has, over the centuries, acquired many connotations: it is associated with power, intrigue and excitement when we spike our food with spicy flavors, when we spice our words with interesting analogies or spice our lives with new experiences. Spice in a pinch or with a few grains can change a whole meal.

"After the year 1500 there was no pepper to be had that was not dyed red with blood."—Voltaire

Many bloody battles were fought over spice trading rights in Southeast Asia amongst the Spanish, Portuguese, Dutch and British traders and adventurers who were looking for *ad loca aromatum*, the location of the spices. The Arabs and Indians who controlled the spice trade until the 15th century kept the location of the Spice Islands a secret, spinning tales of their exact position to protect the huge profits they were making. Spices like pepper sold for up to 16 times the original price by the time they arrived in Europe because of the many times they changed hands en route to the Mediterranean.

The first and perhaps most famous of the explorers in search of bounty (another word for spice) was Christopher Columbus. Had Columbus sailed east instead of west his story would have been quite different. Vasco Da Gama and Magellan reached the pepper coast of Malabar first and shattered the Arab Indian monopoly over the spice trade. The most highly sought after spices—pepper, cloves, cinnamon and nutmeg—were finally available to the world. Hemphill, the spice expert, describes the basic difference between spice and herb or fruits (as in chili). He describes herbs as the leaves of a plant; their fruit, when dried, can appear as buds (cloves), as bark (cassia) or as seeds (coriander) or stamens (saffron). When dried, these fruit and seeds are all called spices.

Spices were used medicinally for years before they were used for cooking. This happened many times in my family home when decoctions of spices and herbs were distilled into medicines. Turmeric was applied as a poultice and ground ginger was rubbed onto chests for colds. Garlic was often roasted and then placed on a fevered temple or ground and chewed for a sore throat, or sometimes added with the Indian resin asafoetida to lentil curries as an anti-flatulent.

Modern research has recently led us to believe that spicy cinnamon will alleviate stress and suggests that tired drivers take a sniff of cinnamon instead of a cup of coffee or tea to stay awake while driving. Today spices are featured heavily in modern-day aromatherapy, cropping up in the most amazing beauty salons and luxury spa baths as they did in Cleopatra's time.

As with anything exotic, there are many myths surrounding the use of spices. One such myth is that spices were used to preserve foods in the heat of the tropics. But mose spices do not have preservative properties—other than turmeric, which is an antiseptic for surface wounds, and also for preserving fish and meat for a few hours.

It is also said that spices were used to mask the odors of rotting meat. This may have been true in Europe, but in tropical Asia, people never cook with old meat. They shop daily and cook with fresh ingredients, especially fish and meat, as there was no refrigeration in the past and there were few leftovers to spoil. Spices were used instead as medicines—boiled in teas and taken as tonics long before they were used for flavor.

There has always been a tremendous interest in spices, so more today as Western countries become multi-cultural, especially in the wake of modern air travel. The huge global interest in Asian food has stirred up a need to experience, taste, contemplate, appreciate and cook with spices and herbs. Coriander and fennel seeds, peppery and lemon-like are used in Indian curries. Even clean tasting galangal and warm perfumed star anise, used mainly in chicken recipes or my double-cooked pork, have found their way into kitchens from London to Sydney. People are willing to experiment with spices in their own kitchens today, perhaps for the first time. The great divide between East and West lies not in the varieties used, but in how the spices are used.

Spices are used in everyday dishes all over Asia. These spices, especially the Indian curry spices like coriander, pepper and cumin, are roasted, fried, heated and ground into pastes and sauces. They are sautéed or barbecued with fish or meats in tandoors or on satay grills. As the tantalizing blend of aromas rises from the heat into the kitchen and passes out through the windows, it announces to neighbors and passing strangers that a fabulous dinner is being prepared. Asians are used to eating perfumed foods and they are masters at creating and blending these scents so that the complete meal comes to the table, seducing the diner with its aromas long before the first mouthful is eaten.

In Asian cooking, spices with all their exotic nuances, cooked in partnership with fresh, green-scented herbs, are used freely across the entire spectrum of dishes—presenting a deliriously hedonistic rainbow of perfumed food flavors.

Use these spices in abundance and have fun with them.

Cardamon ~

The aroma of cardamom, reminiscent of cups of chai masala tea brewing, is the India I remember, especially the spice gardens in Kerala. Chai tea is best made with a tea bag, a cardamom pod and heated milk—a treat for visitors and friends at Christmas.

Cardamom, the small oval seed pod of a ginger-like plant, has a special meaning to me, as it was the spice used in all our Christmas cakes. The ritual of Christmas baking began a month beforehand. Spices were assembled; dried fruits and candied cherries were chopped on boards over newspapers spread on the floor. We had a team of friends who came over to help. The spices were then ground, and the time-consuming task of separating the cardamom seeds from the pods was often assigned to the most important person, my mother, who would arrive regally accompanied by bottles of pickles from Malaysia. The miniscule seeds escaped easily, and she chewed more than she saved for the cake. Cardamon is the breath freshener of Asians, and it always reminds me of her hoard of cardamom seeds that she often chewed.

Today I use cardamom along with cinnamon or cassia to flavor and add aroma to dishes. It is amazing what one tiny bit of ground cardamom can do to lift the flavor of rice with ghee and saffron into a royal dish. No wonder that European spice traders chased after these precious spices with such determination. Curry and meat dishes are lifted with the flavor of whole cardamom pods, which can be removed before serving or left in as a chunky surprise to the diner, who may enjoy this power-packed punch while chewing on a morsel of meat.

Purchasing: Cardamom pods are available whole or split and the seeds are sold loose or ground. It is best to buy the whole pods and grind the seeds yourself as ground cardamom loses its aroma quickly. There are two varieties of small cardamom, each the size of a fingernail. The pale green variety is the better quality one; the beige variety has been bleached to make it white as this is the preferred color for consumers. So always look for green pods when buying cardamom. The larger, almond-shaped pods, known as black or brown cardamom, are dark brown and have a milder aroma compared to the smaller green pods. These are grown in Cambodia, Vietnam and Laos for cooking.
Culinary uses: There are three ways of using cardamom: as whole pods, as whole seeds or by grinding the seeds to a fine powder. Each has its own merits, but common sense prevails. For a stronger flavor, use roughly pounded seeds in curries or stews. Finely ground cardamom is used in desserts, pastry mixes and Indian sweets. Whole pods are used in many dishes in cuisines from Egyptian to African to Asian.
Preparation: Lightly crack open the whole pods before using. If using the seeds, peel the pod to extract the small, dark seeds inside and then grind them in a mortar. Sift the ground seeds

and grind further for a fine powder.
Storing: Store leftover cardamom in a dark cool place in air-tight containers.
Substitutes: Equal parts of ground nutmeg and cloves or cloves and cinnamon

Cinnamon and cassia~

Enter a bakeshop and you will often encounter the delicious aroma of cinnamon and cassia. Inhale more deeply and you will feel hungry. This is a programmed taste memory from childhood—the memory of Christmas cookies, mother's kitchen and the curries of Asia.

The bark of the fine-textured cinnamon tree found in Sri Lanka has a subtle, slightly sweet aroma—almost a delicate rose-like pungency. The dried inner bark harvested from an evergreen tree that is native to Sri Lanka and southern India comes in brittle rolls that you can almost crush between your fingers, and because of its subtle aroma, it is used in cakes, egg custards and puddings without other spices that might clash with it.

Somewhat confusingly, the spice commonly sold in Southeast Asia as cinnamon is often not true cinnamon but cassia, another closely related species. Cassia bark is a coarser version of the thinner bark of the cinnamon plant that grows in China and Southeast Asia. Chew it and you will taste a certain pungency. Both cinnamon and cassia belong to the laurel family although the latter, with a dark brown and rough texture, is a heavier bark from a larger tree. It is important to differentiate the two, since cinnamon has an aroma that is delicate whereas cassia is much stronger.

Purchasing: Available year-round, both cinnamon and cassia are commonly sold in sticks or in powdered form. True cinnamon can be distinguished from cassia by its lighter color and finer powder. Always buy just the quantity you need as this spice loses its fragrance quickly. Scrape the sticks and sniff them: fresh cinnamon or cassia should emit a pleasant aroma.
Culinary uses: Both cinnamon and cassia have similar uses, but cinnamon is used more in desserts, cakes, icing and even in coffee blends because of its delicate flavor and aroma. Whole pieces of cassia bark are generally used to flavor meats, rice and curry dishes.
Preparation: Lightly heat the amount needed before using, being careful not to scorch it.
Storing: Store in a dark cool place in an airtight container.
Substitutes: Nutmeg or allspice.

Cloves ~

Fly into any big city in Indonesia and on the tarmac you are assaulted by an aroma of the tropics—not the smell of durians or mangoes, but the pungent and rather exciting aroma of cloves. No, they are not cooking them, but smoking them. The aroma of kretek, the Indonesian ground clove cigarettes, is an aroma that will spark many flavor memories of dinners in Bali under swaying palm trees next to brown sand beaches.

The clove was an essential spice that brought the West to the East. There have been more wars fought over the use of cloves than any other spice. First the Portuguese and Spanish explorers came, then the British with Queen Elizabeth's dashing sea captain, Sir Francis Drake, and finally the Dutch. It is a wonder that this tiny little spice, packing such a punch, could survive so many power struggles.

A native of the Moluccas, today the clove is the largest spice export for Indonesia. With a unique shape that resembles a small nail, the clove is actually the unopened flower bud of an attractive tropical tree—the buds are picked before they flower and sun-dried to a brownish black. This spice is warm, pungent, peppery and numbing in flavor and has a very strong aroma that is a mix of cardamon and camphor. To me, it is reminiscent of Christmas cakes and good cheer.

Purchasing: Cloves are sold whole or in powdered form in Asian markets. Like most other spices, it is better to buy whole cloves and grind them yourself as the ground spice loses its aroma quickly. Always grind them in small quantities. Look for well-formed cloves with no bruised ends. They should look darker at the base, light at the top and have a fresh aroma.

Culinary uses: This is a spice that can easily overpower a dish, so always use it sparingly. Cloves are used in many ways—whole in curries and to enhance the flavor of meats and main dishes and ground in spice mixes, desserts and cakes. Try a couple of cloves in a cup of brewed coffee for a change or use it as my recipes suggest—Basmati Rice with Spiced Chicken and Yogurt (page 160) or Plump Apricots with Rum Cream and Clove Syrup (page 194). You can also make the expensive aroma of clove pomanders for very little: prick an orange with a pin and stud it with cloves all around, then leave the clove-studded orange to dry thoroughly before putting it in a linen drawer.

Preparation: Like cardamom, it is better to use freshly ground cloves for the best aroma and flavor. As cloves have natural oil, an electric grinder is an ideal mean to grind them. However, if you have to work with a mortar or coffee grinder, grind small amounts of cloves at a time, then sift and grind again until fine. This may be a bit time consuming but the final result is worth the effort, especially when used in Christmas cakes and puddings.

Storing: Store whole cloves in an airtight container in a dark cool place and grind only the amount that you need; replenish when needed. Cloves lose their scent and taste after three years, but they have a longer shelf life than the other sweet spices like cardamom and cinnamon. I keep my cloves in the refrigerator.

Substitutes: Allspice can be used in place of ground cloves.

Coriander seeds ～

Coriander seeds, the small round beige seeds of the coriander plant (see page 20), have a distinct lemony aroma with back notes of musk that remain on the palate long after the meal is digested. These seeds, when dry-roasted and ground, are the main flavoring ingredient in Asian curries as the mild flavor adds balance to other more strongly-scented spices like cardamom and nutmeg.

The grinding of a curry paste always begins with this spice. During my teen years, the task of making curry pastes began long before school. First I would roast a handful of coriander seeds in a shallow skillet to dry them and "reboot" the flavor. Then I would transfer the seeds to the waiting granite grinding stone, and drag the elongated pestle that looked like a large cucumber back and forth over the seeds so they would gradually release their fresh, lemony aroma. The seeds would pulverize quickly as dried chili peppers and a smidgen of turmeric were added with a few drops of water. When dry-roasted coriander seeds are ground with roasted cumin and fennel, you get the basis of a traditional Malaysian and Indonesian mixture known as *ketumbar jintan*.

Although coriander seeds are used in most Asian cuisines, they must have originated in the Mediterranean area and traveled to the East as there is evidence of the use of this spice in Egyptian tombs 3000 years ago.

Purchasing: Coriander seeds are available whole or ground in Asian food stores. It is always better to buy whole seeds and grind them yourself as ground coriander loses its flavor and aroma quickly. Look for seeds that are creamy brown, either round or slightly oval in shape.

Culinary uses: Whole coriander seeds are used in pickling and in some drinks. Ground coriander is used in curries, baked foods, soups and stews and in many spice blends, notably curry powder and garam masala. Coriander seeds can be used in three strengths—when a mild flavor is required, add them whole or sauté them with other spices. For a more pronounced, lemon–aniseed flavor, grind the seeds and add them to curries. For a particularly intense flavor, dry-roast the seeds in a pan until fragrant, cool and grind them to a powder, then use. Ground roasted coriander is added to curries, pickles and meat or fish marinades, especially satay.

Preparation: Dry-roast the seeds before using. Coriander seeds are naturally soft and do not grind well unless dry-roasted first, which also refreshes their flavor and aromas. Grind the seeds in a mortar or spice grinder. You may have to sift a quantity and grind the coarser bits again to get a fine powder for a curry mix. It is worth the trouble.

Storing: Store whole seeds in an airtight container in a dark cool place and they will keep almost indefinitely. Dry-roast and grind the seeds as needed. For optimum flavor, store the seeds for no more than a year.

Substitutes: Equal parts of fennel and cumin with a pinch of turmeric.

Cumin ~

The enduring perfume of cumin in curry dishes adds not only spice flavors but an aroma that beguiles and teases the senses. The curry you enjoy may contain a confusing gamut of spices but the musky scent of cumin is probably the most distinctive and addictive one. Once you have tasted cumin and used it in your food on a daily basis, its sensuality will be with you for life.

The cumin plant is an annual that grows up to 3 feet (1 meter) tall. It has feathery leaves and tiny fruit seeds. The seeds have a range of colors but the best cumin is the dull green variety.

Dried cumin seeds are elongated, almost like the hull of a boat, hairy and brownish in color with a striped pattern containing nine ridges and a tiny stalk attached to the end. Closely resembling caraway or fennel seed in appearance, cumin is lighter and slightly larger than caraway but smaller and narrower than fennel.

In Southeast Asia, cumin has a distinctive spicy sweet liquorice and lemon-ginger taste and aroma, and next to coriander seeds it is the most important spice—added to many curries and pickles. It is my favorite spice and I use it in abundance, adding more of it to my curries than coriander seeds, which is more than the normal proportion recommended by curry gurus all over the world. It is the aroma of cumin that strikes first as the meat is raised to your mouth. And it is the aroma that keeps you coming back for more.

Medicinally, cumin has been said to have strong curative properties and is used to aid indigestion and colic. When added to boiling water with honey, it is used to soothe sore throats, colds and fevers.

Purchasing: There are two varieties of cumin—the small and brown variety which is the true cumin, and the small dark seeds called nigella or *kolonji* in Tamil. Caraway seeds are sometimes referred to as cumin but they are quite different. The confusion arises because both have the same Tamil name *jeera*. Whole and ground cumin are widely available in supermarkets or Asian food stores. As much as possible, always buy whole seeds and then freshly grind them. Buy a little at a time, because the aromas and flavors are quickly lost.

Culinary uses: Like coriander seeds, cumin is used whole or ground, either plain or roasted to draw out the sweetness of dishes. It is a common ingredient in most curry powders, many savory spice mixes, marinades and sauces, and is used in stews, grills and meat dishes and to flavor rice or couscous. It can also be sprinkled on salads. The seeds are dry-roasted and then ground for use in curries. In a typical curry, the amount of coriander seeds is double that of cumin and fennel. For instance, 2 tablespoons of coriander seeds and $1/2$ tablespoon each of cumin and fennel are the usual proportions.

Preparation: For optimum aroma and flavor, cumin seeds should be lightly dry-roasted before using whole or ground. To dry-roast cumin seeds, heat a skillet and roast the seeds over low heat until fragrant, 3-5 minutes. Alternatively, place in a dish and microwave for 1 minute on high, constantly checking to make sure the seeds are not burning. Cumin seeds can be easily ground in a mortar or spice grinder.

Storing: Store whole or ground cumin in an air-tight container in a dark, cool place. For longer storage, keep whole.

Substitutes: Fennel or aniseed.

Fennel ～

The fruity anise-like aroma of fennel accompanies every dish to which this spice is added. Cooked as it is, fennel imparts a light lemony aroma, but when dry-roasted, the aroma becomes sweet and gives a dill-like taste. It is a versatile spice commonly used in conjunction with cumin and coriander. However, when used on its own, it has a sweetness that tantalizes, notably in the famous satay sauce of Southeast Asia.

As a spice, the name "fennel" refers to the dried seeds of the fennel plant, although the plant itself is used as both a herb and a vegetable.

The spice is elongated with an oval almond shape and is greenish to yellowish-brown in color, looking very similar to cumin but larger and lighter in color. It has a very distinctive, sweet taste with an aroma of aniseed and lemon and a whiff of dill. It has a much softer aroma than the gutsy cumin.

Fennel is used on its own to flavor many fish dishes, but most people associate it with a mix of other spices. The Cashew Nut Satay Sauce (see page 151) that accompanies my grilled meat skewers is best made with fennel and coriander, rather than with cumin.

The sweetness of fennel enhances the sweet taste of grilled meat, which is also usually marinated with turmeric, chili, soy sauce, sugar and salt and the presence of sugar caramelizing the meat and spices creates an aromatic treat.

Fennel is my favorite spice with fish, especially a warm salmon salad with hot cubeb pepper and pickled white onions.

Purchasing: Whole and ground fennel are sold in Asian markets. Identify fresh seeds by taking a bite of one or crush it between your palms. The aroma indicates freshness. The seeds should be bought in small quantities because the aroma and flavor deteriorate with time.

Culinary uses: Use whole or ground fennel, roasted or plain, as with coriander seeds. Adjust the amount according to the strength. Fresh fennel with its sweet lemony flavor and aroma is very gentle on the palate, but does not have as much flavor as the dry-roasted ground fennel. The latter is used in Southeast Asian curry pastes and Indian curries when an obvious fennel taste is needed in the blend. Ground fennel is an ingredient in Chinese five spice powder. Fresh fennel is used to flavor breads, cakes and sweets. The Vietnamese use fennel or dill leaves for an interesting fish dish where fresh fennel leaves are added to a fish broth cooked on a table-top stove.

Preparation: Fennel should be dry-roasted before adding it to fish dishes. Otherwise use it in its natural state.

Storing: Store fennel in an air-tight container in a cool, dark place.

Substitutes: Aniseed or cumin.

Galangal ~ blue ginger

The refreshing aroma of galangal acts in combination with and as a contrast to lemongrass in many recipes in this book. It has a beautiful gingery scent and helps to tenderize meat, especially when it is slow-cooked in my favorite Rendang recipe. Used sparingly, it will provide a wonderful perfume and flavor to your dishes.

Most Southeast Asians are familiar with galangal not only in foods but (as with many herbs) for its curative properties. A slice of galangal rubbed over an irritating tropical infection clears the skin in a matter of days.

I use galangal in most curries where I use lemongrass. It is the yin that partners the yang in an artistic curry paste blend to create entertainment for the palate. Cooked in soups, especially in Vietnamese *pho* beef soups, the aroma and gingery taste of galangal is more apparent than the lighter lemongrass, which is added at the end. In Southeast Asian laksas, curries and sambals, it is the lemongrass that hits and is recognized instantaneously, while the galangal remains in the background, but without it the dish would be lacking.

Looking at galangal, one can easily mistake it for young ginger, for both are pinkish-cream roots that grow in knobs and put out spiky shoots. But look closer at the galangal, scratch the skin and a distinctive rose and iodine-like aroma hits you. Scratch it and your nail does not easily penetrate the skin as it would with ginger. This rhizome feels woody and solid, and is firmer and more flavorful compared to ginger.

Purchasing: Look for fresh, unwrinkled galangal roots in Asian markets.

Culinary uses: Although galangal looks like ginger, they are not interchangeable. Galangal may be used in two ways—added to soups in slices or processed in curry pastes and spice mixes. I have used galangal in a shrimp and coconut pickle recipe, where you may not taste the galangal, but it gives the shrimp an interesting lift. When galangal is ground with garlic, lemongrass, chili peppers and onions, it creates an explosion of incredible flavors. Galangal is seldom used on its own except when added to soups such as Vietnamese *pho* and Thai *tomyum*. Use galangal as instructed in the recipe.

Preparation: Scrape off the skin using a sharp knife, then chop or slice and use as instructed. As mature galangal is very tough, slice the pieces thinly first before grinding or processing them into a paste with other spices.

Storing: Wrap in newspaper or a cloth and refrigerate for up to 2 weeks. Alternatively, slice thinly or grind into a paste and freeze in a plastic bag or container. This is convenient for quick cooking but should not be kept for more than a month.

Substitute: Young ginger.

Ginger ~

The aroma of ginger is warm, peppery and subtly rose-like; it is the comfort spice for most Southeast Asians. Ginger cooked with chicken seduces, and ginger juice squeezed into fish sambals and stews with lime enlivens a dish.

Visit a tiny village anywhere in Southeast Asia and you will encounter the aroma of ginger wafting through the windows of huts, homes and restaurants as millions begin stir-frying, sautéing and steaming their fish and vegetables or grilling their meats. It is the next most important stir-frying spice after garlic. Young ginger, fresh and pink, soft and juicy is added in slices to delicately spiced fish dishes. Old ginger, knobbly-kneed like old men with arthritic joints, has a stronger flavor and is used in curries and teas. Both are equally important but used in different ways. Chinese and Southeast Asian cooks are more inclined to use young ginger, which by the way can be grown at home, while Indians prefer old ginger, which has a more mature flavor and stronger aroma. Old ginger is used medicinally to calm the stomach and to combat nausea; it is the spice used for colds and coughs to "heat" the body and drive away the cooling properties (yin elements). My amah would slice ginger and place one slice on each temple whenever she had a headache. Ginger is sliced, pounded, grated and sometimes juiced and mixed into soups and stir-fries.

I use ginger to fry chicken with soy sauce, and ginger juice is used as a marinade to tenderize the chicken and lend an aroma before cooking. The aroma of ginger always conjuress up for me this picture of a golden brown chicken slowly frying in a sizzling hot pan with wonderful fragrances wafting all around me, in my nostrils and throughout the house. It is the aroma of home in Southeast Asia, but also the aroma of the world. What would Chinese New Year be without ginger wine?

Purchasing: Fresh ginger is sold as young or old roots in the market. Young ginger is lighter in color, less "spicy" and juicier than mature roots. It has pink tips, sometimes with sections of the shoots left intact. Always look for plump and firm roots.
Culinary uses: Ginger is used in everything from dips and marinades to soups, stews, curries and drinks. The young ginger, with a fresher and less predominant flavor, is used sliced in delicate stir-fries and softer flavored dishes, and as a garnish. It is also used with vinegar to make those delicious red ginger pickles, a condiment served with Japanese and Chinese dishes. The old ginger, having a more pronounced flavor that is almost hot, and a pithy, fibrous texture, is often combined with chili peppers, garlic and lemongrass to make a sambal, which is sautéed slowly with meat or fish curries. I recently tasted a wonderful fruit juice made by processing fresh beetroot, carrot and 1 in (3 cm) of ginger together in a blender. A truly healthy drink that not only warms the chest, but also the spirit.
Preparation: Using a knife, scrape the skin from the ginger root, then chop or slice it and use as instructed. For ginger juice, peel and grate the ginger using a grater, then transfer to a fine sieve and press down with the back of a spoon to extract the ginger juice. If using drier mature ginger, it may be necessary to add a little water to the ginger and mix it before straining.
Storing: Store fresh ginger whole in an open container in a dry place.
Substitutes: Ground ginger.

Pepper and sichuan pepper ∽

The quest for spices was the main reason explorers traveled to Asia and initially the main trade was in pepper, one of the earliest spices known to the West. Before the 1500s much of the pepper arriving in Europe was either carried on camel caravans overland or on trading ships mainly by the Arabs who had dominated the spice trade since the Middle Ages. By the time the spices arrived at the spice markets of Venice they had changed hands many times and would cost 16 times their original price. The West wanted to break this monopoly by finding a direct route to the Spice Islands of the East. When Vasco De Gama eventually arrived in Calicut his actions and of those following him, eventually changed the course of history and reconfigured Asia. It was said that Italian housewives would dole spices out to their servants in minute quantities and they were kept under lock and key. Spices were highly regarded in Europe because they added flavor to meats and seemed to make people feel more healthy.

Although black pepper has been grown in Asia for many years, in most Southeast Asian dishes white pepper is preferred to the stronger black pepper. Both are from the same peppercorn but the white pepper has been husked and is therefore not as strong. In the West, black pepper is sprinkled over food at the table. One of the reasons the waiter produces the pepper mill with a flourish is not only to create drama but because the aromatic oils in peppercorns are released when the spice is ground. And it is this aroma that the nose enjoys before the palate tastes the flavor.

Black pepper is the fruit of the pepper vine. The berries are harvested whilst still unripe and dried on mats in the sun until they become the dark peppercorns we know. Dark green peppercorns still on the vine are available in brine and have a different taste; peppery but not as strong. White pepper is made by husking ripe berries picked when they are red or orange, then soaking them in running water, washing again and drying them. Black pepper is the whole berry with the husk left on, which has a stronger taste.

The shiny aromatic black seeds with magenta husks known as Sichuan pepper are not true peppercorns but the berries of a bush found in the Sichuan region of China. They have a subtle warming taste and a lemon-lime aroma that lingers on the tongue and produces a slight numbing effect similar to that of cloves when chewed. When dry-roasted and crushed, they add a warm spicy flavor to roast chicken and to duck and pork dishes. Sichuan pepper is available in clear pepper shakers in Japanese supermarkets and is used as a last minute garnish for heavy vegetarian or meaty soups. It is also ground with pepper and salt to make a fragrant Chinese table dip for roast duck.

Purchasing: Peppercorns should be bought in small quantities to retain their freshness, which can be ascertained by biting into one. Fresh white peppercorns should make you sneeze.
Culinary uses: Black peppercorns are added to dishes at the end of the cooking process, while white peppercorns are normally ground and added during the cooking process.
Preparation: I have in some of these recipes ground black pepper into salads to give a bite that would normally be substituted

with chili. The flavors are different; chili is sweet, while pepper is rustic.
Storing: Always buy in small quantities and store in a cool, dark place.
Substitutes: The obvious substitute for pepper is to use a touch of chili, either in dried powdered form, or chili flakes. But if you prefer a milder peppery taste, try ground, dry-roasted Sichuan pepper instead.

Saffron ~

Hold several tiny strands of scented saffron with their perfume of lilies and crocuses in your hand and you could well be Cleopatra, who was said to bathe in milk perfumed with saffron. Remember that you are holding one of the most romantic (and expensive) spices in the world.

Saffron is the stigma of a crocus flower that grows in the Middle East and Northern India. Each stigma is so tiny that it takes more than 250,000 flowers to produce one pound (500 grams) of saffron. The flower blooms in autumn only for 2 weeks, when it has to be picked by hand. No wonder saffron is so expensive, for it requires so much work to produce.

The subtle aroma of saffron when added to milk or to a delicately spiced rice dish is something one never forgets. Breathe deeply and you will smell roses, lavender and jasmine. In the Middle East, saffron has been used for centuries by princes and kings to perfume food, drinks and even linen.

In the spice markets of Asia, these delicate threads are often kept in cloth bags, which is quite unusual. Others normally store them carefully in wooden boxes. In Southeast Asia, unless it is specifically stated that saffron should be used, cooks tend to substitute turmeric for a cheaper alternative. The two are miles apart and if possible should never be interchanged.

Purchasing: Look for a reputable saffron merchant, or you will probably be given something else. I was duped into buying a whole bundle of reddish-green petal-like bits in Indonesia, which the trader swore was saffron. I later found out it was not. Look for even-colored threads with vivid dark-gold and red hues, some curly and some with a thicker head. They are sold whole in tiny plastic boxes or ground into an orange powder. Avoid powdered saffron, which is often adulterated with other flavorings. Beware of imitations—turmeric powder is quite often sold as saffron. The best saffron comes from Iran, Spain and Kashmir. Buy only a small amount and use it sparingly.

Culinary uses: Saffron imparts a warm sunshine yellow color and subtle jasmine-like perfume to any dish it is cooked in. I use saffron mainly in my rice dishes, but also in pasta sauces, custards and other desserts where subtle flavors and aromas add to the sunshine shades of the stamens. It is best added to rice after soaking a few threads in warmed milk to release its color. Dry-roasting a few threads of saffron heightens the perfumes making it crisp to easily crumble into any dish. It is interesting to note that in India saffron is added to the baby's first taste of milk.

Preparation: To extract the maximum flavor from saffron, lightly dry-roast the strands in a small pan over very low heat, then soaked them in warm milk for 5–10 minutes, then add both the saffron and the milk to the dish.

Storing: Store in the refrigerator in a sealed, dry container to ensure freshness.

Substitutes: For color, use about four times as much ground turmeric or twice the quantity of marigold blossoms. For flavor, substitute about eight times as much safflower, although the taste is usually inferior.

Star anise ～

Star anise, often seen as the star of our food, does not only have a classic shape and a warm amber-like color, it also has a warm cinnamon and aniseed aroma which traditionally flavors pork and duck dishes in its countries of origin, especially China and Vietnam. This spice has always been associated with slow-cooked meat dishes, soups and rich festival dishes. I find its aroma most comforting and wonderful as it counteracts the small amount of fat or oiliness in my favorite pork dish, Sweet Soy Pork with Mushrooms and Star Anise (*Tau Yew Bak*—page 174).

This spice is actually the seed pod of a small oriental tree. As its name suggests, it is star-shaped, usually with eight radiating pointed sections. These hard sections reveal small, shiny black seeds when they are split open. This spice is one of the essential ingredients in Chinese five spice powder, an important spice mix used in Chinese cooking to season braised meat dishes. The Chinese also use it to marble eggs in tea. It is an essential ingredient in the beef stock in Vietnamese *pho* beef soup. I use star anise in slow-cooked soy meat dishes and chili hotpots. Try using it in slow-simmered meat stews and crock-cooked dishes with pork, chicken or lamb.

Star anise is always sold as whole pods in its dried form and its use has spread from East Asia to the rest of the world today. (It also contains the principal ingredient used to make Tamiflu, one of the leading anti-flu drugs). I have noticed that the use of this spice in lamb dishes takes away the sometimes gamey flavor by creating a delicate spectrum of aromas that strengthens the top notes of any other spice or herb flavoring the dish. It is used with great success in my Chicken Rice recipe—page 162.

Purchasing: Like most other spices, these seed pods are available both whole and ground in Asian markets. Look for perfect stars although broken bits are as effective when used. Do not confuse this spice with aniseed, which is different.

Culinary uses: Star anise is used in the East in the same way as aniseed in the West. It is rich and pungent and should only be used in small quantities. One pod is more than enough to flavor an entire pork dish, or a duck stir-fry. Use it whole in cooking or ground into a paste and then added to dishes. It is a good idea to remove the small seeds in the pods as these do not add any extra flavor.

Preparation: No preparation is required for star anise itself but you have to decide if you want the spices whole or pounded for cooking. Use them whole if you require aroma alone, but if you want the peppery taste and sweetish cinnamon aroma, pound the star anise roughly to retain larger pieces so they may be removed before serving. The tiny seeds in the star may be removed before pounding, as they do not add any flavor.

Storing: Star anise has a long shelf life and keeps well, but I prefer to buy it in small amounts, storing it in an air-tight container in a cool, dark place.

Substitutes: Substitute equal parts of cloves and cinnamon.

Turmeric ~

Freshly ground turmeric has the aroma of roses, similar to rose oil. I grow my own turmeric plants in Sydney and harvest the roots which look like short, fat orange caterpillars. They are dried in the sun for 30 days, then ground in a coffee grinder. The aroma is unmistakably rose-like. Turmeric is a legendary spice used as a tenderizer. With other spices, turmeric creates a tempting perfume.

The rhizome of a ginger-like plant, this root resembles ginger but is much smaller and thinner, and the caterpillar-shaped tubers are covered with a thin brownish skin that lets the bright orange-yellow flesh inside show through. Although turmeric is widely used in India and outside Asia in its dried ground form, the fresh root is preferred in Southeast Asia for its fragrance, flavor and bright yellow color.

Turmeric is also used as a natural dye for fabrics and is an important medicinal herb. It has in fact been used as an antiseptic by Chinese and Indian medical practitioners long before it was used for cooking. I remember reading a book on the Indian rajahs and their hunting habits. They took with them a couple of assistants, guns, spears, their trusty horses and turmeric, either ground or fresh. The "kill" was smeared with ground turmeric and salt in the forests so it would still be fresh when they arrived back at their palaces. Don't be surprised to find women with yellow face packs in some smaller villages in India where the names of Estée Lauder or Lancôme do not mean anything. Continued use of a mask of fresh turmeric on the face is believed to be effective in removing facial hair and keeping the skin smooth and clear, although this is not recommended unless you want a yellow face.

Purchasing: Both fresh roots and ground turmeric are sold in Asian markets. Look for firm fresh rhizomes with few brown patches. However, if you are making an Indian curry, it is more convenient to use ground turmeric. Always buy ground turmeric in small quantities as its flavor diminishes with time.
Culinary uses: Turmeric is always used in very small amounts, to color and flavor dishes and to mask unwanted aromas. It is used in curries, marinades, rice dishes and pickles. This spice should be used sparingly, especially when fresh, for it is quite bitter. In an Indian curry mix, the quantity of turmeric is often only five percent of the total spice blend. In Asia, it is used as a cheaper substitute for saffron when cooking yellow rice.

When used in this way, the cook usually compensates for the missing saffron aroma with the addition of cloves, cardamom and cinnamon.
Preparation: Scrap off the skin using a sharp knife, then chop or slice and use as instructed. Take care not to get the juice on your clothing as it will stain permanently.
Storing: Wrap fresh roots in paper towels or a cloth and refrigerate for up to 2–3 weeks. Store ground turmeric in an air-tight container in a cool, dry place.
Substitute: When fresh turmeric root is not available, use ground turmeric.

Chicken satay with fragrant spices and coconut

Chicken Satay is everyone's favorite—delicate barbecued morsels with an enticing fragrance of caramelized palm sugar, coconut cream and grilling chicken. A food fit for the Gods!.

1 lb (500 g) boneless chicken thigh fillets, sliced into 20 long, narrow strips
20 bamboo skewers, soaked in water for 1 hour to prevent them from burning
1/4 cup (60 ml) coconut cream
2 tablespoons oil
2 teaspoons shaved palm sugar or dark brown sugar
Cucumber slices, to serve
Onion wedges, to serve
1 portion Cashew Nut Satay Sauce (below)

MARINADE
1 tablespoon Amah's Curry Powder (page 108)
2 tablespoons Lemongrass Paste (page 242)
1 teaspoon ground turmeric
1 teaspoon cumin, dry-roasted and ground
3 tablespoons shaved palm sugar or dark brown sugar, mixed with 1/2 cup (125 ml) hot water

Prepare the Amah's Curry Powder and Lemongrass Paste by following the recipes on pages 108 and 242. Combine these with the other Marinade ingredients in a shallow dish and mix well. Thread each chicken strip on a soaked bamboo skewer, in a zig-zag pattern. Place all the skewers in the dish with the Marinade, coating the chicken pieces well with the Marinade. Cover and refrigerate for at least 2 hours.

Prepare the Cashew Nut Satay Sauce by following the recipe below.

Make a basting sauce by combining the coconut cream, oil and palm sugar in a small bowl and mixing well. Set aside.

Grill the skewers on a preheated pan grill, under a broiler or over a charcoal fire for 2–3 minutes on each side until cooked, constantly basting with the basting sauce. When they are done, arrange the satays on a platter on a bed of sliced cucumber and onion wedges, and serve hot with bowls of the Satay Sauce.

MAKES: *20 satays*   PREPARATION TIME: *45 mins + marination time*
COOKING TIME : *20 mins*

Cashew nut satay sauce

Most satay sauces use peanuts. As many people have peanut allergies, I have created an alternative version using dry-roasted cashew nuts instead, but you can substitute peanuts if you prefer.

3 tablespoons oil
3 cloves garlic, minced
1 onion, finely chopped
8 candlenuts or macadamia nuts
1 stalk lemongrass, thick part only, outer layers discarded, inner part sliced
2 tablespoons Meat Curry Powder (page 242)
1 tablespoon Sambal Oelek Chili (page 240)
1 tablespoon tamarind pulp, mashed with 1/2 cup (125 ml) water, strained to obtain juice
1 cup (120 g) raw cashew nuts or peanuts
2 tablespoons milk powder
2 cups (500 ml) hot water
1 1/2 tablespoons sugar
2 tablespoons plum sauce
1 teaspoon salt, or to taste

Prepare the Sambal Oelek Chili Paste and Meat Curry Powder by following the recipes on page 240 and 242.

Dry-roast the cashews or peanuts in a skillet over low heat, stirring continuously for 2–3 minutes until they are a golden color and cooked. Then coarsely grind them in a mortar or blender and set aside. Heat the oil in a wok and stir-fry the garlic, onion and lemongrass over medium heat until fragrant, 1–2 minutes. Add the curry powder, sambal and tamarind juice and bring to a boil, then simmer uncovered for about 2 minutes. Stir in the cashew nuts or peanuts, milk powder and hot water and cook over medium-low heat until the sauce thickens, 3–5 minutes. Reduce the heat to low, season with the sugar, plum sauce and salt and remove from the heat.

MAKES: *2 cups (500 ml)*   PREPARATION TIME: *30 mins*
COOKING TIME: *10 mins*

1 lb (500 g) swordfish or baby shark steaks, skinned and thinly sliced
1 cup (250 ml) water, or more to cover the fish
Pinch of salt and ground white pepper
2 tablespoons oil
2 onions, finely diced and mixed with
   $^1/_2$ teaspoon salt
6 cloves garlic, finely chopped
1 tablespoon cumin seeds, dry-roasted and ground in a mortar
$^1/_2$ teaspoon ground turmeric
2 teaspoons ground red pepper
1 cup (100 g) unsweetened dried grated (desiccated) coconut, dry-roasted (page 43)
1 teaspoon garam masala
1 teaspoon salt, or to taste
1 teaspoons ground white pepper
Lettuce or witlof leaves, to serve
1 tablespoon fresh lime juice
Fresh curry leaves and coriander leaves (cilantro), to garnish
Lemon wedges, to serve

Flaked fish salad with spices and coconut

This favorite Sri Lankan Jaffna Tamil salad of fried fish shreds has the seductive spicy aroma of sautéed onion, garlic, dry-roasted coconut and toasted cumin—an unbeatable combination of lemony sweet scents that appeals to the primitive brain in all of us. When you hold a lettuce cup of the salad in your palm, you are inhaling all the aromas of Sri Lankan Jaffna Tamil cuisine.

In a saucepan, cover the fish with the water and add a pinch of salt and pepper. Poach the fish over medium heat until it turns opaque, 5–10 minutes. Alternatively, steam the fish in a steamer over rapidly boiling water for about 10 minutes. Remove the fish and drain, then pat dry with paper towels. Place the fish on a platter and use a fork to flake the flesh into small pieces, removing any bones or cartilage. Set aside.

Heat the oil in a wok and stir-fry the onion and garlic over medium heat until fragrant and golden brown, 3–5 minutes. Turn off the heat, add the flaked fish and toss until the fish blends well with the onion and garlic. Add the cumin, turmeric and ground red pepper, and continue tossing. Finally add the roasted grated coconut and garam masala, mix thoroughly and season with the salt and pepper.

Arrange the lettuce or witlof leaves on individual serving plates and top with a portion of the salad. Sprinkle a little lime juice over the top, garnish with curry and coriander leaves and serve immediately with lemon wedges.

SERVES: *6*   PREPARATION TIME: *30 mins*   COOKING TIME: *15 mins*

10 oz (300 g) dried rice stick noodles
1 onion, sliced
6 oz (150 g) beef sirloin, very thinly sliced
Ground white pepper, to taste

STOCK
1 1/2 lbs (750 g) beef bones, hock or shin,
    fat trimmed
2 star anise pods, bruised
2 in (5 cm) fresh ginger, peeled and
    bruised
2 in (5 cm) fresh galangal root, peeled and
    bruised
5 Asian shallots, peeled
1 onion, peeled
10 cups (2 1/2 liters) water
3 green onions, sliced or chopped
1 stick cassia or cinnamon (1 in/3 cm)

4 dried black Chinese mushrooms, soaked
    in hot water until soft, stems removed,
    caps sliced
1 lb (500 g) stewing beef or chuck steak,
    fat trimmed, sliced into chunks
2 tablespoons fish sauce
1 teaspoon sugar
1 teaspoon salt, or to taste
1/2 teaspoon ground white pepper

ACCOMPANIMENTS
Fish sauce
Hoisin sauce
Lime wedges
Sliced red finger-length chili peppers or
    bottled sweet chili sauce
Fresh Thai basil or coriander leaves (cilantro)
Bean sprouts, tails trimmed

Beef noodle soup with fragrant herbs ~ *Pho*

All the delicate aromas of Vietnamese food are contained in this classic *pho* (pronounced "fir") soup. As a steaming bowl is placed in front of you, bend down and inhale the wonderfully complex fragrances of the slow-cooked beef stock, with back notes of star anise, peppery ginger and refreshing, minty galangal. As you sip the first spoonful, the perfume of sweet cassia enters your nostrils—a coffee-like hit that is both sweet and pungent. This is the iconic breakfast, lunch and dinner dish of the Vietnamese, with a slow-cooked stock that perfumes the whole kitchen and its surroundings. Served with a large bowlful of crisp Vietnamese mint, Thai basil and perilla leaves, then topped with crunchy raw beansprouts, *pho* soup is my panacea for all ills.

Prepare the Stock first. Preheat the oven to 350°F (180°C). Combine the beef bones, star anise, ginger, galangal, shallots and onion in a baking dish, and bake for 20 mins until fragrant. Alternatively, roast the star anise, ginger, galangal, shallots and onion, separately, by holding them with tongs over a flame until they are slightly burned on all sides. Transfer to a large stockpot, add the water and bring to a boil over high heat, skimming off any foam that floats to the surface. Continue boiling and skimming, and topping up with more hot water as the stock reduces, until it is clear of residue. This may take up to 1 hour.

    Add the green onions, cinnamon and mushroom to the clear Stock, and return to a boil. Lower the heat to medium and simmer half-covered for 1 hour. Finally add the chuck steak to the Stock and simmer for 3 minutes, then season with the fish sauce, sugar, salt and pepper. Remove from the heat and strain. Thinly slice the chuck beef and keep the clear Stock warm over very low heat. Discard the beef bones and spices.

    Bring a saucepan of water to a boil and cook the rice noodles until soft, 5–7 minutes. Remove from the heat and rinse with cold water, then drain. Divide the noodles equally into 6–8 serving bowls and top with the onion slices and cooked and raw beef slices. Return the Stock to a boil and ladle boiling Stock into each bowl (the raw beef will partially cook in the boiling Stock). Sprinkle with ground pepper and serve hot with small bowls of the Accompaniments on the side.

SERVES: *6–8*   PREPARATION TIME: *30 mins*   COOKING TIME: *2 hours*

1 cup (200 g) uncooked short-grain rice

6 cups (1½ liters) water

1 tablespoon oil

2 cloves garlic, minced

8 oz (250 g) ground pork or 10 oz (300 g) white fish fillets, cubed

4 tablespoons chopped Chinese pickled mustard greens (*kiam chye*)

1 tablespoon grated fresh young ginger

2 teaspoons soy sauce

Salt, to taste

Sesame oil, to drizzle

2 green onions, thinly sliced

3 tablespoons preserved Chinese cabbage (*tang chye*)

Chopped red bell pepper or roasted dried shrimp, to serve

Sprigs of coriander leaves (cilantro), to garnish

Ground white pepper, to taste

Chinese rice congee with all the trimmings

Chok (the Cantonese word for rice congee), is the ultimate comfort food cooked by grandmothers for their grandchildren when they start teething, or a dish brought to your bedside when you are down with a heavy cold. The soft rice served with brined mustard green shreds is subtly aromatic on its own and it can be dressed up with the inviting perfumes of fresh ginger, sesame oil and golden-fried garlic.

Wash the rice in a couple of changes of water until the water runs clear (page 159). Place in a large saucepan with the water and bring to boil, then simmer half-covered over medium heat for 30–40 minutes, stirring occasionally and topping it up with boiling water as necessary. When the rice is soft and mushy, remove from the heat and set aside.

Heat the oil in a large saucepan and sauté the garlic over medium heat until fragrant and golden, about 1 minute. Add the cooked rice and stir to combine. Add the ground pork or chicken in small bits and stir in the pickled vegetable, ginger and soy sauce. Cook the congee for about 5 minutes, stirring from time to time. Season with salt to taste and remove from the heat. Ladle into individual serving bowls, drizzle with sesame oil on top and sprinkle with green onion, preserved Chinese cabbage and chopped bell pepper or dried shrimp. Garnish with coriander sprigs. Sprinkle with ground white pepper and serve hot.

Note: Instead of ground pork or chicken, white fish fillets cut into cubes also work well with this recipe. If you like, you can roll the ground meat and add it to the porridge in the form of meatballs.

SERVES: *6* **PREPARATION TIME:** *20 mins* **COOKING TIME:** *45 mins*

5–10 saffron threads

1 tablespoon warm milk with $^1/_4$ teaspoon ground turmeric added

1 cup (250 g) uncooked Basmati or long-grain rice

1 tablespoon oil

$^1/_4$ cup (30 g) dry-roasted cashew nuts

1 onion, halved and thinly sliced

2 cardamom pods, crushed and peeled

2 cloves, slightly crushed

1 cup (250 ml) coconut milk, mixed with 2 cups (500 ml) water, or 3 cups (750 ml) Chicken Stock (page 245)

$^1/_2$ teaspoon salt, or to taste

Saffron rice with cloves and cashews

The subtle perfume of saffron, crocus stamens is infused into this golden rice dish which is also strengthened by the sweet aroma of cloves. Given their differences, the warm pungency of cloves works well with light saffron to produce an amazingly scented rice dish.

Prepare the Chicken Stock by following the recipe on page 245.

Place the saffron threads in a small bowl and cover with the warm milk and turmeric mixture. Allow to soak for 10 minutes.

Wash the rice in a container by covering it with cold water and stirring it, then draining off the water. Repeat this several times until the water drains clear (this removes some of the starch from the rice). Set aside.

Heat the oil in a large skillet and sauté the cashew nuts over medium heat until golden, 1–2 minutes. Turn off the heat and remove the nuts from the skillet, leaving the oil.

Reheat the oil and sauté the sliced onion, cardamom and cloves over medium heat until fragrant, 1–2 minutes. Add the rice and toss for about 5 minutes, until the rice grains become opaque. Remove from the heat and transfer the rice mixture to a large saucepan. Pour in the diluted coconut milk or Chicken Stock until the level is $1^1/_2$ in ($3^1/_2$ cm) above the rice. Stir in the saffron threads with milk and add the salt.

Cook the rice half-covered over medium–high heat until all the liquid is absorbed, 8–10 minutes (cook for a further 3 minutes if the rice is still wet). Reduce the heat to low, cover the pan tightly and turn off the heat. Allow the rice to steam for 10 minutes with the cover on. Fluff the rice with a fork and serve hot with a curry dish.

SERVES: *4*   PREPARATION TIME: *20 mins*   COOKING TIME: *20 mins*

1¹/₃ lbs (600 g) boneless chicken fillets,
    fat trimmed, sliced into bite-sized chunks
¹/₂ teaspoon salt
¹/₂ tablespoon fresh lime juice
3 tablespoons ghee or butter
2 medium onions, finely sliced
2 cups (450 g) uncooked basmati rice,
    washed and drained, then dried on paper
    towels
5 whole cloves
1 stick cinnamon (3 in/8 cm), broken into
    pieces
5 cardamom pods
1 tablespoon minced garlic
1 tablespoon ginger juice (pressed from
    grated fresh ginger)

1 tablespoon Amah's Curry Powder
    (page 108)
¹/₂ tablespoon garam masala
1 tablespoon ground pomegranate seeds
1¹/₂ cups (375 ml) Chicken Stock (page 245)
3 tablespoons plain yogurt
4-5 saffron threads, soaked in 2 tablespoons
    warm milk
1¹/₂ teaspoons salt
¹/₂ teaspoon ground white pepper
¹/₄ teaspoon rose water (optional)
Sprigs of coriander leaves (cilantro),
    to garnish
Saffron threads, to garnish (optional)

Basmati rice with spiced chicken and yogurt

Sit back and inhale! This dish is one to be savored slowly while allowing your senses to separate and identify each aroma and flavor. I normally serve it with a light yogurt raita and a light vegetarian korma so that the scents do not run rampant. To prepare this dish, you will need a strong, heavy-based pan where the rice can be sautéed and cooked slowly.

Prepare the Amah's Curry Powder and Chicken Stock by following the recipes on pages 108 and 245.

In a bowl, combine the chicken pieces with the salt and lime juice and mix well, then marinate for 10 minutes. Rinse the chicken and drain.

Heat 1 tablespoon of the ghee or butter in a large skillet and sauté half of the onion slices over medium heat until golden brown, 1–2 minutes. Add the rice and half of each of the spices and stir until fragrant, 1–2 minutes. Remove from the heat and cool.

Heat the remaining ghee or butter in a large heavy-based saucepan and sauté the remaining onion slices over medium heat until golden brown, 1–2 minutes. Add the garlic and ginger juice and sauté for 30 seconds, then stir in the remaining spices and mix until fragrant. Add the chicken pieces, curry powder, garam masala, ground pomegranate seeds, mix well and cook for 1–2 minutes. Remove from the heat.

In a bowl, combine the Chicken Stock, yogurt, saffron and milk, mix well and season with the salt and pepper.

Layer the spiced rice and a layer of the chicken in the bottom of a rice cooker. Continue placing more layers of rice and chicken until they have been used up. Slowly pour in the Chicken Stock mixture until it is about 2 in (5 cm) above the level of the rice or chicken, then gently stir in the rose water (if using). Cover and cook as you would normal rice.

If using a pot to cook the rice, lay the ingredients in the pot in the same manner and cover tightly. Cook over medium heat for about 10 minutes until all the liquid has evaporated, then reduce the heat to low and simmer for 5 more minutes. Remove from the heat. Spoon the spiced chicken rice onto individual serving plates, garnish with coriander leaves and saffron if desired, and serve immediately.

SERVES: 6   PREPARATION TIME: 45 mins   COOKING TIME: 30 mins

1 fresh chicken (2 lbs/1 kg), with skin on
2 cups (400 g) uncooked long-grain rice, washed (page 244) and drained well
2 star anise pods
1 in (3 cm) fresh ginger, peeled and sliced
6 cloves garlic, peeled
2 teaspoons sesame oil
6 cups (1½ liters) Chicken Stock (page 245)
3 green onions
2 teaspoons preserved Chinese cabbage (*tang chye*), plus 1 more tablespoon for the soup
Salt and ground white pepper, to taste
1 teaspoon sesame oil, to rub into the chicken
Black soy sauce

GARLIC GINGER MIX
4 cloves garlic, peeled
1 in (3 cm) fresh ginger, peeled and sliced

GARLIC CHILI SAUCE
¼ cup (60 ml) bottled garlic chili sauce
1 tablespoon vinegar

ACCOMPANIMENTS
Sliced cucumber
Sliced tomatoes (optional)
Sliced red chili peppers
Green onion strips

Chicken rice with fresh chili ginger sauce

Lift the lid while cooking and breathe in deeply the tempting aroma, especially if you are using jasmine rice and a full-bodied chicken stock. The brothy chicken aroma is layered into the dish with star anise, ginger and nutty sesame oil when the chicken is served, making it an enticing and satisfying dish for your family or guests.

Prepare the Chicken Stock by following the recipe on page 245.

Clean the chicken well, removing the fat from under the skin and back. Dice the chicken fat and melt it in a skillet over high heat. Pour the chicken fat over the washed rice and mix well.

Grind the star anise, ginger and garlic in a food processor or a mortar until fine. Rub the paste over the entire body of the chicken and inside the body cavity.

Heat the sesame oil in a wok and stir-fry the fat-coated rice over medium heat until fragrant, 3–5 minutes. Set aside.

Bring the Chicken Stock to a boil in a pot. Add the chicken, green onions, preserved Chinese cabbage, salt and pepper, and return to a boil. Reduce the heat to medium and simmer uncovered, skimming off the foam from the stock, until the chicken is just cooked, 3–4 minutes. Remove from the heat. Remove the chicken from the stock and strain it, discarding the solids. Rub the sesame oil over the chicken and set aside. Cut the chicken into bite-sized pieces just before serving.

To cook the rice, place the stir-fried rice, 2½ cups (625 ml) of the reserved stock and salt to taste in the rice cooker. The stock should be 1–1½ in (3–4 cm) above the rice level. Switch on the rice cooker and allow to cook. Alternatively, boil in a saucepan for 1–2 minutes, then cover the pan and simmer over low heat for about 20 minutes until all the water has been absorbed and the rice is cooked. Turn off the heat and allow the rice to sit for 5–10 minutes before removing the lid. If desired, add a little sesame oil to the cooked rice, then fluff with a fork to separate the grains before serving.

Prepare the Garlic Ginger Mix by grinding the garlic and ginger to a paste in a mortar. Prepare the Garlic Chili Sauce by mixing the ingredients together.

To prepare the soup, boil the remaining stock and preserved Chinese cabbage for about 2 minutes. Remove from the heat and ladle into individual serving bowls.

To serve, place the chicken rice on serving plates. Arrange the chicken pieces and Accompaniments on top. Serve immediately with the soup, Garlic Ginger Mix, Garlic Chili Sauce, green onions and black soy sauce on the side.

SERVES: *4–6*   **PREPARATION TIME:** *45 mins*   **COOKING TIME:** *30 mins*

1 cup (180 g) dried couscous
1 cup (250 ml) boiling water
1¹/₂ tablespoons olive oil
¹/₂ onion, finely chopped
1 teaspoon black mustard seeds
3 stalks fresh curry leaves; leaves plucked
    from the stalks
³/₄ cup (100 g) sundried tomatoes in olive oil,
    drained and sliced into thin strips
2–3 black olives, chopped
1 teaspoon dry-roasted ground coriander
1 teaspoon ground red pepper, or to taste
Fresh juice of 2 limes
1 teaspoon grated lime rind
¹/₂ cup (60 g) roasted cashew nuts, chopped
1 teaspoon salt, or to taste
¹/₂ teaspoon ground white pepper

Tomato and olive couscous with curry leaves

This recipe, like many of my other recipes, started from a simple Uppama dish we used to make in Malaysia. I had no coarse semolina, so I used couscous instead. When it turned out well, I continued adding other ingredients from my kitchen. The large bottle of sundried tomatoes seemed too good to miss, and I added black olives and lime juice, not forgetting the essential Uppama ingredients—black mustard seeds and curry leaves. Call it fusion if you will; the flavors are a refreshing change to the usual.

Combine the couscous, boiling water and ¹/₂ tablespoon of the oil in a large bowl and mix well, then cover and allow to soak for 5 minutes. In the last 1 minute, stir the mixture with a fork to separate the grains.

Heat the oil in a wok and stir-fry the onion over medium heat until fragrant and tender, 1–2 minutes. Move the onion to the sides of the wok, add the mustard seeds and stir-fry until they pop, then stir in the curry leaves.

Add the couscous, sundried tomato strips, chopped olives, ground coriander and red pepper, and toss for 2–3 minutes until well combined, adding extra olive oil if the mixture appears too dry. Stir in the lime juice, grated lime rind and cashew nuts and season with the salt and pepper. Remove from the heat, transfer to a serving bowl and serve with an iceberg lettuce salad with fresh onions.

SERVES: 4   PREPARATION TIME: 20 mins   COOKING TIME: 5 mins

1 fresh duck (about 3$\frac{1}{2}$ lbs/1$\frac{1}{2}$ kg)
2 teaspoons Chinese rice wine
1 teaspoon oil
2 in (5 cm) fresh galangal root (blue ginger),
  peeled and thinly sliced
10 Asian shallots, peeled but left whole
$\frac{1}{4}$ cup (50 g) crushed raw rock sugar
1 stick cinnamon (about 3 in/8 cm)
2 star anise pods
6 cloves
1 tablespoon black soy sauce

Sweet blue ginger duck with star anise

This is one of my favorite aromatic recipes for duck. It is heady with the aromas of star anise, cinnamon and the clean fresh fragrance of galangal that not only adds fragrance, but also tenderizes the meat until succulent—a recipe from my friend, Pauline Loh.

Clean the duck and rinse well. Trim off the neck, wing tips, tail and webs. Sprinkle the duck with the Chinese rice wine and rub well over the entire body including the cavity. Set aside.

Heat the oil in a wok and stir-fry the galangal slices and whole shallots over medium heat until browned and fragrant, 1–2 minutes. Add the rock sugar and spices and stir until the sugar melts and begins to caramelize.

Place the whole duck in the wok, increase the heat to high and brown the duck on all sides for about 2 minutes, turning the duck using 2 spatulas. Add the black soy sauce and pour in enough water to cover the duck halfway.

Cook the duck for 30–40 minutes, turning it often. The shallots will melt and thicken the sauce while the duck is cooking. Reduce the heat to low, turn the duck, then cover and simmer for 30 minutes, adding a little water if the duck starts to dry out. Cook uncovered for another 15 minutes and remove from the heat. Remove the duck from the wok and slice into bite-sized pieces, then transfer to a serving platter. Skim off the fat from the surface of the duck gravy and transfer to a serving bowl. Spoon some duck gravy over the duck pieces and serve with steamed rice and the duck gravy on the side.

SERVES: 6   PREPARATION TIME: *15 mins*   COOKING TIME: *1 hour 30 mins*

3 lbs (1¹/₄ kg) duck breasts and legs
2 tablespoons black soy sauce
1 teaspoon ginger juice (pressed from grated fresh ginger)
2 cups (500 ml) oil, for frying
6 dried shiitake mushrooms, soaked in hot water until soft and drained, stems discarded, caps halved
1 stick cinnamon (3 in/8 cm)
2 star anise pods, roughly ground in a mortar

¹/₄ cup (20 g) dried woodear or cloud ear fungus, soaked in hot water until soft then drained, hard bits removed
1¹/₂ tablespoons soy sauce
1 tablespoon sake or dry sherry (optional)
¹/₄ cup (60 ml) Chinese rice wine
1 teaspoon vinegar
3 green onions, finely sliced
1 mandarin orange, peeled and segmented
2 tablespoons dried cranberries, to garnish

Black soy duck with orange and cranberries

The duck is aromatic, crisp skinned and sinfully tasty. Sniff into the mushroomy spice sauce that is earth-cooked into the duck flesh and enjoy a truly orgasmic experience.

Prepare the duck first by rubbing the black soy sauce and ginger juice into the duck pieces. Allow to marinate for 2 hours, hanging up if possible.

Heat 1 tablespoon of oil in a wok and stir-fry the mushrooms over medium heat until fragrant, 1–2 minutes. Remove from the heat and set aside.

Preheat the oven to 375°F (190°C).

Heat the remaining oil in the wok and fry the duck over medium heat until golden brown and crispy. Remove from the heat and transfer to a large heatproof casserole dish. Add the cinnamon, star anise and enough boiling water to just cover. Place the dish on the stove and cook the duck over low heat for about 15 minutes or until the sauce is reduced. Remove from the heat and stir in the mushrooms, woodear fungus and soy sauce. Cover the casserole with aluminum foil and bake in the oven for about 1 hour. Remove the duck from the oven, skim off the fat from the surface of the sauce and add the sake or sherry (if using), Chinese rice wine and vinegar. Return the duck to the oven. Lower the temperature to 320°F (160°C) and bake for 15 more minutes. Remove from the heat.

Stir in the green onion and cook the duck on the stove uncovered over low heat for another 15–20 minutes or until the duck is tender and the sauce thickens. Add the orange segments and remove from the heat. Transfer to a serving platter, garnish with the cranberries and serve with Nonya Pickled Vegetables with Dried Shrimp (page 220).

SERVES: *6*   **PREPARATION TIME:** *1 hour*   **COOKING TIME:** *1 hour 45 mins*

Lamb baked with dates, tomatoes and cumin

The perfume of Arabia came to Africa as it did to India. It was food lingering fragrances of honey-like saffron, chocolate-like cassia, smoky paprika, sweet dates and clove-like bay leaves. The dish originates from Cape Town. It was given to me by a Cape Malay cook.

1½ lbs (700 g) boneless lamb, fat trimmed
2 teaspoons dry-roasted ground cumin
Pinch of salt
1 tablespoon freshly ground black pepper
¼ cup (60 ml) olive oil
2 onions, finely diced
3 cloves garlic, finely chopped
2 carrots, peeled, halved and sliced
  diagonally
1 parsnip, peeled and sliced diagonally
12 saffron threads, soaked in 1 tablespoon
  warm milk
1 teaspoon chopped fresh bay leaf
1 teaspoon chopped fresh coriander leaves
  (cilantro)
⅓ cup (50 g) roasted almonds
1 cup (250 ml) dry red wine or tamarind
  juice (strained from 2 tablespoons pulp
  mashed with 1 cup [250 ml] water)
One 14-oz (400-g) can whole tomatoes
1 cup (100 g) dried dates, soaked in water
  until soft, then drained and halved
Salt and ground white pepper, to taste

Debone the lamb and trim off any fat, then place in a large bowl. Mix the cumin, salt and pepper in a small bowl and rub the mixture into the lamb with your fingers. Allow to marinate for 1 hour.

Preheat the oven to 350°F (180°C).

Heat the oil in a wok and stir-fry the lamb over high heat for 2–3 minutes until lightly browned. Remove the lamb from the pan and set aside. Reheat the oil and stir-fry the onion and garlic over medium heat for 1–2 minutes. Add the carrot, parsnip, saffron in milk, bay leaf, coriander leaves and almonds and stir-fry for 1–2 minutes. Pour in the wine or tamarind juice and bring to a boil, then simmer uncovered for 1–2 minutes until the gravy thickens.

Stir in the tomatoes, dates and stir-fried lamb and mix well, then transfer to a casserole dish and bake in the oven for about 50 minutes until the lamb is tender. Remove from the heat, adjust the taste with salt and pepper, and serve hot with Saffron Rice with Cloves and Cashews (page 159) or mashed potatoes.

SERVES: 6   PREPARATION TIME: *45 mins + marination time*
COOKING TIME: *1 hour 15 mins*

Grilled beef steak with asian spices

Maximum flavor with minimum fuss, this recipe is guaranteed for success as long as good quality tenderloin is well marinated, grilled quickly and sliced across the grain. Cooked this way, beef is the consummate meal that satisfies.

1½ lbs (700 g) beef tenderloin
2 tablespoons fresh lime juice
2 tablespoons soy sauce
1 tablespoon cumin seeds, dry-roasted and
  coarsely ground in a mortar
2 teaspoons coriander seeds, dry-roasted
  and ground in a mortar
1½ teaspoons salt
1 tablespoon oil
Fresh juice of ½ lime

Combine the lime juice and soy sauce, then pour this over the beef and coat well with the mixture. Allow to marinate for at least 20 minutes.

Mix the cumin, coriander and salt in a small bowl and rub the mixture into both sides of the beef. Lightly brush with oil and grill the beef on a preheated pan grill or under a broiler for about 3 minutes on each side until cooked, turning often. Remove from the heat.

Slice the grilled beef into thick slices. Arrange on a serving platter, sprinkle with lime juice and serve hot with a salad.

SERVES: 4   PREPARATION TIME: *10 mins*   COOKING TIME: *15 mins*

2–4 sirloin steaks (8 oz/250 g each)
1 tablespoon oyster sauce
1 tablespoon ginger juice (pressed from
    grated fresh ginger)
$1/2$ teaspoon ground white pepper
Oil, for grilling
Blanched broccoli, to serve

SWEET ONION JAM
1 tablespoon oil
2 medium onions, thinly sliced
2 teaspoons Sambal Oelek Chili Paste
    (page 240)
$1/2$ cup (125 ml) Chinese rice wine
1 tablespoon shaved palm sugar
1 teaspoon salt, or to taste

MASHED SWEET POTATOES
2–3 sweet potatoes, peeled, or $1/2$ small
    pumpkin, deseeded and peeled
1 tablespoon butter
$1/2$ teaspoon sugar (optional)
$1/2$ teaspoon freshly ground black pepper

Barbecued beef steaks with sweet onion jam

The smoky, mouth-watering aroma of grilling meat spluttering on a barbecue with pepper and ginger awaken the tastebuds in anticipation of a good meal. The trick of layering the textures builds up the aromas and flavors—spicy meat and sweet onion jam served with roasted sweet potatoes and crunchy greens.

Prepare the Sambal Oelek Chili Paste by following the recipe on page 240.

Place the beef in a bowl, add the oyster sauce, ginger juice and pepper and rub well into the beef. Allow to marinate for 20 minutes.

Prepare the Sweet Onion Jam by heating the oil in a saucepan and sautéing the onion over low heat until light brown, 3–5 minutes. Stir in the Sambal Oelek, cover and cook for 3–4 minutes. Add the Chinese rice wine and palm sugar, mix well and simmer uncovered for 15 minutes until the sauce is thick and the onion is soft. Season with the salt and remove from the heat. Transfer to a serving bowl and set aside.

To make the Mashed Sweet Potatoes, poke holes in the sweet potatoes or pumpkin with the sharp tip of a knife to allow steam to escape and then microwave until soft, 15–20 minutes on high. Remove from the heat and mash with a spoon. Add the butter, sugar, salt and black pepper and mix well. Set aside.

Brush the marinated beef with a little oil on both sides and grill on a preheated pan grill or under a broiler for 2 minutes, then turn over and grill the other side for 1 minute. Grill for 1 minute on each side if you want the steaks rare. Arrange the beef on a bed of blanched broccoli on individual serving plates and top with the Sweet Onion Jam. Serve immediately with a bowl of Mashed Sweet Potatoes on the side.

SERVES: *2–4*   **PREPARATION TIME:** *45 mins*   **COOKING TIME:** *1 hour*

COOKING WITH AROMATIC ASIAN SPICES

1 tablespoon oil

6 cloves garlic, bruised

1 lb (500 g) pork belly, skin removed and discarded, cubed

1 lb (500 g) pork ribs or 10 oz (300 g) pork shoulder, sliced into pieces

3 star anise pods, roughly ground in a mortar

1/2 teaspoon Sichuan pepper (optional)

2 tablespoons chili black bean sauce

2 tablespoons Sambal Oelek Chili Paste (page 240) or other sweet chili paste

1/2 cup (125 ml) cup sweet caramelized soy sauce, or *kecap manis*

3 cups (750 ml) water

2 teaspoons shaved palm sugar or dark brown sugar

1/3 cup (100 ml) sweet Chinese black vinegar

2 tablespoons Chinese rice wine

8 dried black Chinese mushrooms, soaked in hot water until soft, drained and stir-fried in 2 teaspoons of oil for 2–3 minutes

Salt, to taste

Crispy Fried Garlic (page 47), to garnish

Green onion curls (page 229), to garnish

SWEET CUCUMBER PICKLES

1/2 cup (125 ml) vinegar

2 tablespoons sugar

1 cucumber, halved lengthwise, cored and thinly sliced

Sweet soy pork with mushrooms and star anise

This caramelized pork dish which is known in Malaysia as *Tau Yew Bak* was a speciality of my Cantonese amah who understood that the flavor and aroma that went hand in hand to create it. Over the years I've improved it by adding black bean sauce and chili and caramelizing the pork so that it becomes a dish with an amazing complexity of flavor. Once I had difficulty getting some air tickets for a television program overseas. I invited the manager of an airline company and served him dinner with this dish. We got the tickets. It may be a coincidence, but this dish has always worked its magic at other times and a colleague of mine dubbed it my "lethal weapon." It might bring you success too!

Prepare the Crispy Fried Garlic and green onion curls by following the recipes on pages 47 and 229.

Prepare the Sweet Cucumber Pickles by combining the vinegar and sugar in a bowl and stirring until the sugar is dissolved. Add the cucumber slices and mix well. Allow to marinate for 2 hours and drain the Pickles just before serving.

Heat the oil in a wok and stir-fry the garlic over high heat until golden and fragrant, about 30 seconds. Add both types of pork, the star anise and Sichuan pepper (if using) and stir-fry for 1–2 minutes. Add the chili black bean sauce, Sambal Oelek and black soy sauce and toss well to coat the pork with the sauce.

Pour in the water and bring the ingredients to a boil. Reduce the heat to medium and simmer covered until the pork is very tender, about 20–30 minutes. Season with the sugar, vinegar and rice wine, and stir in the mushrooms. Half cover the pan and simmer over low heat for 1 hour, until the pork is tender and the sauce is thick but not completely dried up. Increase the heat to medium, season with salt to taste and stir-fry the pork to coat it evenly with the sauce. Remove from the heat.

Transfer the pork to a serving bowl and sprinkle with the Crispy Fried Garlic. Garnish with green onion curls and serve immediately with steamed rice and the Sweet Cucumber Pickles on the side.

SERVES: *6–8*   **PREPARATION TIME:** *45 mins + marination time*   **COOKING TIME:** *1 hour 10 mins*

½ cup (125 ml) mirin
1 cup (250 ml) water
4 boneless skinless chicken breasts (about
   1 lb/500 g total)
Chopped garlic chives, to garnish
Orange Clove Sauce (page 179), to serve

SICHUAN PEPPER OIL
2 teaspoons sesame oil
2 teaspoons sichuan pepper

Poached chicken breasts with sichuan pepper oil

The fragrance of this dish leaps up at you even before the cooking is completed. It begins with the mushroomy mirin broth that poaches the chicken, and then moves on to a pungent, peppery and anise-flavored oil that seeps into the chicken, providing a seductive spice hit with every bite. When the chicken is served chilled, the aromas are more pronounced.

Prepare the Orange Clove Sauce by following the recipe on page 179. Set aside.

Bring the mirin and water to a boil in a saucepan. Add the chicken breasts and poach for 2–3 minutes until cooked. Remove from the heat and drain, then arrange the chicken breasts on a serving platter.

Mix the Sichuan Pepper Oil ingredients in a small bowl, then drizzle over the chicken breasts. Chill the chicken breasts in the refrigerator until ready to serve. Garnish with chopped garlic chives and serve the chicken breasts with a bowl of Orange Clove Sauce on the side.

Note: This chicken dish can be served on its own or with any of the leafy salads in the book.

SERVES: *4*   **PREPARATION TIME:** *10 mins*   **COOKING TIME:** *5 mins*

2 fresh medium crabs (each 1 lb/500 g),
   scrubbed and rinsed well
1 teaspoon ground paprika
$1/_4$ teaspoon ground cumin
$1/_4$ teaspoon salt
$1/_2$ teaspoon ground white pepper
$1/_2$ teaspoon cornstarch
1 teaspoon oil
1 medium onion, diced
4 oz (125 g) small fresh shrimp, peeled and
   chopped
2 teaspoons minced green onion
1 red finger-length chili pepper, deseeded
   and minced
1 egg, lightly beaten
$1/_2$ cup (40 g) breadcrumbs
Pinch of ground nutmeg, to sprinkle on top

Stuffed crabs baked in their shells

This dish beckons with aromatic spices such as paprika and cumin baked with the crab meat in their shells. It makes a wonderful meal; truly a dish to savor and enjoy. If empty crab shells aren't available, simply turn it into baked crab cakes. The time taken to prepare this scented dish will definitely be repaid by the compliments received.

Scrub and clean the crabs well. Detach the claws from each crab. Lift off the outer shell and reserve it for use as a casing. Scrape out any roe and discard the gills. Rinse well and quarter the crabs with a cleaver. Crack the claws with a mallet. Place all the crab pieces in a heatproof dish and place the dish in a bamboo steamer.

    Half-fill a wok with water and bring to a rapid boil. Place the steamer with the crab over the boiling water and steam for 5–10 minutes until cooked. Remove from the heat and cool. Reserve the crab stock and remove the crab meat from the shells. In a bowl, combine the crab meat with the paprika, cumin, salt and pepper and mix well.

    Heat the oil in a wok and stir-fry the onion over medium heat until fragrant and soft, 1–2 minutes. Add the shrimp and green onion and stir-fry for 1 minute. Add the crab meat mixture and 2 tablespoons of the crab stock (saved from steaming the crabs) and toss for 1 minute. Remove from the heat and stir in half of the beaten egg.

    Clean the reserved crab shells and fill them with the crab and shrimp mixture. Brush the top with the remaining egg and sprinkle with the breadcrumbs. Place the filled crab shells on a baking pan and bake in a preheated oven for 10 minutes at 350°F (180°C). Remove from the heat, sprinkle with the ground nutmeg and serve immediately.

SERVES: *2*   PREPARATION TIME: *1 hour*   COOKING TIME: *30 mins*

1 lb (500 g) freshly shucked scallops
Pinch of salt
1 tablespoon olive oil
$^1/_4$ cup (30 g) chopped roasted pistachios
Rind of 1 orange, blanched in boiling water
    until soft, drained and sliced into shreds

ORANGE CLOVE SAUCE
1 tablespoon olive oil
1 onion, finely diced
1 tablespoon Thai Orange Curry Paste
    (page 241)
1 tablespoon tamarind pulp, mashed with
    $^1/_2$ cup (125 ml) water and strained to
    obtain juice
$^1/_2$ cup (125 ml) fresh orange juice
$^1/_2$ teaspoon ground cloves
1 tablespoon honey
1 tablespoon orange marmalade
1 tablespoon shaved palm sugar or dark
    brown sugar
Salt, to taste

Seared scallops with orange clove sauce

Plump and juicy scallops served with a sauce of orange and cloves, lends a fruity fragrance and middle eastern flavors to this divine combination in a recipe that is Thai in origin.

Prepare the Thai Orange Curry Paste by following the recipe on page 241.

Prepare the Orange Clove Sauce by heating the oil in a wok and stir-frying the onion until golden and tender, 1–2 minutes. Add the Curry Paste and tamarind juice and bring to a boil. Reduce the heat to low and simmer uncovered for about 5 minutes. Remove from the heat and strain, discarding the solids. Return the strained sauce to the wok. Add all the other ingredients and bring to a boil, then simmer uncovered over low heat for 5–10 minutes until the sauce has thickened. Season with the sugar and salt to taste and remove from the heat. Set aside.

Place the scallops in a large bowl, sprinkle with salt and mix well, then set aside for 5 minutes. Heat the oil in a skillet and sear the scallops until opaque and cooked, 2–3 minutes on each side depending on the size of the scallops. Do not overcook them.

Arrange the cooked scallops on individual serving platters lined with lettuce leaves (if using). Drizzle the Orange Clove Sauce over the scallops and garnish with the pistachios and orange rind shreds. Serve immediately.

SERVES: *6*   **PREPARATION TIME:** *20 mins*   **COOKING TIME:** *30 mins*

Fish hotpot with coconut broth and dill

The famous Vietnamese Ca Qua hotpot brings the bubbling fragrance of coconut and the strong aromas of fennel, turmeric and dill to the dinner table. The fish added to the soup strengthens the flavors, leaving the diner satiated. I had the best Ca Qua in a restaurant in Hanoi, where I climbed up the dark stairs into a huge room completely filled with trestle tables and diners all eating this one dish served to them by eager waitresses chasing up and down the stairs, making sure the hotpots were full of beautiful soups and herbs that were constantly replenished. The meal was quite an experienece.

COCONUT BROTH

1 tablespoon oil
$^{1}/_{2}$ teaspoon dried shrimp paste, dry-roasted
2 cloves garlic, minced
$^{1}/_{2}$ teaspoon fennel seeds, dry-roasted and ground, or $^{1}/_{4}$ teaspoon ground fennel
$^{1}/_{2}$ teaspoon chili paste, or to taste
2 cups (500 ml) coconut milk
1 cup (250 ml) water
$^{1}/_{2}$ teaspoon ground turmeric
$^{1}/_{3}$ cup (100 ml) coconut cream
1 teaspoon fish sauce
2 teaspoons fresh lime juice
1 teaspoon salt
$^{1}/_{2}$ teaspoon ground white pepper

ACCOMPANIMENTS

1 lb (500 g) firm white fish fillets (sea bream, John dory or whiting), sliced
Dried rice vermicelli, soaked in warm water until soft and drained

GARNISHES AND SAUCES

Crushed roasted unsalted peanuts
Thinly sliced green onions
Sprigs of dill
Fish sauce
Soy sauce
Bottled chili sauce

Prepare the Coconut Broth by heating the oil in a wok and stir-frying the shrimp paste and garlic over medium heat until fragrant, about 1 minute. Add the fennel and chili paste and stir-fry for 1 minute. Stir in the coconut milk, water and turmeric and bring to a simmer. Cook for 2–3 minutes for the flavors to integrate, then pour in the coconut cream, season with the fish sauce, lime juice, salt and pepper to taste, and bring the broth to a slow boil.

Transfer the Coconut Broth to a hotpot or fondue pot on the dining table and keep it simmering over very low heat. Arrange platters of the Accompaniments and Garnishes, and bowls of the Sauces around the hotpot. Invite your guests to dip and cook the fish in the Coconut Broth, then fill a bowl with the noodles, ladle the Coconut Broth over them and eat with the Garnishes and Sauces.

Note: If you don't wish to go to the trouble of cooking this at the table, simply add the fish pieces to the simmering broth at the final stage and allow it to cook for 1–2 minutes, then serve the noodles and fish with Coconut Broth in individual bowls with the Accompaniments and Garnishes on the side for each guest to add by themselves. More freshly ground fennel may be sprinkled on top of the soup for additional fragrance.

SERVES: *4*   PREPARATION TIME: *15 mins*   COOKING TIME: *5 mins*

COOKING WITH AROMATIC ASIAN SPICES

3 fresh lobsters (each 1 lb/500 g) or 3 lbs
   (1¹/₃ kg) fresh crayfish
¹/₂ cup (125 ml) oil
5 tablespoons butter
7 cloves garlic, crushed
1 teaspoon black peppercorns, coarsely
   cracked in a mortar or spice grinder
1 tablespoon rice vinegar
1 tablespoon sugar
¹/₂ teaspoon salt, or to taste
Salmon roe, to garnish

MARINADE
1 teaspoon coarsely ground black
   peppercorns
2 tablespoons soy sauce
¹/₂ tablespoon sugar

Black pepper lobster tails with garlic butter

A seafood dish that is a gastronomic delight and a triumph for the cook as the pepper-spiked lobster is lowered into hot butter and tossed quickly. The sweetness of butter and sizzling lobster quickly wafts into the dining room enticing all within reach.

If using live lobsters, freeze them for 1 hour, then lay on the chopping board and cut through the head along the point between the eyes with the back of a cleaver or a sharp knife to quickly kill them. Omit the freezing step if using frozen lobsters. Twist off the claws and detach the tails from the heads by inserting a knife into the gap between the tail and head. Crack the claws with a cracker or hammer, and quarter each lobster tail. Discard the heads. If using crayfish, rinse and scrub them well to remove the mud. Detach the bodies from the heads by twisting off the head of each crayfish. Discard the heads and halve each crayfish. Pat dry the lobster or crayfish pieces with paper towels.

Combine the Marinade ingredients in a bowl and mix well. Pour the Marinade over the lobster or crayfish pieces and mix until well coated. Allow to marinate for at least 1 hour.

Heat the oil in a wok until hot. In small batches, stir-fry the lobster or crayfish pieces over medium heat until red and crispy, 2–3 minutes. Remove from the heat and drain on paper towels, keeping warm.

In another wok, melt the butter over medium heat and then stir-fry the garlic until golden brown and fragrant, 1–2 minutes. Add the cracked black pepper and mix well. Add the fried lobster or crayfish pieces and toss until well coated. Season with the rice vinegar, sugar and salt, and remove from the heat. Transfer to a serving platter and sprinkle with the salmon roe. Serve hot.

SERVES: *4–6*   **PREPARATION TIME:** *20 mins + 1 hour to marinate*   **COOKING TIME:** *10 mins*

1 lb (500 g) baby potatoes, peeled
2 teaspoons cumin seeds
1 teaspoon fennel seeds
1 tablespoon oil
2 cloves garlic, minced
1 tablespoon Sambal Oelek Chili Paste
   (page 240) or 2 red finger-length chili
   peppers, deseeded and sliced
3 sprigs curry leaves; leaves plucked from the
   stalks
1 tablespoon tomato paste
1 tablespoon tamarind pulp, mashed with
   4 tablespoons water and strained to obtain
   juice
$^{1}/_{2}$ cup (30 g) dried methi leaves or dill
1 tablespoon sundried tomatoes, chopped
$^{1}/_{2}$ teaspoon salt, or to taste
$^{1}/_{4}$ teaspoon ground white pepper

Herbed potatoes with sundried tomatoes

Potatoes are skillfully cooked to perfection with sour-sweet tamarind, citrusy cumin, anise-like fennel and peppery curry leaves. The result is a combination which releases an aroma most inviting to the senses of the mouth. This South Indian dish is proof that a vegetarian dish can be more imaginative and tastier than a meat dish.

Prepare the Sambal Oelek Chili Paste by following the recipe on page 240.

Bring a pot of water to a boil, add the potatoes and boil for 5–10 minutes until cooked. Remove from the heat and drain.

Dry-roast the cumin and fennel seeds in a skillet over low heat for 3–5 minutes until fragrant. Remove from the heat, cool and grind to a powder in a mortar.

Heat the oil in a wok over medium heat and stir-fry the garlic until golden and fragrant, 1–2 minutes. Add the spice mixture, Sambal Oelek or chili, and curry leaves, and stir-fry for 1 minute. Stir in the tomato paste and tamarind juice, and bring the mixture to a boil. Add the cooked potatoes, methi leaves or dill and sundried tomatoes and mix well. Season with the salt and pepper and remove from the heat. Transfer to a serving platter and serve hot with a curried lamb or beef dish.

SERVES: *4*   PREPARATION TIME: *25 mins*   COOKING TIME: *20 mins*

1¹/₂ lbs (700 g) slender Asian eggplants
2 teaspoons salt
¹/₂ tablespoon grated fresh turmeric root, or
  ¹/₂ teaspoon ground turmeric
1 cup (250 ml) light olive oil, for frying
¹/₄ cup (30 g) raw cashew nuts, dry-roasted

SPICE PASTE
2 teaspoons cumin seeds, dry-roasted
1 teaspoon fennel seeds, dry-roasted
2 in (5 cm) fresh ginger, peeled and sliced
5 cloves garlic, peeled
2 stalks lemongrass, thick bottom part only,
  outer layers discarded, inner part sliced
2 onions, peeled and quartered
3 tablespoons extra virgin olive oil
2 tablespoons Fish Curry Powder (page 242)
1 tablespoon black mustard seeds, roughly
  crushed in a mortar
2 teaspoons ground red pepper
¹/₂ cup (125 ml) white vinegar
2 tablespoon shaved palm sugar or dark
  brown sugar

Eggplant sambal with black mustard and cashews

This aromatic sambal with an aroma of heady garlic, lime-like lemongrass and cumin has an additional layer of aromatic fennel and pungent mustard. The slow-cooking makes it possible for all the spice aromas to be separately enjoyed and the vinegar heightens the spice scents. This is a wonderful pickled sambal with exceptional fragrance and taste.

Prepare the Fish Curry Powder by following the recipe on page 242.

Cut the eggplants into 1 in (3 cm) thick slices. Combine the salt and grated turmeric in a small bowl and mix well. Brush the eggplant slices with the mixture and set aside for 10 minutes, then press between paper towels to dry them.

Heat the olive oil in a skillet and in small batches, fry the eggplant slices over medium heat until light brown, 1–2 minutes on each side. Remove from the heat and drain on paper towels.

To prepare the Spice Paste, grind the cumin and fennel seeds in a spice grinder until fine. Combine with the ginger, garlic, lemongrass and onion, and grind to a smooth paste in a mortar or food processor. Heat the olive oil in a skillet and sauté the ground paste over medium heat until fragrant, 2–3 minutes. Add the Fish Curry Powder and continue to sauté for 1 more minute. Move the spice mixture to the sides of the pan, increase the heat to high, add the mustard seeds and cook until they begin to pop, then combine them with the spice mixture from the sides of the pan and mix well. Stir in the ground red pepper and season with the vinegar and sugar.

Add the cashew nuts and fried eggplant slices and toss until the eggplant is coated well with the sauce, taking care not to tear the pieces. Adjust the taste and remove from the heat. Serve hot or cold. This dish is especially tasty when served with baked ham, moussaka and crisp lettuce, or with steamed or fried fish.

SERVES: *6*   PREPARATION TIME: *45 mins*   COOKING TIME: *15 mins*

10 oz (300 g) young okra, stems trimmed
1 teaspoon cornstarch
$^{1}/_{2}$ teaspoon ground turmeric
$^{1}/_{4}$ cup (60 ml) plain yogurt
$^{1}/_{2}$ teaspoon ground red pepper

FILLING
5 tablespoons dried shrimp, dry-roasted
   and crushed (see note)
1 tablespoon dried mango powder
   (*amchoor*), or $^{1}/_{2}$ teaspoon tamarind
   pulp mixed with as little water as
   possible to make a paste
1 tablespoon grated fresh ginger
2 tablespoons Sambal Oelek Chili Paste
   (page 240), or Chili Jam (page 244)
1 tablespoon unsweetened dried grated
   (desiccated) coconut, dry-roasted in a
   pan until golden (page 43)
1 teaspoon Dijon mustard
2 teaspoons sugar, or to taste
Pinch of salt, or to taste
3 teaspoons water

Okra stuffed with dried shrimp and coconut

Dry-roasted and cooked dried shrimp take on an inviting fragrance of nutty fried fish. In this recipe, the aromatic addition of shrimp stuffing with buttery roasted coconut and the spike of ginger transform the plain okra, giving it life.

Prepare the Sambal Oelek Chili Paste by following the recipe on page 240.

Rinse the okra well, then drain and dry with paper towels. Make a slit along the side of each okra with a sharp knife, making sure not to cut through it and that the slit does not continue until the tip. Carefully remove the seeds and pith. Set aside. Combine all the Filling ingredients in a bowl and mix well. Stuff each okra by gently opening up the slit and filling it with 1 teaspoon of the Filling, using a fork or chopstick to press it in.

Preheat the oven to 320°F (160°C).

Mix the cornstarch and turmeric together on a plate. Roll each stuffed okra in the turmeric mixture to coat well, then place them on a baking sheet and bake in the oven for 20 minutes. Remove from the heat and arrange in a serving plate in a shallow yogurt bath. Sprinkle with ground red pepper and and serve immediately.

Note: Dry-roast the dried shrimp by placing them in a shallow dish and microwave on high for 2 minutes. Remove from the oven, stir well and return to microwave for 1 more minute until crisp. Grind or crush them by placing them between sheets of baking paper and roll them with a rolling pin, or pulse them quickly a few times in a blender or food processor.

SERVES: *4*   **PREPARATION TIME:** *30 mins*   **COOKING TIME:** *20 mins*

1¹/₃ lbs (600 g) slender Asian eggplants
¹/₂ teaspoon salt
Pinch of ground turmeric
6 cloves garlic, peeled
1 small onion or 6 Asian shallots, peeled
¹/₂ cup (125 ml) extra virgin olive oil, for
   brushing
2 tomatoes, deseeded and diced
Fresh juice of 2 limes
³/₄ cup (30 g) finely chopped coriander
   leaves (cilantro)
Dash of bottled sweet chili sauce
1¹/₂ teaspoons salt
¹/₄ teaspoon ground white pepper
1 green finger-length chili pepper,
   deseeded and minced, to garnish
   (optional)
1 tablespoon coconut cream, to garnish

Eggplant salad with tomato and coriander

The baked or grilled eggplant in this delicious salad triggers off childhood memories of eggs whipped into a lunchtime omelet after school. The two have similar inviting aromas and in a strange way I feel I can smell the purple color especially when it is presented in all its jewel-like regal glory.

Halve each eggplant lengthwise. Rub the salt and ground turmeric into the exposed sides with your fingers.

Preheat the oven to 350°F (180°C).

Place the eggplant halves, garlic and onion or shallots in a baking dish and brush them all with the olive oil then bake in the oven for 15 minutes, turning the garlic and onion or shallots often. Alternatively, grill them all on a pan grill or under a broiler for 2–3 minutes. Remove from the heat and set aside to cool. Using a spoon, scoop out the eggplant flesh from the skins and discard the skins.

Roughly mash the eggplant flesh, garlic and onion or shallots in a salad bowl, then add all the other ingredients except the green chili pepper and coconut cream, and mix well. Just before serving, sprinkle minced green chili pepper (if using) and swirl coconut cream on top of the salad.

SERVES: 4–6   PREPARATION TIME: 20 mins   COOKING TIME: 15 mins

Semolina halva with almonds and cardamom

With each step of this recipe, we are creating aromas. The dry-roasted semolina comes first, followed by a caramelized syrup and finally the sweetish cardamom is added to give this fragrant dessert the scent of Persian cuisine.

1 cup (250 ml) milk
1 cup (250 ml) water
1 teaspoon cardamom seeds, lightly crushed
³/₄ cup (150 g) sugar
¹/₂ cup (100 g) butter
1 cup (185 g) large-grain semolina
¹/₄ cup (50 g) sultana raisins
2 tablespoons raw sliced almonds, dry-roasted
¹/₄ cup (60 ml) golden syrup (optional)

SERVES: *6–8*

PREPARATION TIME: *40 mins*

Bring the milk, water and cardamom to a boil in a saucepan. Remove from the heat, add the sugar and stir until the sugar is dissolved. Set aside and allow to cool slightly.

In a wok, melt the butter over medium heat and stir-fry the semolina until golden brown and fragrant. Do not allow the wok to get too hot or the semolina will burn. Add the sultanas and stir-fry for another 1 minute. Reduce the heat to low, pour in the milk mixture and simmer for 4–5 minutes, stirring quickly, until the liquid has reduced. Remove from the heat.

Pour the cooked mixture into a buttered 8-in (20-cm) pie plate. Smooth the surface with the back of a buttered spoon and slice into diamond shapes using a knife or cookie cutter. Arrange on a serving platter and decorate each piece with the almond slices. Drizzle with the golden syrup (if using) and serve warm or cold with coffee.

Note: This dish keeps for a week in the refrigerator wrapped in plastic wrap. Before serving, bring refrigerated halva to room temperature or warm gently in a microwave or an oven.

Spiced mangoes in yogurt and honey

The heady "honey and peaches" aroma of ripe mangoes blend naturally with a smooth natural yogurt base. This dessert is enticingly garnished with drizzled honey and the subtle aromas of sprinkled golden saffron threads. A hint of cardamom ties the dish together as it strengthens the yogurt.

1 cup (250 ml) thick plain yogurt
2 cardamom pods, skins removed and seeds ground to a powder, or 1 teaspoon ground cardamom
2 tablespoons honey
1 tablespoon golden syrup
2 ripe mangoes, peeled, pitted and thinly sliced into sheaths
Warm honey, to serve
Few strands of saffron, soaked in 1 teaspoon yogurt, to garnish

In a mixing bowl, combine the yogurt, ground cardamom, honey and golden syrup and whip until well blended.

To serve, spoon the whipped yogurt mixture into serving bowls and lay 2 mango sheaths on top, then drizzle with some warm honey over them and garnish with the saffron strands.

SERVES: *4*   PREPARATION TIME: *15 mins*

Kulfi ice cream with cardamom and pistachios

A classic North Indian dessert, this is yet another quickie recipe created out of desperation. Use good quality ice cream and delicately dry-roasted pistachio nuts. Experiment with the melony aroma of the rum or Midori liqueur and allow the lemony cardamom to dazzle the senses.

1 quart (1 liter) good quality vanilla ice cream, half-thawed
1 cup (250 ml) heavy cream, whipped with 1 tablespoon confectioner's (icing) sugar
2 cups (250 g) roasted unsalted shelled pistachio nuts, finely chopped
2 teaspoons ground cardamom
2 tablespoons rum or Midori liqueur (optional)

In a large bowl, combine the half-thawed ice cream, heavy cream and icing sugar and mix well, then add the chopped pistachios (reserving some as a garnish) and cardamom. Just before freezing, add the liqueur (if using). Pour into dessert molds and freeze in the freezer until firm.

To serve, turn the ice cream out onto serving dishes and sprinkle with the reserved chopped pistachios.

SERVES: *4–6*   PREPARATION TIME: *10 mins + freezing time*

Cardamom cake with rum and passionfruit

The combination of mild lemony cardamom and sweet rum gives a surprisingly fragrant aroma and a rich nutty flavor to this simple recipe. I have added tart passionfruit to the syrup to temper its sweetness. Serve this cake after a curry or salad meal. Any cardamom in the curry will be pleasantly reflected in this dessert, completing the meal in style.

$^3/_4$ cup (150 g) powdered icing sugar, plus 1 tablespoon to dust over the cake
$^3/_4$ cup (200 g) butter
4 eggs
$^2/_3$ cup (100 g) ground almonds or hazelnuts
$1^3/_4$ cups (200 g) self-raising flour, sifted
2 teaspoons ground cardamom
Fresh juice from 2 limes

RUM AND PASSIONFRUIT SYRUP
$^1/_2$ cup (100 g) sugar
1 cup (250 ml) water
Juice of 6 fresh or canned passionfruits
3 lime leaves, torn
Fresh juice of 2 limes
8 cardamom pods, cracked
2 tablespoons rum

SERVES: *6–8*

PREPARATION TIME: *30 mins*

COOKING TIME: *45 mins*

Preheat the oven to 325°F (160°C). Lightly butter a 10-in (25-cm) round cake pan or line it with parchment paper and set aside.

Combine the sugar and butter and beat with a mixer or wooden spoon until light and fluffy. Add the eggs, one at a time, beating well between each addition, then fold in all the other ingredients.

Spoon the mixture into the prepared cake pan and bake in the oven for about 45 minutes or until the cake springs back when touched. Remove from the oven and prick it all over with a fine skewer. Leave the cake in the pan for 10 minutes, then turn it out onto a serving platter.

To make the Rum and Passionfruit Syrup, combine the sugar and water in a saucepan and heat over low heat, stirring until the sugar is dissolved. Stir in all the other ingredients except the rum and bring to a boil, then simmer uncovered for a few minutes over medium heat. Remove from the heat and strain, discarding the solids. Add the rum and mix well.

Drizzle the Rum and Passionfruit Syrup over the cake and dust the top with the confectioner's sugar.

Note: For a non-alcoholic version, simply leave out the rum. You may substitute with more sugar syrup.

Plump apricots with rum cream and clove syrup

The dessert encapsulates all the heady perfumes of Arabia in each mouthful of apricot, clove cream and pistachio. It is a no-fuss recipe that can be made ahead of time and put together at the very last minute for maximum effect.

24 dried apricots, soaked in warm water for 2 hours until soft
1¹/₂ cups (180 g) finely chopped unsalted pistachio nuts

CLOVE SYRUP
1 cup (200 g) sugar
3 cups (750 ml) water
6 cloves, lightly pounded
1 tablespoon fresh lime juice

RUM CREAM
1¹/₂ cups (375 ml) heavy whipping cream
2 tablespoons confectioner's (icing) sugar
Pinch of ground cloves
1 tablespoon rum
¹/₄ teaspoon salt

Prepare the Clove Syrup by bringing all the ingredients exept the lime juice to a boil over high heat in a saucepan, stirring them until the sugar is fully dissolved. Before the syrup begins to thicken, add the lime juice to prevent the sugar from caramelizing. Continue to boil for 3–5 minutes until the syrup reaches a silky consistency.

To make the Rum Cream, beat the cream in a bowl with an electric mixer until it begins to thickens. With the motor running, add the sugar gradually, then all the other ingredients and continue to beat until stiff peaks form. Chill in the refrigerator until ready to serve.

To serve, arrange half the apricots in a single layer on a serving platter and smear them with the chilled Rum Cream. Top with the remaining apricots and sprinkle with the chopped pistachios. Drizzle some Clove Syrup over them.

SERVES: *6*   **PREPARATION TIME:** *30 mins*   **COOKING TIME:** *5 mins*

Green mango and saffron lassi

A lassi is a refreshingly tangy drink made with yogurt. This one, made with green mangoes, is different. Although lacking the ripe pineapple-honey mango aromas, it is fragrant with the luxurious honeysuckle of unripe mango and saffron reminiscent of Middle Eastern souks—one can imagine drinking this in gilded tents surrounded by rich treasures, served by a genie in a bottle.

2 unripe green mangoes (about 12 oz/350 g total), peeled, pitted and diced
2 cups (500 ml) water
¹/₂ cup (100 g) sugar
Salt, to taste
2 cups (500 ml) chilled milk
8–10 threads saffron, soaked in 2 tablespoons warm milk for 30 minutes, plus additional saffron threads, to garnish

MAKES: *4 glasses*

PREPARATION TIME: *10 mins + 4 hours to chill*

COOKING TIME: *5 mins*

In a saucepan, bring the mango pieces and water to a simmer and cook over medium heat until the mango pulp softens, 2–3 minutes. Add the sugar and stir until the sugar dissolves. Remove from the heat and process the mango mixture to a purée in a food processor. Strain the purée into a jug and stir in the salt to taste, then chill in the refrigerator for at least 4 hours.

To serve, process the chilled milk, saffron milk mixture and chilled mango purée until well blended. Pour into individual serving glasses and garnish each one with a saffron thread.

Note: If you find the green mangoes too tart, adjust the taste by adding more sugar to the purée.

8 ripe baby bananas or 4 ripe regular
   bananas, peeled
$^1/_2$ cup (125 ml) low fat fresh milk
1 tablespoon butter
2 tablespoons fresh lime juice
$^3/_4$ cup (100 g) self-raising flour, sifted
4 tablespoons rice flour, sifted
$^1/_2$ teaspoon ground cinnamon
$^1/_4$ cup (60 ml) oil, for frying

SUGAR SYRUP
$^1/_2$ cup (100 g) sugar
$^1/_4$ cup (60 ml) water
$^1/_2$ teaspoon ginger juice (optional)

Isaac's baby banana cinnamon pancakes

Bananas make surprisingly tasty tiny pancakes or pikelets, which can be prepared beforehand as the lime juice keeps them from darkening. The aroma of bananas and butter cooking makes the whole family salivate and makes up for the lack of sophistication in this simple dish—a favorite of my grandson Isaac, a six-year-old cook in his own right.

Prepare the Sugar Syrup first by bringing the ingredients to a boil in a small saucepan and stirring until the sugar is dissolved. Remove from the heat and set aside to cool. This makes about $^1/_2$ cup (125 ml) of Sugar Syrup. Alternatively, microwave the mixture for 3 minutes on medium, remove and stir until the sugar is dissolved, then return to microwave for 1 more minute.

Process the bananas, milk, butter and lime juice in a food processor until smooth, then add the flours and continue processing to a smooth batter. Stir in the ground cinnamon and set aside for at least 1 hour.

Heat the oil in a skillet until hot. Spoon 1 tablespoon of the batter into the hot oil, at the same time turning the skillet to form the batter into a thin round pancake. Fry the pancake over medium heat for 1–2 minutes until it begins to brown, then turn over and fry the other side for 30 seconds. Remove from the heat and drain on paper towels. Repeat to fry the remaining batter in the same manner. Serve the pancakes hot with the Sugar Syrup on the side.

SERVES: *4-6*   **PREPARATION TIME:** *15 mins*   **COOKING TIME:** *20 mins*

'When heat is applied to these complex seasonings, the alluring aromas of the individual ingredients are unleashed in an amazing chemistry of flavor.'

Cooking with
aromatic asian seasonings

Asian cuisines depend on fragrant sauces, pastes and wines for marination—which give foods an interesting dimension and edge. When heat is applied to these complex seasonings, the alluring aromas of the individual ingredients are unleashed in an amazing chemistry of flavor.

Asian sauces and seasonings give foods life as they enhance, complement and sometimes alter the taste of the dishes we serve. When we consider the wide range of Asian seasonings that are available throughout the whole of Asia—each one different and distinctive to either a particular country or even to a particular dish, it simply overwhelms the mind. And when these are combined, added or blended with other Asian spices and flavorings, they ascend to yet another level, creating a symphony of flavors, aromas and textures on the palate. Unlike western concepts of saucing, where a stock is reduced from cooking juices, Asians rely on many time-honored traditional sauces and seasonings that are purchased and always consistent.

Sometimes the mere whiff of an aromatic sauce is enough to touch off a chain reaction of food memories from the past to induce a craving for a particular dish. There are many particular aromas and identity triggers. Sauces from Southeast Asia are generally tinged with the heat of chili peppers and the pungency of fish or shrimp paste. The Nonya cooks of Malaysia use a thick fermented black shrimp paste, sweet and fecund, called *petis* or *hae koh*, which is mixed into a spicy dressing for their electrifying *rojak* vegetable salad (Crisp *Rojak Salad with Spicy Sweet Dressing*, page 98). Rice wines are used in Chinese communities all over Asia as marinades and added to sauces that tenderize meats while imparting a delicate aroma to the dish. Japanese miso, which comes in a delicate range of truffle-like flavors, and sake, used for marinating or for drinking, both originated from China but developed their own unique Japanese flavors with a flair and precision that is typically Japanese.

There are five flavors the eastern cook is generally aware of: sweet, sour, salty, bitter and spicy. When I was a young girl we were taught to recognize the fifth flavor as spiciness but in a modern analysis of the taste spectrum, the Japanese have identified this fifth taste as *umami*—which translates as a brothiness or great mouth-feel. In its natural state, *umami* occurs in foods like tomatoes, eggplant, *belacan* (dried shrimp paste) and in miso. It creates an astringent, soup-like taste, stimulating the mucus membranes of the mouth and tastebuds, tempting the diner to eat more.

Seasonings in the form of sauces and pastes add to our enjoyment of foods but identifying them can sometimes be a problem. Walk into an Asian supermarket where a variety of Asian cuisines are represented and you will be met with a gastronomic kaleidoscope as you pass row upon row of different sauces with unusual names and subtle variations. Think soy sauce and you will find at least a dozen different varieties from Korean brews to Malaysian *kecap manis*—a caramelized version. Think chili pastes, and you will find at least ten stir-fry starters: including chili sauce with black beans or a spicy paste ideal for a chili crab dish. Think oyster sauce and you are likely to find four or five different varieties including a mushroom oyster sauce for vegetarians.

I have found the black and bean pastes and the red chili pastes from China invaluable whenever I am making dumplings or pork dishes. Then there are the soy sauces brewed with wheat that were initially developed in China but later traveled to Korea, Japan and Southeast Asia. Each has its own particular aroma and flavor guaranteed to create interest and add punch to a meal. The solution is to try several different types until you find one that suits you best and use it as your own.

The Chinese are the sauce experts and have produced the most exotic seasonings for their everyday meals as well as their elaborate gourmet dinners—when everything from a chicken wing to a bird's nest or pig's ear is transformed into an amazing dish through the use of sauces.

The fermented golden rice wines from Southern China, and the stronger distilled wines from the North are used in many variations—for marination or as delicate glazes over steamed fish, prawns or chicken. A well-known example is the drunken chicken, steamed in soy sauce, sesame oil and wine, fast-cooled in ice to preserve that fine layer of gelatin under the skin, and then glazed with wine, to finish.

The dark Chinkiang vinegars, aged for 3 weeks, are sweetish-sour and used as a dip with northern dumplings, while similar dark vinegars, aged to perfection, are ideal for slow-cooked meats and tofu dishes.

Asian sauce and spice paste producers today are attempting to bridge the medical diet gap with sauces which are gluten-free or wheat-free for people with certain types of allergies, so that everyone can enjoy tasty, well-seasoned meals. But it is best to be reminded that seasonings and sauces are only meant to complement foods and should be used with reserve, as less is more. When everything comes together in a dish, there is a perfect harmony of aromas and tastes that elevates any dish to haute cuisine status.

Here are some recipes using ready-made sauces and seasonings that will allow you to create a whole repertoire of interesting new dishes in your kitchen at home.

Chinese black vinegar ~

This is a rich vinegar with great character, aromatic sweetness and spice on the nose, that is seductive even before it is tasted. Chinese black vinegars are very similar in color and aroma to the Italian balsamic vinegars, except there is a slight overriding aroma of soy and five spice powder, where the western vinegars have more wine aromas. Star anise and cassia are added to this rice vinegar while it is fermenting. The mixture is then stored in large brown ceramic vats and the aromas are left to mingle for at least four or five years, allowing a pleasant infusion of flavors into the vinegar.

This dark brown sweet vinegar is brewed from corn, salt and maltose. It is much more flavorful than plain white rice vinegar and has a pungent, sweet aroma and flavor. Open the bottle or jar and sniff deeply, you will understand that the flavor and aroma is unparalleled. If this vinegar is not unavailable, it is possible to substitute balsamic vinegar, although the flavors and aromas will be slightly different.

Pork and chicken are tenderized when marinated with this vinegar and it retains some deep sweet-sour maltose flavors. Once you use this to marinate your food or cook with it, it will be hard to do without it. The use of this vinegar is almost addictive. So if you find a brand that has all these qualities, preferably a dark vinegar in a jar, stock up on it, as it keeps forever.

This vinegar is rather special when cooked with pork when it produces a special flavor that is unparalleled. I used it for my caramelized pork dish—Sweet Soy Pork with Mushrooms and Star Anise, page 174.

Purchasing: Look for bottles or jars labeled as dark vinegar or Chinese black vinegar in Asian grocery stores or well-stocked supermarkets. There are many different brands with very different flavors and names. Some are sweeter or more sour than sours. A trustworthy brand is "Greatwall" vinegar. The green bottle normally has a red label.
Culinary uses: Chinese black rice vinegar is used in marinades, in braised pork and poultry dishes, and as a dipping sauce

straight out of the bottle. It is a favorite dipping sauce for serving pork and shrimp pot-stickers, steamed shrimp and chicken dumplings.
Storing: Once open, it can keep for at least a year stored in a cool place covered well. It will keep much longer refrigerated. Clean dry spoons should always be used.
Substitute: Red rice vinegar added with sugar or good quality balsamic vinegar makes a good substitute.

Fermented soybean pastes ⁓

Pick one ingredient that is common to all Asian cuisines and that injects an incomparable flavor and taste and it would invariably be the fermented soybean. It is often undetectable in a chef's repertoire of ingredients alongside of the better-known garlic, onions, chili and lemongrass. And while the latter often steal the limelight, looking flatteringly bright and exotic, the humble soybean sits in its salted, fermented state waiting to be spooned into a dish while cooking. The lowly status of the fermented soybean belies its importance in Asian cooking as it is cheap and sometimes looks downright unappetizing, yet when mashed and cooked, it adds an indescribable flavor reminiscent of smoked mushrooms cooked in garlic.

The small salted and fermented black beans found in ancient Chinese tombs remain the oldest recorded soy product in China's history. The Chinese still use the original method of producing these beans, although the packaging in plastic packets or glass jars is different today. Salted fermented soybeans pack yeasty flavors that can be used in stir-fries with beef or pork or cooked into the famous Chili Crab with chili paste (see Chili Crabs with Ginger and Garlic Chives, page 64).

These fermented beans appear in many guises, but if you prefer a pure black bean flavor, just rely on the basic beans, mashed into a paste, or used whole. Black bean sauce is, according to Chinese writer Deh Ta-Hsiung, a Hong Kong invention concocted for Western palates.

The basic **brown bean paste**, often confusingly labeled as **"yellow beans,"** is fermented from sweeter yellow soybeans which are less intense and have a maltier flavor closer to the taste I try to achieve in my cooking. They appear toffee-colored, whole or semi-mashed, the size of a little finger nail. The Koreans produce a sweeter but similar paste called *doenjang*, and in Vietnamese or Thai supermarkets these bean pastes come fermented and freshly-packed in clear plastic containers. Try these as they are superior in quality and refrigerate well.

There are other interesting varieties of fermented soybeans sold in the form of bottled sauces combined with spices and seasonings. **Hoisin sauce** with star anise and red coloring added is one variety (see page 202). Some other successful combinations pair several addictive flavors—for example chili and garlic with the fermented soybean. *Guilin lajiao jiang,* is an example of a black bean chili sauce produced in China (the word *lajiao* means chili). Japanese miso paste is another form of fermented bean paste which may be used as a substitute if the Chinese bean pastes are unavailable. Other varieties have added sugar and five spice powder and come from China, Japan and Korea. Especially interesting is the Korean *gochujang*, a sweet bean paste with red pepper and garlic guaranteed to knock the socks off any diner.

When buying fermented bean pastes, trust your eyes, and ask the shop owner, or simply buy them and experiment. Labels may deceive as a sauce may be labeled "Black Bean Chili" whereas the beans inside may be yellow to golden malt in color.

Despite the daunting array of strange jars on the shelf, it is well worth trying several of them until you find ones that suit your palate.

1. Mashed brown bean paste 2. Salted yellow beans 3. Whole fermented yellow beans 4. Korean sweet brown bean paste similar to miso
5. *Gochujang*—Korean fermented bean paste with added chili
6. Whole salted black beans

Purchasing: The best brown bean paste is a golden toffee-colored paste, with an earthy mushroom and yeasty aroma that becomes addictive when foods are cooked in the beans. It comes in varieties and you may find this paste in glass jars, earthenware jars, or sometimes in plastic box containers. The consistency can be half-mashed, smooth, or at other times mixed with chili (called hot bean paste). Look for one that has a pure golden color in the condiment section of Asian markets. Whole fermented honey-colored beans are so soft that you can mash them with a fork as you cook them. The black soybean is small, dark and shiny. Soak in water for 6–8 hours and then boil in slightly salted water. The beans may then be mashed or pureed and used as a sweetened filling for Chinese pastries as *dau sa* or used whole in salads. They are also used in making the salted or fermented beans and the black bean sauce. Fermented soybeans are whole beans fermented in a brownish liquor made from soybeans, water, salt and sugar. Sometimes chili and garlic are added to this fermenting paste or sauce for flavor and texture. The chili jam has elements of all these things put together: fermented soy bean, chili, garlic, sugar and an addition of shredded dried prawns. Each Miso variety has a specific flavor and purpose. It is best to pick the Shiro Miso available in vacuum sealed plastic bags or the *akamiso* or red miso for use in fish and seafood dishes.

Culinary uses: Any bean paste goes well as a stir-fry base. Brown bean paste, which has a distinct, nutty yeasty aroma and flavor, when sautéed with garlic gives out a wonderful, aromatic burst. It can also be used to add flavor for steamed dishes, especially steamed fish, and as a table condiment for dipping. Black bean paste has a powerful aroma and it is commonly used sparingly to enhance the flavor of fish or beef. Miso comes in a variety of tastes, color tones and textures. The Japanese use it not so much as a flavoring but for color and texture as it enriches and thickens soups, stews and stir-fries.

Chili jam is a Western name for a mixture of black bean and chili sauce. This is made from the sediment produced from manufacturing soy sauce. If shrimp paste is added to the sauce, it results in a lovely dried shrimp flavored paste. The aromas and flavors are distinctive—hot, sweet and pungent—and a little goes a long way.

Preparation: Always spoon the bean paste from the jar using a clean, dry spoon. Mash whole beans with the back of the spoon before adding it to the dish. If using canned bean paste, drain and empty into a jar, then store or use as instructed. Whole salted black beans must be washed to remove extra salt before using.

Storing: Always check the used-by date. If the bean paste comes in a can, decant it into a glass or plastic jar and refrigerate. Glass jars and earthenware jars are the best. Always use a clean dry spoon and keep the lid on tightly after each use. When stored properly, bean paste will keep indefinitely. If mold builds up, discard the bean paste immediately. Always refrigerate miso and use a clean, dry spoon when taking portions for use.

Substitutes: Hoisin sauce may be used even though the taste is not the same.

Black bean pastes

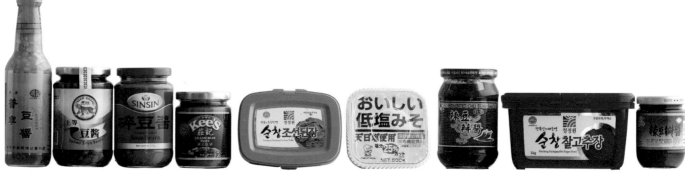

Brown bean pastes   Brown miso   Miso   Korean hot bean pastes

Fish sauces ⁓

A thin and salty translucent golden liquid which is indispensable in Southeast Asian cooking, fish sauce has the fresh and tangy aroma of the sea, which amazingly dissipates on cooking. The taste it brings to Thai and other Southeast Asian dishes has created a whole generation of aficionados who are addicted to its use. The earliest mention of fish sauce in Roman records was a similar product called *garum*. Interestingly enough, *garam* is the Indonesian or Malay word for salt. There must have been some sort of link between the use of sea salt and salty fish sauce in Asia from very early times.

The gastronomic impact of this sauce is similar to the use of the flavor enhancer MSG, although it does not have any of the negative effects of MSG. The flavor of fish sauce in any dish certainly outweighs any reservations as to its use in cooking and in salad dressings.

Fish sauce, known as *nam pla* in Thai and *nuoc cham* in Vietnamese, is produced by layering salt with fish or shrimp in earthenware vats and allowing it to ferment in the brine solution for about six months. The fermented liquid is slowly siphoned off, filtered and bottled. The flavor and aroma of a fish sauce can vary greatly depending on the quality of fish that is used, and the care that is taken to make it. A top-quality fish sauce is very expensive, just like a good olive oil or vinegar. The ideal aroma to look for is a fresh whiff of fermented fish and the sea. If the aroma is too strong for you, try another brand. Fish sauce does not necessarily have to smell strong. And it is good to remember that once cooked into a dish, the strong aromas evaporate, leaving only beautiful flavors. Enter a good Vietnamese or Thai restaurant and you will find tables laid out not only with plates and chopsticks, but a tray filled with sauces such as hoisin, oyster, chili sauce, sesame oil and most certainly a little bottle of amber-colored fish sauce. You can mix any combination of these sauces into a tiny saucer and use it as a dipping sauce. For example, a little bit of fish sauce with some sliced chili and a splash of soy sauce will result in a marvelous concoction that goes very well with dumplings, noodle dishes or seafood. It is interesting that unlike Western meals, each mouthful of an Asian meal can taste different depending on the sauces the food was dipped in.

Fish sauce is used throughout Southeast Asia. The Chinese also use fish sauce, but the Chinese variety is quite different from the common Southeast Asian one and isn't as readily available. The Chinese have now taken to using Vietnamese fish sauce whenever necessary, as it is easier to obtain and more tasty.

Purchasing: Bottles of fish sauce from various countries are available in Asian food stores and well-stocked supermarkets. Look for clear amber-colored fish sauce, which is an indication of the best flavor and aroma. The sauce is high in vitamin C and presents well if it is clear. The Viet Huong brand, with a pink label, is preferred by the Vietnamese for use as a dipping sauce rather than for cooking because it has a less "fishy" aroma and a clearer, more intense color. The favored sauce for cooking is the green-labeled Squid or "Sotong" brand from Thailand.

Culinary uses: Fish sauce is used by most Asians for seasoning and marinades, while the more expensive variety is used in soups and as dipping sauces on its own or added with chili and chopped garlic.

Storing: Wipe the lid and the top of the bottle clean after each use and store it in a cool, dark place. Fish sauce lasts for a year or two but should not be used if it clouds or crystallizes.

Substitute: Soy sauce with a bit of oyster sauce makes the best substitute.

Hoisin sauce ∼

Hoisin sauce is a Chinese sauce recognized and used throughout Asia as the universal barbecue sauce. It is made from red rice brewed with soybean paste, garlic, sugar, five spice powder and some star anise. Depending on the region of production, basic hoisin sauce is usually very sweet although some brands have a spicier version, with more chili paste added. For instance, a Sichuan pepper flavored hoisin sauce is produced in Sichuan to match their spicy dishes. In other areas, a tiny amount of sweet potato starch may be added to thicken the sauce for use as a basting marinade for barbecues.

The color of hoisin sauce varies from brand to brand. Traditional hoisin sauce ranges from a reddish brown to a dark mahogany color due to the use of annatto seeds. Others may appear honey colored and less piquant.

Hoisin sauce is used as a table condiment, in meat marinades and as a flavoring agent for sauces. It is famously known as the dipping sauce for Peking Duck and for roast chicken or pork barbecues, and is sometimes labelled as a dark *char siew* barbecue sauce for roast pork or duck. In Malaysia, a thin coating of hoisin or thick sweet soy sauce (*tim cheong*) is spread onto spring roll wrappers before they are filled with delicious pork, shrimp and water chestnut filling. A variety of hoisin, sweeter than the common type, is the main "hero sauce" on Vietnamese dining tables, served alongside soy sauce and chili sauce as the condiment for *pho* (Beef Noodle Soup with Fragrant Herbs—see page 155).

Purchasing: Hoisin sauce is sold in bottles, jars or cans in Asian markets and supermarkets. There are many varieties of hoisin sauce, so read the labels and decide if you want a spicier version or a mild, sweet one for your use. Choose sauce bottles that come in smaller amounts so you will not need to store it for so long.
Culinary uses: Hoisin sauce may be used as a basting sauce for roasting duck, chicken and other meats. It is especially good with pork ribs. The dark red hoisin, also marketed as Chinese barbecue sauce, is used to glaze the reddish brown ducks seen in barbecue meat shops in Chinatown. A wonderful combination of hoisin sauce, oyster sauce and soy sauce in equal parts makes a great sauce for stir-frying. This combination of sauces also works well in a simple fried rice, adding

both color and flavor. Because hoisin can be overpowering, particularly if you're new to Asian cuisine, it's recommended that you add only a bit at a time to experiment with the flavor or dilute the flavor by adding a little water or oil before adding it to a recipe.
Storing: Hoisin sauce keeps well only when refrigerated after opening so it is best to buy a small jar or bottle and replenish with fresh supplies as needed. If you are spooning hoisin from a jar, use a clean dry spoon. Be sure to wipe the neck and lid of the bottle with a paper towel before refrigerating.
Substitute: Chinese barbecue sauce or a mix of oyster sauce and tomato sauce may be substituted, although this combination never works as well as true hoisin sauce.

Mirin ~ sweet Japanese rice wine

A strong, sweet rice wine with a smoky woody flavor of mushrooms that lifts any dish, mirin is used extensively in Japan and now the world over. It is brewed from sweet sticky (glutinous) short-grained rice and matured for at least five years before it is bottled and sold commercially. The main characteristic of mirin is a sweet aroma which comes from the addition of corn syrup and alcohol, reminding one of pineapples with a light touch of vinegar and a hint of brandy.

The method of manufacture varies according to the region. Traditional methods are still used in the more remote parts of Japan, but there are many factories that have moved into the 21st century using modern brewing and bottling techniques. There are many types of mirin; some are almost good enough to be drunk as an alcoholic beverage like sake, while cheaper varieties are only used for cooking.

I was shown how to make sushi rice a few years ago and was adventurous enough to travel to Japan to learn from the masters. The main ingredients are Japanese rice (short grained and round) with a sticky texture that can easily be rolled into shapes and wrapped with nori or egg. Before any of the shaping can happen the hot rice is always mixed with sugar and mirin, which gives it a wonderful fragrance and sheen. The sweetness of the mirin gives sushi the distinctive taste which is today familiar to all of us.

Mirin is different from any of the other rice wines I have tasted and is more similar to sherry than to sake. It is this sweetish characteristic that appeals.

Purchasing: Mirin is normally found in Japanese stores, but any good Asian store will stock it, because like me, many Asians have learnt to use mirin in place of other rice wines. Look for a gold-colored mirin with low alcohol content (below 14%). A reliable brand is Kikkoman which comes in a clear, small bottle with a red cap. Mirin should never be used for drinking as it is a cooking wine. Some types of mirin are pale, almost whitish in color.

Culinary uses: Mirin is used as a marinade to tenderize meat or can be added to a salad dressing. It is one of the main ingredients in sukiyaki sauce that you serve with a sukiyaki platter of beef and vegetables. To make this sauce, combine 2 cups (500 ml) of dashi stock with 1/2 cup (125 ml) of mirin and 1/2 cup (125 ml) of black soy sauce and mix well. Mirin is also an ideal glaze for teppanyaki grilled meats, and can be added to soups and sauces for extra flavor. If you are serving a meat dish with rice, it makes sense to use mirin as a marinade for the meat. When making tempura, if the vegetables are marinated in mirin before they are battered and deep-fried, you will get a crispness and sweetness that lift the vegetables, giving them a lovely flavor.

Storing: Mirin has an indefinite shelf life, especially if treated kindly. It stores best when refrigerated. Do not use it if it turns cloudy or crystallizes.

Substitute: Sherry or white wine or sake with a little sugar added, or Shaoxing wine with added sugar makes a good substitute.

Oyster sauce and abalone sauce ~

Oyster sauce is one of the earliest sauces used in Chinese cooking, brewed from the natural salting of fish or oysters in seaside areas. For centuries, oyster sauce has been an indispensable seasoning sauce that is added to many different types of dishes. In an amazing transformation of flavors, the fishy taste of the sauce dissipates when it is cooked, leaving only an aroma and flavor so elegant and tasty that it is used by cooks now throughout the whole of Asia.

Today this sauce is made from dried oysters mixed with salt and sugar that caramelizes into a flavorsome end product. Oyster sauce is invaluable as a stir-fry sauce for greens, as a table condiment and for marinating or barbecuing meats, although the sugar in the sauce may cause some caramelization if left unattended. Different strengths of oyster sauce are available in the market, some made for vegetarians without any seafood added in the brewing process. This works well to give the effect of oyster sauce although the flavors are not as rich. Chinese broccoli or *kailan* quick-fried or blanched and then served with garlic and oyster sauce is a stylish and flavorsome favorite in Chinese cuisine.

Abalone sauce is a similar seafood sauce made from pure abalone extract rather than oysters. It is a rich and delicious sauce used for steaming, stir-frying, marinating and dipping.

Purchasing: To shop for the best oyster sauce, look for a rich, thick, dark brown sauce with a strong oyster flavor. Check the label to see what it contains—many oyster sauces contain added MSG. Vegetarian oyster sauce is flavored with gluten and mushrooms rather than oyster extract. There are fewer types of abalone sauce but most of them come in large-necked jars and squat bottles that allow the cook to spoon amounts directly from the jar. Look for a pleasant shrimp-like aroma when the jar is opened.

Culinary uses: Use oyster sauce for stir-fries, for seasoning grilled and barbecued meats and when stir-frying vegetables. Oyster sauce works best when cooked with sautéed garlic.

The slightly fishy aroma dissipates on cooking, leaving a fabulous flavor. Abalone sauces can be used in noodle dishes where seafood is added, Cantonese style and thickened with egg white or cornstarch, steamed crab dishes and prawn stir-fries especially with the dried egg noodles.

Storing: Refrigerate after opening. Be sure to wipe the neck and lid of the bottle with a paper towel before refrigerating.

Substitute: Fish sauce mixed with *kecap manis* or sweet soy sauce is a good substitute for oyster sauce. The best substitute for abalone sauce is oyster sauce blended with a teaspoon of dried shrimp which have been soaked in boiling water and pounded.

Oyster sauce

Abalone sauce

Vegetarian oyster sauce

Rice wines ~ white rice wine, Shaoxing and sake

The main difference between Asian wines and the wines found in the West is that they are distilled or fermented from grains rather than fruit. These wines, usually made from rice but sometimes from other grains such as sorghum or millet, are believed to have been invented 4000 years ago when Yidi, a consort of the king from the first Chinese dynasty, perfected the method of distilling a yellow liquor from millet before rice became popular. Traditionally, Asian wines are consumed together with food although Japanese sake has a different social context in Japan.

The most common Chinese rice wine is the Chinese Shaoxing, which is fermented from sticky glutinous rice, yeast and water. A finely aged golden Shaoxing wine can be expensive, and can release the fruity flavors of a sweet Muscat wine. Some inferior qualities may taste chemical and almost vinegary. The best known Shaoxing wine is Hua Tiao Chiew, which refers to the flower pattern carved on the urns in which this brew is aged. Shaoxing is available in most Asian stores and investing in a better quality Shaoxing wine will enhance your cooking.

Chinese white rice wine, *baijiu*, is clear with a pleasant yeasty aroma. There are two main types, *huangjiu*, a rice wine fermented with yeast, and the stronger *shaojiu*, heat-distilled from glutinous rice. Use this wine for marinating meats, making salad dressings, for thinning chili dipping sauces and to give a lift to marinating sauces in cooking. It is best kept refrigerated.

The Japanese white rice wine sake, to quote the Japanese food expert, Hosking, is double fermented and fairly strong as it has a general alcohol content of 16%. As with all wines the world over, the varieties of sake are amazing. The more delicate sakes, sold in small porcelain vase-shaped jars, are snapped up by aficionados before ever reaching the open market. The service of sake is a whole culture unto itself as tradition dictates whether it should be served hot or cold. For cooking, sake can be used as a dressing for delicate steamed fish, or a few drops may be added to a soup to give it a zing. The lower grades of sake may be used for cooking, but another refreshing alternative is the sweet cooking sake, mirin, traditionally used to flavor sushi rice and sauces (see page 203).

In earlier times, the Japanese brewed a special sake called *binjinshu* when virgins chewed the rice and spat the "virgin rice" into containers as the starter. Today sake is brewed from polished glutinous rice and the difference between the better quality and ordinary sakes depend on the degree of polishing of the rice grains and the varieties of rice used. Sake and rice wine are clear but quality, taste and aroma differentiate the two.

Purchasing: When buying Shaoxing wine, look for a dark brown or green bottle. Check that the label is in good condition; it should have a clear Shaoxing wine label or a floral design. White rice wine made in Zhejiang is a good choice. If you are in an Asian store, it is better to ask for it by the ethnic name or write the name down as this will help the shop assistant understand what you are asking for. There are three main grades of sake. The best, *ginjoshu*, the epitome of the sake brewer's art, is made in limited quantities and never reaches the market. *Honzozukuri* is a sake that has a rich flavor. There is some added alcohol but it must never exceed 25%. There are sweet and dry sakes as they range from bone dry to fairly sweet and there is an official grade of sweetness and dryness running from -10 to +10 but other factors including acidity affect the individual tastes. The only way to find out about sake is to engage in some serious tasting.
Culinary uses: Chinese rice wine makes a very good addition to your kitchen cupboard so always keep it handy. It is great in salad dressings, marinades and dipping sauces, mixed with oyster or hoisin sauce, or even used in Western dishes such as pasta sauces. Use just a small amount to avoid overpowering the other flavors.
Storing: Store bottles of rice wine in the refrigerator and remember to wipe the lid and bottle neck clean after each use.

It is best to store sake in the refrigerator once opened.
Substitute: A good sherry or mirin can be substituted.

Plum sauce and lemon sauce ~

Plum sauce is a sweet and tart Chinese sauce made from small, sour Chinese plums preserved with sugar and molasses until it becomes light and aromatic. It develops a light apricot color or in some cases appears reddish. This sauce adds an aromatic fruitiness to marinades and meat and fish dishes and is commonly used as a dipping sauce. A version of this plum sauce is the sweet, dark *tim cheong*—a dark thick hoisin sauce which sometimes has plum sauce in it, used to brush on Chinese spring roll wrappers before the filling is added.

Lemon sauce is a delicate mixture of lime or lemon oil and tangerine peel cooked with sugar and ginger. The flavors differ from brand to brand—some contain white pepper while others contain a little tamarind, a touch of star anise or a light chili seasoning. It is generally thickened with sweet potato starch. Lemon sauce is often used as a marinade for seafood or with stir-fries (especially with Chinese cabbage). I often use this sauce, with or without chili sauce added, as a light dipping sauce.

Purchasing: Most plum sauces are dependable so you have to choose whether you want a dark, stronger sauce or a light milder one for your dish. This may depend on whether you are preparing meat or fish in your recipe. It is best to buy smaller quantities rather than large bottles as they don't keep well.
Culinary uses: Use as a marinade with lime juice brushed onto fish before grilling, or as a caramelizing glaze for steaks. Plum and chili sauce in equal amounts forms a good dipping sauce

for finger foods. Try it in stir-fries, brushed onto satay skewers or added to pork when cooking a sweet and sour dish.
Storing: Refrigerate after opening to keep the sauce fresh.
Substitute: Fried onions added to a bottle of plum jam is a great substitute for plum sauce. If it is too sweet add a tablespoon of lime juice. The lighter colored plum sauce is similar to lemon sauce and can be used as a substitute for the latter, but add a little bit of lemon juice.

Sesame oil ~

Sesame oil is extracted from tiny white or black sesame seeds. The sesame fruit has to be fully ripe before the capsules containing the seeds split open and eject the seeds—a process enshrined in the Arabian tale of Ali Baba whose cave doors spring open to reveal a rich treasure trove inside only when the magic words "open sesame" are uttered. Sesame seeds and their oils were very precious even then and some of the oil jars where his brother the thief hid may have contained sesame oil.

Sesame oil comes in a range of colors—from clear to orange to red or dark amber—depending on the method used for extraction. It is prized for its antioxidant properties and stability. Sesame oil burns easily because of its heavy texture and is mostly used as a flavoring oil rather than for frying. The nutty and smoky taste of sesame oil adds depth to many vegetarian and herbal dishes. In many parts of Asia it is normally added right at the end to finish a dish.

Purchasing: Look for bottles of sesame oil in most supermarkets. The best sesame oil is Korean, which is extremely flavorful and can be quite expensive.
Culinary uses: Chinese and Koreans use sesame oil extensively in stir-fries, for flavoring at the end of the cooking cycle, and as a garnish or marinade. A few drops of sesame oil are often added to finish a dish, especially steamed fish dishes and soups. You might want to try adding a few drops of sesame oil to

fried rice or at the end of cooking any stir-fried dish in this book. The aroma will waft through your kitchen, making a memorable impression. But always bear in mind that less is more, especially for first-time users.
Storing: Once open, a cool and dark pantry is the best place to store sesame oil and it will keep indefinitely.
Substitute: Dry-roasted sesame seeds that are ground and added to regular cooking oil.

Shrimp pastes ~ dried and wet

All the aromas of Southeast Asia come together in this paste. Fresh shrimp, fish and krill are used to make this basic paste which is added to almost every dish. Dry-roasted dried shrimp paste is aromatic, yeasty and smoky, reminiscent of barbecued fish and shrimp. Unforgettable for its taste and strong aroma especially when blended with chili and garlic, it is definitely an acquired taste that some non-Asians simply cannot stand, just as many Asians do not like strong cheeses.

I have traveled all over Asia in search of the best shrimp paste and the finest I have ever used is from the Portuguese settlement in Malacca.

Each Southeast Asian country produces its own version. It is known as *belacan* in Malaysia, *trasi* in Indonesia and *kapi* in Thailand. In Burma, I came across a huge cake of shrimp paste and the woman who was selling it cut out a large triangular chunk for me and wrapped it in a lotus leaf. This paste was almost cloudy with pink lumps in it. Upon closer inspection, the lumps turned out to be chunks of shrimp fermenting in between the fish. These fermenting chunks tasted fabulous when cooked, but the strong aroma of the raw paste infused every part of me—clothes, hair, fingers and even my running shoes. Dried shrimp paste is like an opiate to people who are accustomed to it. It is widely used in Malaysia, Singapore, Cambodia, Laos, Burma, Thailand and the Philippines. I use Malaysian *belacan* in most of my recipes that call for dried shrimp paste. If this is not available, other types of dried shrimp paste work equally well.

Wet shrimp paste, *petis* or *hae koh*, is a liquid shrimp paste sold in jars and has much stronger fish taste than the dried version, however it is easier to use as it can be spooned into a wok or a pot. The wet shrimp paste can be added to dishes straight from the bottle but it is better to give it a zap in the microwave for a minute or two to enhance the aromas. If you have to choose between dried or wet shrimp paste, choose the dried one as it keeps forever.

1. Wet shrimp paste 2. Dried shrimp paste in a block 3. Dry-roasted crumbled shrimp paste

Purchasing: There is a large variety of dried shrimp pastes to choose from. Malaysian or Indonesian dried shrimp paste is usually sold as a dark brown compressed block wrapped with paper and plastic, although a powdered form is also available nowadays in small jars or shakers. The Thai variety, known as *kapi*, is usually sold in small plastic containers. The color can vary from a pinkish or purplish grey to a dark greyish brown with a consistency from soft and pasty to dry and hard, depending on how long the fermented shrimp were allowed to dry in the sun.

Culinary uses: Some shrimp pastes are thickened with rice bran or flour, while others are ground into a powder. Although they smell atrocious while they are being dry-roasted, the aromas dissipate when the shrimp paste is added to a dish and cooked. The aroma has been likened to that of a strong-smelling cheese. If you are not accustomed to it, begin with a smaller amount so you can develop a taste for it gradually.

Preparation: Dried shrimp paste should always be dry-roasted before using. You can dry-roast a solid chunk by holding it with a pair of tongs or wrapping it in foil and roasting it over a flame to dissipate the fishy aromas. Or you can dry-roast it in a microwave oven for 1 minute on high.

Storing: Store in the refrigerator wrapped in a sealed plastic bag or plastic container. It keeps indefinitely this way.

Substitute: Fish sauce with some oyster sauce added if necessary.

Dried shrimp paste

Ground dried shrimp paste

Wet shrimp paste (*petis* or *hae koh*)

Soy sauces ~

The yeasty, salty aroma of soy sauce whets the appetite as it lifts the flavor of meats, vegetables and seafood cooked with it. This is true of all soy sauces—especially the sauces brewed with added wheat that appear in my repertoire of Asian dishes cooked at home. When I was growing up, we did not have the wide range of soy sauces we have today. Then we only used thick soy and thin soy, which we called white soy due to its lighter color. We had two large bottles in the kitchen, one for each type of soy, and two little bottles that sat on our dining table along with a bottle of home-made chili sauce. For our breakfast a few drops of soy sauce were drizzled onto half-boiled eggs which we slurped from little saucers. I'm not sure why runny eggs were so important in our diet but the soy sauce certainly made them delicious! Soy sauce was used in everything we cooked—a little dash with vegetables as they were stir-fried, a light marinade of thin soy for steamed fish, a big spoonful in our nightly bowl of *kai chok* or chicken congee, and even a splash into our fiery chili chicken, just to take the bite off the chili. Today I have a dozen different types of soy sauce in my kitchen; the choice is astounding.

Basic soy sauce is made from ground soybeans, roasted wheat and a mold "starter." After fermentation, salt is added with lactobacillus and yeast and the liquid is aged and mellowed like wine, and then strained and bottled. Look for the wheat content on the bottle to be sure the soy is traditionally fermented in the slow and time-honored fashion. A factory-brewed soy sauce concocted in a hurry will not have wheat. Imitations made with hydrolyzed vegetable proteins and caramelized sugar have an unpleasant metallic flavor.

There are four grades of soy sauce—thin (also called light or just regular soy sauce), medium, thick (or black) and mushroom soy. Thin or light soy sauces are clear and golden brown in color and slightly salty in flavor, with a yeasty aroma. Medium soy sauces are darker and slightly thicker than light soy sauce, with a sweet and wheaty flavor. Thick soy sauces are thick and black and also come in a very sweet variety with added malt sugar. Mushroom soy sauces are flavored with straw mushrooms; they are dark brown, rich, thick, smoky and flavorful.

Light soy sauces are the ones used for marinades, as dips, and for flavoring white meat and seafood. Thick soy sauces are used for color and smoky flavors, normally added at the end of cooking. They are used for barbecued and stewed meat. For a noodle dish, I use a little light soy sauce as a marinade for the meat or shrimp and then add the thick or mushroom soy sauce at the end of cooking for extra flavor.

Originally transported to Japan by Chinese Buddhists, soy sauce has been highly refined in Japan into a seasoning that is superior to many other soy sauces known generally as shoyu. There are many types of Japanese soy sauce, but a better quality one called Kanaro Shoyu is superior with slightly less salt and sweetness but more flavor.

Sweet Indonesian soy, called *kecap manis*, is dark and pours like molasses. It has large quantities of added malt sugar and is used to caramelize meats and give it a shine.

Light soy sauces

Dark soy sauces

Mushroom soy sauces

Purchasing: Try to purchase soy sauce in glass bottles rather than plastic bottles and preferably in small quantities. If you don't use it often, buy smaller bottles and replenish often as soy sauce has an unpleasant taste if it sits in the cupboard too long and the solids settle to the bottom of the bottle.

Storing: Wipe the bottle clean after each use and store in a cool, dark place. It has a long life, but should not be used if the sauce crystallizes or thickens at the bottom of the bottle.

Other specialty soy sauces

Caramel soy sauce (sweet thick soy). This is a thick, sweet sauce which can be used as a marinade for barbecues and as a sauce for thick caramelized pork stews and fried noodles.

Gen-en-shoyu (Japanese low-salt soy). A milder Japanese soy sauce which is brewed in the traditional manner, after which 43% of the salt is removed. This is best for people with special diets.

Kecap manis (sweet thick soy). This is a dark, sweet, reddish black thick soy sauce used specifically for Indonesian and Malaysian cooking. The sugar content and unusual flavor comes from palm sugar with star anise and sometimes garlic. The sauce has a mellow, smoked tofu flavor and is used as a basic ingredient. It is sweeter than ordinary soy sauce and used for rice stick noodle dishes (especially *char kway teow*) to flavor and color meat dishes or for cooking red meat.

Koikuchi shoyu (salt reduced thin soy). This is the most widely-used soy sauce in Japan, brewed with cooked soybeans and roasted wheat. It has a low salt content for special diets.

Lu soy or **lu shui** (spicy lime soy). This is a master sauce made from soy, ginger, five spice powder and sugar and gives food a dark-brown color. It makes a good salad dressing when blended with vinegar, some chili and lime juice.

Mitsukane (Korean sweet and aromatic). This is a Korean soy sauce, which is less salty than Chinese and Japanese soy sauces, but sweeter and has a definite malty aroma from the brewing process.

Mushroom soy sauce. Mushroom soy is an aromatic, yeasty and earthy soy. It is sometimes known as black Chinese mustard, consisting of thick strips of dark-grey mushrooms in a thick, glistening, black, textured soy sauce. I find this sauce useful in stir-fries and noodle dishes when fresh mushrooms are unavailable. This sauce can also be used to flavor spring roll fillings— pieces of mushroom give a touch of authenticity and texture.

Tamari shoyu (miso soy). This is a Japanese soy sauce made from the liquid leftover from the fermentation process in the making of miso. It is made only with soybeans, unlike regular soy sauce which is a mixture of soybeans and wheat, and is used especially in sushi restaurants.

Tim cheong (sweet thick soy). *Tim cheong* is used in Malaysia and Singapore to sweeten spring rolls and noodles. This is a thick, black soy sauce, rich with black bean paste and used to brush fresh spring roll wrappers before the filling is placed in and rolled into the fabulous *poh piah*.

Toyo mansi (Filipino sweet soy). This is an interesting and tasty Filipino soy sauce brewed with kalamansi lime juice and used with other soy sauces as a flavoring. It makes an interesting dip or salad dressing.

Sweet soy sauces (*kecap manis*)

Japanese soy sauces

Seafood soy sauces

1 small or $^1/_2$ large watermelon, green rind only
$^1/_2$ cup (100 g) thinly shaved barbecued pork
1 onion, halved and finely sliced
$^1/_2$ bunch (50 g) baby spinach, arugula or
  pennywort leaves
$^1/_2$ ginger flower, thinly sliced
3 red finger-length chili peppers, deseeded
  and sliced
1 tablespoon grated fresh young ginger

SWEET THAI DRESSING
1 tablespoon fish sauce
1 teaspoon shaved palm sugar or dark brown
  sugar mixed with 1 tablespoon warm water
  and chilled
Freshly squeezed juice of 1 lime
$^1/_2$ teaspoon salt
$^1/_2$ teaspoon ground white pepper

Watermelon rind salad with sweet thai dressing

The colors of this salad are exceptional—pinkish white pieces melding into undertones of green and white. Tossed with a bundle of ginger floral scents, the humble watermelon rind looks exotic and spells cool summer evenings and light airy meals.

Peel the outer skin from the watermelon and slice the red flesh from the outer green rind. Reserve the red watermelon flesh for Mint Vodka Collins with Watermelon Fingers (page 81).

Cut the green rind into small chunks or shave it into thin curled strips, then place in a large salad bowl with all the other ingredients. Mix the Dressing ingredients together well in a small bowl, pour the Dressing over the salad and toss until well combined. Serve immediately with Crisp Barbecued Pork Marinated in Sweet Soy (page 227).

SERVES: *6*   **PREPARATION TIME:** *20 mins*

24 fresh scallops, in their shells
Nori and red shiso shreds, to garnish
Salt and pepper, to taste

GINGER MIRIN DRESSING
3 cloves garlic, minced
2 tablespoons finely grated young ginger
2 tablespoons mirin or sherry mixed with
　1 teaspoon miso sauce
2 teaspoons sesame oil

Grilled fresh scallops with ginger mirin dressing

The anise-like aroma of the shiso or perilla leaves which I first encountered in Japan a decade ago creates a fragrant counterpoint to the light and buttery sweet scallops when flash-cooked with mirin or sherry. A feast for all the senses.

Shuck each scallop and discard the top shell. Rinse well under running water to remove any trapped dirt, then drain and dry with paper towels. Arrange the scallops in their bottom shells on a platter.

Combine the Ginger Mirin Dressing ingredients in a bowl and mix well.

Spoon $^1/_2$–1 teaspoon of the Dressing over each scallop in its shell, then gently grill the scallops on a pan grill or under a preheated broiler using medium heat for 2–3 minutes until they have just turn opaque. Do not overcook the scallops. Remove from the heat and transfer the scallops in their shells to a serving platter. Garnish with the nori and shiso shreds, and serve hot with salt and pepper to taste.

Note: The Ginger Mirin Dressing also goes well with steamed fish or shrimp.

SERVES: *6 or Makes 24*　　**PREPARATION TIME:** *30 mins*　　**COOKING TIME:** *3 mins*

1 lb (500 g) fresh shrimp, peeled and
   deveined
$^1/_2$ teaspoon salt
$^1/_3$ cup (60 g) diced pork fat or butter
2 teaspoons sugar
6 cloves garlic
1 egg, white and yolk separated
1 teaspoon cornstarch
1 teaspoon fish sauce
1 teaspoon ground white pepper
12 fresh or canned sugar cane sticks or
   lemongrass stems (each cut to 5 in/12 cm
   long, peeled and rinsed)
$^1/_4$ cup (60 ml) water, mixed with
   2 teaspoons sugar, for glazing
Lettuce leaves, to serve

SWEET CHILI DIPPING SAUCE
1 tablespoon bottled sweet chili sauce
2 teaspoons fish sauce
2 tablespoons shaved palm sugar or dark
   brown sugar

Grilled shrimp on a stick with sweet chili dip

You are attracted to the enticing aromas of buttery rich shrimp and sweet sugar cane or lemongrass as it grills on street-side braziers while spitting fat and caramelizing aromas. You eat with your eyes, nose and ears before sinking your teeth into a fragrant mouthful. Street food at its best in Vietnam.

Place the shrimp in a bowl, sprinkle with the salt, then rub the salt into the shrimp with your fingers. In a separate bowl, rub the sugar into the pork fat and let it stand for 30 minutes. Omit this step if using butter. Process the shrimp, sweetened pork fat or butter and sugar and garlic in a food processor until smooth and well combined. Transfer the processed mixture to a bowl and mix well with the egg white, cornstarch, fish sauce and pepper.

To make the skewers, wet your hands and divide the shrimp mixture into 12 equal portions. Flatten each portion and wrap it around the middle of a sugar cane stick or lemongrass stem, pressing firmly so the shrimp mixture sticks. Continue to make the other skewers in the same manner with the remaining ingredients.

Prepare the Sweet Chili Dipping Sauce by combining all the ingredients in a serving bowl and mixing well. Set aside.

Grill the shrimp skewers on a preheated pan grill or under a broiler or over a charcoal fire, brushing with the sugar water mixture (to glaze them) and turning often, for about 5 minutes or until cooked. Remove from the heat, arrange on a serving platter lined with lettuce leaves and serve with a bowl of the Sweet Chili Dipping Sauce on the side.

MAKES: *12 skewers*   **PREPARATION TIME:** *30 mins*   **COOKING TIME:** *15 mins*

Fresh seafood salad with sesame lime dressing

Yusheng is a seafood feast lit by sparks of stray light on silky white squid, lime-tinged crystalline shrimp and freshly filleted sweet fish—a salty, fresh combination of aromas, colors, textures and flavors that is a Singapore original. I temper this feast of the senses with a nutty and truffle-like dressing balanced with special Shaoxing rice wine that has the surprising raisin-like perfume of a rich port wine.

6 fresh medium squids (10 oz/300 g total)
10 oz (300 g) fresh sashimi grade fish
    fillets (salmon, tuna or white fish)
10 oz (300 g) fresh medium shrimp, peeled
    and deveined, tails left on
1/2 cup (125 ml) fresh lime juice
1 cup (100 g) snowpeas, trimmed and
    sliced in half lengthwise
10 asparagus spears, tough ends trimmed
1 stalk celery, thinly sliced diagonally
1 red bell pepper, cut in half, cored,
    deseeded and sliced
1/2 cup (20 g) dried woodear or cloud ear
    fungus, soaked in hot water until soft,
    hard bits trimmed, drained well
1 teaspoon grated lime rind

SESAME LIME DRESSING
3/4 cup (200 ml) Chicken Stock (page 244)
2 tablespoons Shaoxing rice wine
1 tablespoon superfine (caster) sugar
1 1/2 teaspoons sesame oil
1 tablespoon oyster or mushroom sauce
2 teaspoons Worcestershire sauce
1 teaspoon fresh lime juice
1/2 teaspoon salt, or to taste
1/4 teaspoon ground white pepper

DIPPING SAUCE
1/4 cup (60 ml) fresh lime juice
1 teaspoon sugar
1 teaspoon bottled sweet chili sauce
2 kaffir lime leaves, cut into thin shreds

SERVES: *6*

PREPARATION TIME: *1 hour 30 mins*

COOKING TIME: *5 mins*

Prepare the Chicken Stock by following the recipe on page 244.

Rinse the squids, pull the heads and innards from the tubelike bodies. Discard the heads but retain the tentacles, and remove the beak from the mouth. Clean the body tubes, removing and discarding the long, thin cartilage inside. Halve each tube lengthwise and rinse the inside well. Using a sharp knife, score the flesh on the inside by making diagonal criss-cross slits across the surface, then slice into bite-sized pieces. Half-fill a saucepan with water and bring to a boil. Poach the squid pieces in the boiling water for about 1 minute, then remove and immediately plunge into a bowl of iced water to stop the cooking process. Set aside.

Place the fish fillets and shrimp in a bowl and pour the lime juice over them. Refrigerate for 15 minutes, turning over once. Remove from the refrigerator and drain off the lime juice. Slice the fish fillets into bite-sized strips. Place all the seafood in a platter and refrigerate until ready to serve.

Half-fill a saucepan with water and bring to a boil. Blanch the snowpeas and asparagus separately for about 1 minute each. Remove from the heat and immediately plunge into iced water to stop the cooking process. Drain well and refrigerate together with the other vegetables, until ready to serve.

To prepare the Sesame Lime Dressing, combine all the ingredients in a bowl and mix well. Make the Dipping Sauce by mixing all the ingredients until the sugar is dissolved and dividing it into several tiny dipping bowls.

To serve, arrange the seafood and vegetables on a large platter and scatter the grated lime rind over the fish pieces. Place the platter with the bowl of the Sesame Lime Dressing in the center of the dining table and tiny bowls of the Dipping Sauce around them. Provide each guest with a pair of chopsticks and a small side plate. Begin by pouring the Dressing over the salad, then invite your guests to toss the ingredients all at once using their chopsticks for health and prosperity.

4–6 dried beancurd skin sheets, each 8 in
   (20 cm) square
2 egg whites, for brushing
Oil, for deep-frying

SWEET BLACK SOY DIPPING SAUCE
$1/2$ cup (125 ml) sweet bottled chili sauce
$1/4$ cup (60 ml) sweet thick soy sauce
   (kecap manis)
$1/4$ cup (60 ml) rice wine
$1/2$ tablespoon Chinese black vinegar, or to
   taste

FILLING
8 oz (250 g) ground fatty pork
8 oz (250 g) ground lean pork
6 fresh or canned water chestnuts, peeled
   and finely diced
$1/2$ teaspoon ground white pepper
$1^1/2$ tablespoons sugar
$1/2$ tablespoon Sambal Oelek Chili Paste
   (page 240) or other sweet chili paste
1 tablespoon black soy sauce
1 teaspoon hoisin sauce
$1/3$ cup (40 g) sticky (glutinous) rice flour

Beancurd skin sausage rolls with sweet soy dip

Loh bak, the beancurd skin rolls are one of the classic favorites, containing a rich pork filling blended with sticky sweet hoisin, salty and yeasty black soy, and crunchy water chestnuts. These rolls create their own flavors and exude a steamy bouquet as they cook in their paper-thin tofu skins. Serve them on their own with a sweet and pungent Chinese vinegar soy dip.

Prepare the Sambal Oelek Chili Paste by following the recipe on page 240.

Prepare the beancurd skin sheets first. Soak 2 clean dish towels in warm water and then squeeze out the water. Lay the damp towels out flat on a work surface and place the beancurd skin sheets in between the two towels for about 10 minutes to soften them, then remove them carefully and brush with the egg white. Cover the softened sheets with a damp towel.

Combine the Sweet Black Soy Dipping Sauce ingredients in a serving bowl and mix well. Set aside

Combine the Filling ingredients in a large bowl and mix well. To make the pork rolls, wet your hands and divide the Filling into 4 equal portions. Roll each portion into a long sausage-like cylinder, about 1 in (3 cm) in diameter and 6 in (15 cm) long. Place a cylinder along one edge of a beancurd skin square. Roll the skin around the Filling, then fold in the sides and roll up tightly, dabbing the inside edge with a little water if necessary and pressing to seal. Continue to make the rolls in the same manner with the remaining ingredients. Place the pork rolls in a heatproof dish.

Half-fill a wok with water and bring to a rapid boil. Place the dish with the pork rolls in a bamboo steamer and set the steamer over the boiling water to steam for about 10 minutes. Remove from the heat and set aside to cool.

Heat the oil in a wok and deep-fry the pork rolls, a few at a time and turning them often, over medium heat for 2–3 minutes, until crispy and golden brown on all sides. Remove from the hot oil and drain on paper towels.

Slice each deep-fried roll into several pieces and arrange them on a serving platter. Serve with the serving bowl of Dipping Sauce on the side.

Note: It's a good idea to prepare extra beancurd skin sheets in case 1 or 2 of them tears during rolling. You can substitute filo pastry if beancurd skin sheets are not available—use 3 filo sheets to make each pork roll. Then bake the rolls instead of steaming and frying them. You will need 12 filo pastry sheets to make this recipe.

SERVES: *6–8*   **PREPARATION TIME:** *1 hour*   **COOKING TIME:** *20 mins*

1/4 cup (60 ml) oil
1 onion, thinly sliced
10 cloves garlic, thinly sliced
2 teaspoons dried shrimp paste, dry-roasted
    and crumbled
1 tablespoon Sambal Oelek Chili Paste
    (page 240) or other sweet chili paste
1/2 teaspoon ground turmeric
1 tablespoon ginger paste (crushed or
    ground from fresh ginger root)
11/2 cups (200 g) dried shrimp, rinsed, dry-
    roasted and coarsely ground in a mortar
    or blender
2 tablespoons fish sauce, or to taste
1–2 tablespoons dry chili flakes
2 teaspoons sugar, or to taste
Pinch of salt, or to taste
Fresh juice of 1/2 lime

Crisp dried shrimp with lime, ginger and chilies

I have had this Burmese Belachaung in many forms and with different heat strengths—some more tart, some less—but all made with the basic dried shrimp which produces a strong, fragrant sambal. I find this dish so tasty that one tends to ask for more, especially when served with crisp-fried fish fillets.

Prepare the Sambal Oelek Chili Paste by following the recipe on page 240.

Heat the oil in a wok and stir-fry the sliced onion over medium heat until crisp and golden brown, 2–3 minutes. Remove from the pan and then do the same with the sliced garlic. Set them both aside. Drain the oil from the wok, leaving about 1 tablespoon.

Reheat the oil in the wok and stir-fry the shrimp paste, Sambal Oelek, turmeric and ginger over medium heat until fragrant, 1–2 minutes. Add the dried shrimp and fish sauce and stir-fry for another 2 minutes until crispy, taking care not to burn the shrimp. Reduce the heat to low and continue stir-frying until the mixture becomes very crispy. Add the chili flakes, stir in the fried onion and garlic and season with sugar and salt to taste. Remove from the heat and transfer the shrimp to a serving bowl, dribble the lime juice over the top and serve with bread.

SERVES: *4*   PREPARATION TIME: *30 mins*   COOKING TIME: *15 mins*

2 cups (8 oz/250 g) dried baby anchovies
(*Ikan bilis*) or whitebait, heads and veins
removed, rinsed and drained
2 teaspoons rice flour, for dusting
1$^1\!/_2$ cups (375 ml) oil, to shallow-fry
1–2 teaspoons ground red pepper, or to
taste
1 teaspooon sweet thick soy sauce
(*kecap manis*)
1 cup (200 g) dry-roasted unsalted peanuts

SUGAR SYRUP
$^1\!/_4$ cup (50 g) sugar
$^1\!/_4$ cup (60 ml) water

Sweet and spicy ikan bilis nibbles with peanuts

Roasting peanuts have a nutty, caramelized aroma. When combined with fried baby anchovies and then tossed with a sugary syrup, they create a unique aroma. These sugared nibbles go very well with the malty sweetness and floral aromas of beer hops, and are a popular accompaniment to beer served in clubs and good restaurants all over Malaysia and Singapore.

Dust the dried anchovies with the rice flour. Heat the oil in a wok until very hot—it is ready when bubbles form around a skewer dipped in it. Fry the anchovies over medium heat until golden brown and crispy, about 1 minute. Remove them from the oil and drain on paper towels.

Make the Sugar Syrup by combining the sugar and water in a small saucepan over medium heat, stirring until the sugar dissolves. Allow it to boil and simmer uncovered for about 1 minute to thicken the syrup slightly. Remove the Syrup from the heat, pour it into a clean wok and heat over medium heat. When the Sugar Syrup bubbles, add the fried anchovies, ground red pepper and sweet thick soy sauce, and toss well to coat the fish with the Syrup. Stir in the peanuts and remove from the heat.

SERVES: *4–6*   PREPARATION TIME: *30 mins*   COOKING TIME: *10 mins*

Nonya pickled vegetables with dried shrimp

The Nonya (Straits Chinese) version of *achar* (a word of Indian origin that means "pickles") is made with crunchy vegetables marinated in a punchy mixture of vinegar and spices that produce delightful sweet and sour aromas and textures. Served in small bowls as a side dish, this *achar* goes well with meat dishes where the aromas of the ginger and sweet chili can be picked up. I use it when serving lamb shanks in a light curry.

14 oz (400 g) green beans, sliced into short lengths
3 baby gherkins or pickling cucumbers, cut into half lengthwise, cored and sliced into small batons
2 carrots, peeled and sliced in the same manner as the cucumbers
3 cups (400 g) tiny cauliflower florets
2 cups (500 ml) white vinegar
Salt, to taste
3 tablespoons oil
1 teaspoon ground turmeric
1 small onion, diced
5 cloves garlic, peeled
1 in (3 cm) fresh ginger, peeled and thinly sliced
2 stalks lemongrass, thick bottom parts only, outer layers discarded, inner parts sliced
1 teaspoon dried shrimp paste
1 teaspoon sugar
Salt, to taste
2 tablespoons dry-roasted sesame seeds

STUFFED CHILIES
3 long Asian chili peppers
2 tablespoons dried shrimp, coarsely ground in a mortar or blender
1 tablespoon Sambal Oelek Chili Paste (page 240) or other sweet chili paste
1 tablespoon shaved palm sugar or dark brown sugar

MAKES: *3 cups*

PREPARATION TIME: *1 hour + 1 hour for the vegetables to stand*

COOKING TIME: *10 mins*

Prepare the Sambal Oelek Chili Paste by following the recipe on page 240.

Sprinkle each type of vegetable with $\frac{1}{2}$ a teaspoon of salt separately and mix well. Allow them to stand for 1 hour, then drain and squeeze out all the liquid from the vegetables. Set aside.

To prepare the Stuffed Chilies, make a slit lengthwise on one side of each chili pepper with a paring knife, but do not cut through. Using a teaspoon, scoop out and discard the pith and seeds from the inside of each pepper to form a pocket for stuffing.

Combine the dried shrimp, Sambal Oelek and sugar in a dish and mix well, then microwave for about 2 minutes until crisp, stopping to stir the mixture every 30 seconds. Stuff 1 teaspoon of the roasted dried shrimp mixture into each pepper and set aside.

Bring the vinegar and a little salt to a boil over medium heat in a saucepan and blanch each of the vegetables separately for 30 seconds to 1 minute. Remove from the heat and drain each vegetable and place in a glass bowl together with the Stuffed Chilies. Reserve the vinegar mixture used for blanching the vegetables.

Heat the oil in a wok and stir-fry the ground turmeric over medium heat for 30 seconds. Add the onion, garlic and ginger and stir-fry until golden brown, 1–2 minutes. Stir in the lemongrass and shrimp paste and toss until fragrant. Add $\frac{1}{4}$ cup (60 ml) of the reserved vinegar mixture and season with the sugar and salt to taste. Bring the vinegar mixture to a boil. The mixture should be reddish yellow and not caramelized. Stir in all the vegetables and Stuffed Chilies and turn off the heat, then toss thoroughly to mix well. Transfer the *achar* to several clean glass jars and sprinkle about 1 teaspoon of the sesame seeds on top of each jar. Seal and store refrigerated for up to 1 year.

COOKING WITH AROMATIC ASIAN SEASONINGS

1/2 cup (125 ml) oil
10 oz (300 g) dried rice stick noodles,
    blanched in boiling water until soft, then
    drained well
2 eggs, slightly beaten
1 onion, finely chopped
5 cloves garlic, minced
7 oz (200 g) lean pork, thinly sliced and
    marinated with 1 tablespoon oyster sauce
2 tablespoons dried shrimp paste, dry-
    roasted and crumbled
1 cake pressed firm tofu (5 oz/150 g), diced
1 red finger-length chili pepper, chopped
2 tablespoons roasted unsalted peanuts,
    crushed
2 tablespoons chopped coriander leaves
    (cilantro)
1/2 cup (30 g) chopped garlic chives
1/2 cup (25 g) bean sprouts, tails trimmed
Lime wedges, to garnish

SWEET CHILI DRESSING
1/2 cup (60 ml) fresh lime juice
1/2 cup (60 ml) Thai fish sauce
2 tablespoons shaved palm sugar or dark
    brown sugar, with 4 tablespoons water
1 tablespoon bottled sweet chilli sauce

Rice noodles with pork and sweet chili dressing

Fresh, wild and wonderful—this dish creates a culinary insurrection on your palate with its unbeatable combination of garlic chives, bean sprouts and coriander leaves, all of which serve to jog your aromatic memory. My friend Simon Goh of Chinta Ria adds a mean chili dressing when he tosses this particular dish as it is cooked in our hometown of Klang. If shrimp paste is not your thing, omit it for it might change your appreciation of this vibrant noodle dish. Glasses of beer, aromatic and floral when chilled, go well with this dish.

Heat the oil in a wok and fry the noodles over medium heat for 1–2 minutes until slightly browned. Remove from the pan and drain on paper towels.

Heat 1 tablespoon of the oil in a skillet until hot. Add the beaten egg, swirling the pan to form a thin omelet. Cook the egg until set. Remove from the heat and set aside to cool. Roll up the omelet and slice into thin shreds.

Heat 1 tablespoon of the oil in a wok over high heat and stir-fry the onion and garlic until golden brown and fragrant, about 30 seconds. Add the pork and stir-fry until cooked, 2–3 minutes. Add the shrimp paste, tofu and chili, and mix well. Remove from the heat.

Make the Sweet Chili Dressing by combining all the ingredients in a bowl and mixing well.

In a large serving platter, combine all the ingredients except the egg and lime wedges. Pour the Dressing over the noodles and toss until well blended. Sprinkle the egg shreds on top and serve with lime wedges.

SERVES: *4-6*　　　PREPARATION TIME: *45 mins*　　　COOKING TIME: *10 mins*

Crab soup with lemongrass, tamarind and mint

A tempting Cambodian soup that begins with buttery crab flavors layered into a seafood stock with creamy mushrooms, citrusy lemon and fragrant kaffir lime—finished off with a spike of burnt chili shrimp paste. The unforgettable fragrance of this soup entices diners with a luxurious tinge of caramelized butter on the palate. A truly orgasmic experience, this soup is not only a feast for the senses but satisfies hungry diners every time.

7 oz (200 g) dried rice noodles

2 cups (100 g) fresh bean sprouts, tails trimmed, or iceberg lettuce leaves torn into shreds (optional)

1/4 cup (10 g) Vietnamese mint (laksa leaves)

Garlic cloves, peeled

Sliced red chili peppers

Lime wedges, to serve

CRAB SOUP

3 lbs (1 1/2 kg) fresh crabs

2–4 red finger-length chili peppers, halved and deseeded

1 teaspoon dried shrimp paste, dry-roasted and crumbled

6 cloves garlic, peeled

2 cups (500 ml) Fish Stock (page 244)

1 cup (250 ml) boiling water

2 stalks lemongrass, thick bottom parts only, dry outer layers discarded, inner parts bruised

1 tablespoon tamarind pulp, mashed with 2 cups (500 ml) water and strained to obtain juice

2 fresh kaffir lime leaves, cut into thin strips

1/2 cup (50 g) enoki mushrooms, trimmed

1/4 cup (50 g) pickled lotus roots or pickled garlic (optional)

2 1/2 tablespoons fish sauce

2 teaspoons sugar

1/2 teaspoon salt, or to taste

1/2 teaspoon ground white pepper

CRISPY FRIED SHALLOTS

2 tablespoons oil

5 small Asian shallots, sliced

Prepare the Fish Stock by following the recipe on page 244.

To prepare the Crab Soup, rinse each crab well and detach the claws. Lift off the outer shell and discard. Scrape out and reserve any roe and discard the gills. Quarter each crab with a cleaver and crack the claws with a mallet. Set aside.

Process the chili peppers, shrimp paste and garlic in a food processor or grind in a mortar until smooth. Combine the paste with the Fish Stock, boiling water, lemongrass and tamarind juice and bring to a boil. Reduce the heat to low, cover and simmer for 3–5 minutes. Add the crab pieces and boil the soup over high heat for about 2 minutes, then reduce the heat to low, cover and cook for another 10 minutes. Add the lime leaves, mushrooms and pickled lotus roots or garlic (if using), and season with the fish sauce, sugar, salt and pepper. Keep the Crab Soup simmering over very low heat until ready to serve.

Prepare the Crispy Fried Shallots by heating the oil in a skillet and sautéing the sliced shallot over medium heat until golden and crispy, 1–2 minutes. Remove from the heat and drain on paper towels. Alternatively, cover the shallot slices with the oil in a dish and microwave for 1 minute on high, then stir and return to microwave for another 1 minute.

Half-fill a saucepan with water and bring to a boil. Add the rice noodles and cook until soft, 2–3 minutes. Remove from the heat and drain well.

To serve, place the noodles in individual serving bowls and add some bean sprouts or lettuce leaves (if using). Ladle the hot Crab Soup into each bowl, distributing the crab pieces evenly. Top with the Vietnamese mint, Crispy Fried Shallots, garlic and sliced chili pepper, and serve immediately with the lime wedges on the side.

SERVES: *4*   PREPARATION TIME: *45 mins*   COOKING TIME: *30 mins*

1 tablespoon oil
1 onion, finely chopped
4 cloves garlic, chopped
2 stalks lemongrass, thick bottom parts only, outer layers discarded, inner parts roughly pounded
1 tablespoon dried chili flakes
Pinch of ground turmeric
1 tablespoon fish sauce
2 tablespoons dry-roasted chickpea flour (besan), mixed with 1 tablespoon water
1 teaspoon salt, or to taste
1 teaspoon freshly ground black pepper
$^1/_2$ cup (20 g) chopped coriander leaves (cilantro)
10 oz (300 g) dried rice noodles, blanched in boiling water until soft

ACCOMPANIMENTS I
1 cup (100 g) sliced fish cakes or cooked fish fingers
$^1/_3$ cup (100 ml) fresh lime juice
2 cups (200 g) sliced cabbage

ACCOMPANIMENTS II (OPTIONAL)
3 tablespoons rice flour, dry-roasted until golden brown
$^1/_2$ cup (20 g) chopped coriander leaves (cilantro)
1 onion, thinly sliced
3 eggs, boiled and quartered
2 teaspoons freshly ground black pepper
Roasted dried chili flakes
Lime wedges
Young lime leaves, thinly sliced

STOCK
$^1/_4$ teaspoon ground turmeric
2 lbs (1 kg) butterfish or catfish fillets
2 stalks lemongrass, thick bottom parts only, dry outer layers discarded, inner parts bruised
$^1/_3$ cup (100 ml) fish sauce
8 cups (2 liters) Fish Stock (page 245)
8 cups (2 liters) water

Fish soup with lemongrass, coriander and lime

Inhale deeply and you will get a bouquet of aromas from this bowl of soup—starting with hit of sweet, crisp garlic, strident and vocal, followed by plentiful fish and lemongrass aromas, almost masking the floral top notes of the kaffir lime. The aromas gradually build up and are reminiscent of earthy dark mushrooms and sour mangoes. This is a meal on its own and is often served as a light lunch or breakfast in Burma.

Prepare the Fish Stock by following the recipe on page 245.

Prepare the Stock by rubbing the ground turmeric into the fish fillets on both sides. Place all the ingredients in a stockpot and bring to a boil over high heat. Continue boiling until the fish is cooked, about 5 minutes. Remove from the heat, strain and reserve the clear Stock. Remove and discard any bones from the fish. Process the deboned fish to a paste in a food processor and set aside.

Heat the oil in a wok and stir-fry the onion, garlic and lemongrass over medium heat until fragrant and golden brown, 2–3 minutes. Add the chili flakes, turmeric and fish sauce and stir-fry for another 1–2 minutes. Stir in the reserved ground fish paste and remove from the heat. Set aside.

Return the clear Stock to a boil over medium heat in a stockpot and stir in the chickpea mixture. Add the stir-fried spice mixture and simmer uncovered over low heat for about 3 minutes until the soup has reduced slightly. Season with the salt and black pepper to taste, and stir in the chopped coriander leaves. Remove from the heat and transfer to a large soup tureen.

To serve, divide the blanched rice noodles into individual serving bowls and place these along with the tureen of soup in the center of the table, surrounded by the Accompaniments. Invite each guest to ladle the hot soup into a bowl of noodles and top with the Accompaniments of their choice.

SERVES: 6-8   PREPARATION TIME: 45 mins   COOKING TIME: 30 mins

COOKING WITH AROMATIC ASIAN SEASONINGS

2 lbs (1 kg) pork belly or thigh
1 teaspoon coarse sea salt
2 star anise, ground
Oil, for brushing
Bottled sweet chili sauce, to serve

MARINADE
2 tablespoons sweet thick soy sauce (*kecap manis*)
1 tablespoon tomato ketchup
2 cloves garlic, minced
2 tablespoons Chinese black vinegar
2 tablespoons plum sauce
1 tablespoon rice wine
2 tablespoons cornstarch
1 tablespoon brown sugar

Crisp barbecued pork marinated in sweet soy

This roast pork is pure heaven—golden brown with a slight burnt edge and a light aroma of star anise that teases the burnt sugar into the roasting meat. You don't have to be a rocket scientist to recreate this tender and sumptuous dish in your own kitchen. Sliced diagonally into thin wafers and added to noodles, pasta, fried rice or a sandwich, your *char siew* will easily transform a simple meal.

Place the pork in a large bowl, sprinkle with the salt and rub the salt into the pork with your fingers. Allow to stand for 2 hours, then pat dry with paper towels. Using a needle, make deep pricks all over the pork.

Combine the Marinade ingredients in a bowl and mix well, then pour the Marinade over the pork and rub it into the meat. Allow the pork to marinate for 1 hour, brushing with a little oil.

Preheat the oven to 400°F (200°C). Place the marinated pork in a baking dish and bake in the oven for 15 minutes. Remove the pork from the oven, drain and reserve the liquid collected in the pan. Reduce the temperature to 340°F (170°C) and return the pork to bake for another 10 minutes. Remove from the oven.

Brush the pork with a little salt and grill on a preheated pan grill or under a broiler for 3–5 minutes until crisp, turning often and basting with the reserved liquid. Remove from the heat and cool. Slice the pork thinly and serve with rice, Cabbage Sautéed with Black Mustard Seeds (page 72) and a bowl of sweet chili sauce on the side.

SERVES: *6*   **PREPARATION TIME:** *20 mins + 3 hours to stand*   **COOKING TIME:** *30 mins*

1¹/₃ lbs (600 g) boneless chicken thighs,
    fat trimmed, cut in half
1 tablespoon soy sauce
1¹/₂ tablespoons oil
3 cloves garlic, minced
1 tablespoon grated fresh ginger
3 green onions, sliced into short lengths
2 tablespoons Chinese rice wine
    (Shaoxing)
1 tablespoon hoisin sauce
¹/₂ tablespoon thick sweet soy sauce
    (kecap manis)
¹/₄ cup (10 g) dried woodear or cloud ear
    fungus, soaked in hot water until soft,
    hard bits removed, drained well
¹/₂ teaspoon salt, or to taste
¹/₄ teaspoon ground white pepper
Green onion curls (see note), to garnish

TEA FLAVORED EGGS
12 quail eggs
1 tablespoon tea leaves
Warm water, to cover
1 teaspoon black soy sauce

Aromatic ginger soy chicken with rice wine

The warm fragrance of ginger and freshly sliced green onion, balanced by floral wine and yeasty soy, creates a memorable combination of flavors and scents to entertain the palate.

Prepare the Tea Flavored Eggs first. Place the eggs in a small saucepan and add enough warm water to cover. Add the tea leaves and bring slowly to a boil over medium–low heat, then simmer uncovered for about 5 minutes. Turn off the heat and remove the eggs from the pan. Roll each egg on a flat work surface to crack the shell on all sides, then return to the saucepan with the tea mixture. Add the black soy sauce, bring the mixture to a boil and simmer over medium–low heat for 3–5 minutes. Turn off the heat, remove the eggs from the pan and plunge them in a bowl of cold water to cool them. Once they are cool, peel the eggs and set aside.

In a large bowl, combine the chicken and soy sauce and mix well. Heat the oil in a wok until smoky and stir-fry the garlic over medium heat until golden and fragrant, about 20 seconds. Stir in the ginger, spring onion and rice wine, then add the chicken and stir-fry for 1–2 minutes. Add the fungus, season with the hoisin sauce and sweet soy sauce, and stir-fry for about 1 minute to mix well. Add a little water if the dish appears dry. Cover and simmer for 3–5 minutes until the sauce thickens and the chicken is well cooked. Season with the salt and pepper to taste and remove from the heat. Transfer to a serving bowl, top with the Tea Flavored Eggs and garnish with green onion curls. Serve immediately with steamed rice or noodles.

Note: To make green onion curls, trim off the bulb of each green onion at the point where the stem begins to turn green. Slice the leaves into 4-in (10-cm) lengths. Using a sharp knife, slice each length into very thin strips length-wise. Soak the strips in a bowl of iced water and refrigerate until they curl up.

SERVES: *6*   **PREPARATION TIME:** *30 mins*   **COOKING TIME:** *20 mins*

1 lb (500 g) boneless chicken thighs, trimmed
$^1/_2$ cup (60 g) all-purpose flour
$^1/_2$ cup (30 g) breadcrumbs
Oil, for deep-frying
$^1/_2$ onion, chopped
2 cloves garlic, minced
5 oz (150 g) fresh shiitake mushrooms, stems
    trimmed, caps sliced (optional)
1 stalk lemongrass, thick bottom part only,
    outer layers discarded, inner part sliced
    and ground in a mortar
$^1/_2$ tablespoon Sambal Oelek Chili Paste
    (page 240) or other sweet chili paste
1 tablespoon brown bean paste (*taucheo*)
1 tablespoon sweet thick soy sauce (*kecap manis*)
$^1/_2$ tablespoon Chinese rice wine
$^1/_2$ tablespoon bottled sweet chili sauce
1 tablespoon sugar
1 tablespoon freshly squeezed lime juice
Salt and ground white pepper, to taste
1 red finger-length chili pepper, deseeded
    and sliced, to garnish
Green onion curls (page 229), to garnish

MARINADE
$^1/_4$ cup (60 ml) Chinese rice wine
$^1/_4$ cup (60 ml) Chinese black vinegar
2 teaspoons sesame oil
1 tablespoon soy sauce

Sweet soy and sambal fried chicken

The quintessential dish of the Nonyas of Malacca, where each dish is given as much attention as the cook can spare to prepare a percussion of spice and herbal aromas overlain with contrasting tastes and textures.

Prepare the Green Onion Curls and Sambal Oelek Chili Paste by following the recipes on page 229 and 240.

Combine the Marinade ingredients in a large bowl and mix well. Add the chicken and mix until well coated. Cover and refrigerate for 3–4 hours, then drain. Combine the flour and breadcrumbs in a zip-lock bag. In batches, place the chicken in the flour mixture, shaking the bag to coat them well with the mixture on all sides. Remove from the bag and set aside on a platter.

Heat the oil in a wok and deep-fry the chicken over medium heat for about 1 minute on each side. Remove from the hot oil and drain on paper towels.

Drain off all but 2 tablespoons of the oil in the wok and stir-fry the onion and garlic until fragrant, about 1 minute. Add the mushroom slices (if using) and stir-fry for 1 minute. Stir in the lemongrass, sambal and bean paste and mix well. Add the deep-fried chicken to the wok and stir-fry for 1–2 minutes. Season with the soy sauce, rice wine, chili sauce, sugar and lemon juice, and stir-fry for 1 more minute. Add the salt and pepper to taste and remove from the heat. Transfer to a serving platter, garnish with red chili slices and green onion curls and serve hot.

SERVES: *4–6*   **PREPARATION TIME:** *30 mins + 3 hours to marinate*   **COOKING TIME:** *15 mins*

COOKING WITH AROMATIC ASIAN SEASONINGS

2 tablespoons olive oil

2 lbs (1 kg) store-bought roasted chicken, cut into bite-sized pieces

8 oz (250 g) streaky smoked pork or bacon, cut into chunks

1 large onion, cut into chunks

$^1/_2$ cup (125 ml) Sambal Oelek Chili Paste (page 240) or other sweet chili paste with dried shrimp paste added

$^1/_2$ tablespoon sweet thick soy sauce (*kecap manis*)

1 tablespoon soy sauce

1 tablespoon tomato paste

3 potatoes, peeled and parboiled, then drained and sliced into chunks

Fresh juice of 1 lime

Quick eurasian curry captain

Savor the mouth-watering European and Asian aromas in this dish of roasted chicken and smoked bacon cooked with spicy sweet soy to create an enticing combination of unusual Portuguese Eurasian flavors. This recipe comes from my sister-in-law's family kitchen, where the exploration of aromas and tastes is always invited.

Prepare the Sambal Oelek Chili Paste by following the recipe on page 240.

Heat 1 tablespoon of the olive oil in a wok and stir-fry the chicken and pork over medium–high heat until crisp, 1–2 minutes. Remove from the heat and set aside. Add the remaining oil to the wok and stir-fry the onion and sambal over medium heat for 1–2 minutes until fragrant. Remove from the heat.

Combine all the ingredients, except the lime juice, in a large saucepan or pot and cook over medium heat for 5–10 minutes, stirring from time to time, until the sauce reduces. Season with the lime juice and remove from the heat. Serve immediately with bread and steamed rice. This dish also goes well with a tasty salad such as Arugula Salad with Tangy Citrus Dressing (page 97).

SERVES: *6–8*   **PREPARATION TIME:** *20 mins*   **COOKING TIME:** *15 mins*

12 oz (350 g) beef tenderloin, thinly sliced
1 tablespoon oil
3 cloves garlic, minced
2 tablespoons Chicken Stock (page 245), or water
1 bunch (8 oz/250 g) Chinese broccoli (*kailan*), stems trimmed
5 dried black Chinese mushrooms, soaked in hot water until soft, drained, stems trimmed
1 tablespoon dried Chinese wolfberries or 5 dried Chinese red dates, rinsed
1 teaspoon freshly ground black pepper
1 red finger-length chili pepper, deseeded and sliced, to garnish

MARINADE
1–2 tablespoons mirin (or rice wine with some sugar added)
$1/_2$ tablespoon mushroom oyster sauce
$1/_2$ tablespoon soy sauce

Beef and black mushrooms with chinese broccoli

The success of this recipe relies on the marination of the meat in fragrant mirin, which evaporates when the dish is stir-fried, leaving a wonderful aroma to beguile the senses. Give the wolfberries a try—they give the dish a slight sweetness and add a celebratory touch of red.

Prepare the Chicken Stock by following the recipe on page 245.

Combine the Marinade ingredients in a large bowl and mix well. Add the beef strips and mix until well coated. Allow the meat to marinate for at least 2 hours or overnight if possible. Drain the beef and reserve the Marinade.

Heat the oil in a wok and stir-fry the garlic over high heat until golden and fragrant, about 30 seconds. Add the marinated beef strips, toss for 1 minute and remove from the heat. Keep warm.

Add the reserved Marinade and all the other ingredients, except the pepper and chili, to the wok and bring to a boil over high heat. Reduce the heat to a simmer, cover and cook for about 1 minute. Season with the pepper and turn off the heat. Return the beef strips to the wok and mix well. Transfer to a serving platter, garnish with the sliced chili and serve immediately with steamed rice.

SERVES: *4–6*   **PREPARATION TIME:** *20 mins + 2 hours to marinate*   **COOKING TIME:** *5 mins*

1/3 cup (100 ml) oil

14 oz (400 g) slender Asian eggplants, thickly sliced diagonally

2 cakes pressed or firm tofu (each 5 oz/150 g), cubed

2 cloves garlic, chopped

1–2 red finger-length chili peppers, deseeded and finely chopped

1 tablespoon brown bean paste (*taucheo*)

2 tablespoons oyster sauce

2 teaspoons bottled Chinese plum sauce

3 green onions, leaves sliced diagonally, to garnish

Eggplant and tofu with sweet spicy bean paste

Eggplant and tofu are interesting and versatile ingredients. I use them in many of my dishes. Brown bean paste is similar to Japanese red miso—it has a nutty and smoky aroma, and when combined with oyster sauce and plum sauce, the result is an amazingly aromatic dish, which goes very well with rice or Quick Tossed Asian Noodles (page 51).

Heat the oil in a wok until hot and fry the eggplant slices in batches over medium heat until golden, 2–3 minutes. Remove from the heat, drain on paper towels and keep warm until ready to use.

Drain off all but 1/4 cup (60 ml) of the oil from the wok. Reheat the oil and shallow-fry the tofu cubes over medium heat until golden and crisp on all sides in the same manner. Remove from the heat and drain on paper towels.

Clean the wok, heat 2 teaspoons of the oil in it and stir-fry the garlic, chili and bean paste over medium heat until fragrant, about 1 minute. Stir in the fried eggplant pieces, the oyster sauce and the plum sauce. Add the fried tofu and toss quickly to combine, then remove from the heat. Transfer to a serving platter, garnish with the green onion and serve hot with steamed rice or noodles.

SERVES: *6*   PREPARATION TIME: *20 mins*   COOKING TIME: *20 mins*

Parsnips and carrots sautéed with rice wine

The kalamansi lime is sweet and fragrant and less tart than regular limes. It combines well with the flavors of sweet parsnips and carrots and the black pepper spikes the dish with energy and warmth. This is truly satisfying when served with an Asian or Moroccan lamb or beef dishes.

2–3 parsnip (1 lb/500 g total), peeled and cut into chunks
1 large carrot, peeled and cut into chunks
1 tablespoon oil
4 cloves garlic, chopped
1 teaspoon minced fresh ginger
2 tablespoon Chinese rice wine or sherry
2 tablespoons Chinese black vinegar
3 tablespoons freshly squeezed kalamansi lime juice or regular lime juice
1 teaspoon sugar
1/2 teaspoon salt, or to taste
1/2 teaspoon ground white pepper

Place the parsnip and carrot chunks in a dish and microwave for about 1 minute to soften them slightly. Remove and set aside.

Heat the oil in a wok and stir-fry the garlic and ginger over medium heat until fragrant and golden, about 1 minute. Add the parsnip and carrot chunks and stir-fry for 1 minute. Deglaze with the rice wine or sherry and season with the vinegar, lime juice, sugar, salt and pepper. Continue to stir-fry for 1–2 more minutes until the vegetables are tender and cooked, adjusting the seasonings as needed. Remove from the heat, transfer to a serving bowl and serve hot with steamed rice.

SERVES: 4   PREPARATION TIME: *15 mins*   COOKING TIME: *5 mins*

Asian greens with shrimp and cashews

Chinese broccoli (*kailan*) and other dark Asian greens have a slightly bitter taste that translates also to a "bitter" aroma. When combined with garlic and the delicious buttery perfume of sautéed shrimp, this dish swells with fragrance, especially when mushrooms and cashews are added.

1 tablespoon oil
2 cloves garlic, minced
12 fresh shrimp, peeled and deveined
12 dried black Chinese mushrooms, soaked in hot water until soft, stems trimmed, caps sliced
1 teaspoon Sambal Oelek chili paste (page 240) or other sweet chili paste
1 bunch Chinese broccoli (*kailan*), stems only, peeled and sliced diagonally
2 cups (200 g) sliced bok choy
2 tablespoons oyster sauce
1/2 teaspoon sesame oil
Salt and ground white pepper, to taste
Roasted cashew nuts, to garnish
Crispy Fried Garlic (page 47), to garnish

Prepare the Crispy Fried Garlic and Sambal Oelek Chili Paste by following the recipes on pages 47 and 240.

Heat the oil in a wok and stir-fry the garlic over medium heat until fragrant and golden, about 1 minute. Add the shrimp, mushroom slices and Sambal Oelek and stir-fry for 1 minute. Add the vegetables and toss well over high heat for 2 minutes until tender. Season with the oyster sauce, sesame oil, salt and pepper to taste, and remove from the heat. Transfer to a serving platter, sprinkle with cashew nuts and Crispy-fried Garlic on top and serve hot with steamed rice.

Note: To prepare as a vegetarian dish, simply omit the shrimp.

SERVES: 4   PREPARATION TIME: *20 mins*   COOKING TIME: *5 mins*

12 fresh oyster mushrooms or honey
   mushrooms, stems trimmed
1$\frac{1}{2}$ lbs (750 g) choy sum, trimmed and cut
   into lengths
1 teaspoon dried green tea leaves
4 cloves garlic, chopped
1 tablespoon oil
2 teaspoons oyster or mushroom sauce
1 teaspoon sesame oil

Chinese greens with mushrooms and oyster sauce

Choy sum is a type of Chinese mustard greens with little yellow flowers, and a crunchy bitterness that you can smell. This vegetable works well as a fragrant stir-fry, especially when nutty sesame oil and yeasty oyster sauce are added. Try this recipe for its aroma, flavor and texture.

Place the mushrooms and choy sum in separate heatproof dishes. Using a 2-tier bamboo steamer, place the dish with the mushrooms in the top tier and the one with the choy sum in the lower tier.

Half-fill a wok with water and bring to a boil. Sprinkle the tea leaves into the boiling water and place the steamer over it. After steaming for 2–3 minutes, remove the choy sum from the steamer. Continue steaming the mushrooms for 1 more minute and remove from the heat.

Heat the oil in a wok and stir-fry the garlic over medium heat until fragrant, about 1 minute. Remove from the heat and drain the fried garlic on paper towels. Arrange the steamed mushrooms on a serving platter and top with the choy sum. Drizzle with the oyster or mushroom sauce and sesame oil and garnish with the crispy-fried garlic. Serve hot with steamed rice.

Note: Instead of steaming, you may want to blanch the mushrooms and choy sum in tea-infused water for a stronger flavor. Half-fill a large saucepan with water and bring to a boil, then add the tea leaves and 1 teaspoon of salt and boil over high heat for 1–2 minutes. Add the mushrooms and choy sum, cover and cook for 1 minute. Remove from the heat and serve as instructed above.

SERVES: 4–6   PREPARATION TIME: 15 mins   COOKING TIME: 10 mins

Basic Recipes

Basics are just that: simple recipes for cooks that will make life simpler in the kitchen. It is what every experienced cook knows and what every beginner would like to know. I have included simple stock recipes and proportions for pastes and curry powder mixes. It all seems like common sense until you have to do it yourself. I have included instructions for cooking rice as I did not know how to do this, when I was married. I produced a fabulous dinner but had to ask my husband to show me how to cook the rice—and he never stopped reminding me about it!

Steamed white rice

Different varieties of rice have different textures when cooked. Jasmine and basmati rice grains are firm and separate while Japanese rice is soft and fluffy. Sticky (glutinous) rice cooks into a dense mass. Before cooking the rice, Asians always rinse it not once but several times, rubbing the grains between their fingers to remove the starchy outer coating on the grains so the rice will be "fluffy" when cooked.

1 cup (200 g) uncooked short-grain rice
1 1/2 cups (375 ml) water

Place the rice in a large bowl and cover it with water. Stir the rice briskly for about 10 seconds, then hold the grains in on one side of the bowl with your hand and carefully pour away the milky water. Repeat this process several times until the water runs clear, then drain the rice. Transfer the washed rice to an electric rice cooker, add the water and switch on the rice cooker. Fluff the cooked rice with a fork to separate the grains before serving.

If you do not have an electric rice cooker, place the rice and water in a heavy saucepan and bring to a boil over medium heat. Let the rice boil for 1–2 minutes, then cover the pan, reduce the heat to low and simmer for 10–15 minutes until all the water has been absorbed and the rice is cooked. Turn off the heat and allow the rice to sit covered for 10 minutes before removing the lid.

MAKES: *2 cups (200 g) cooked white rice*
PREPARATION TIME: *5 mins*   COOKING TIME: *15 mins*

Sambal oelek chili paste

The action of grinding a chili paste is "oelek" or "ulek" in Malay. Commercial brands like the Indonesian ABC brand are good, but this sauce is so simple to make that you should try it. If you have a blender it becomes a simple process, but remember to bring it to the boiling point and cool before storing. (see photo above)

1 onion, peeled and sliced
5 cloves garlic, peeled
1 in (2 1/2 cm) fresh ginger, peeled and thinly sliced
12 red finger-length chili peppers, halved and deseeded
2 tablespoons oil
1 teaspoon shaved palm sugar or dark brown sugar
1/3 cup (100 ml) vinegar
1/4 teaspoon salt, to taste

Grind the onion, garlic, ginger and chili peppers in a food processor or mortar to a smooth paste. Heat the oil in a skillet and sauté the ground paste over medium heat until fragrant, 3–5 minutes, seasoning with the sugar, vinegar and salt.

Remove from the heat and cool, then store refrigerated in a sealed jar for up to 2 months.

MAKES: *1 cup*   PREPARATION TIME: *10 mins*
COOKING TIME: *5 mins*

Thai orange curry paste

A versatile curry paste for chicken, fish or scallops. This is a lighter but tastier curry paste which is simple to make especially if you have larger and sweeter red chilies. I would suggest making double the quantity and freezing the extra for later use. (see photo below)

10 dried red finger-length chili peppers, stems discarded, soaked in hot water until soft
1 teaspoon salt
5 small Asian shallots, peeled
1 tablespoon dried shrimp paste, dry-roasted (page 207)
1 teaspoon rice vinegar

Grind the dried chilies in a food processor or mortar until smooth, then add all the other ingredients and grind until well blended. Store frozen in a sealed jar.

MAKES: *1 cup*   **PREPARATION TIME:** *15 mins*

Aromatic nonya spice paste

This curry paste is the classic Nonya standby. Use it as base for many Nonya curries and laksa dishes. Double the quantity as a time-saving exercise and use it as a stir-fry starter for vegetables and soups instead of starting with chopped garlic and onions. (see photo above)

1 medium onion, chopped
2 stalks lemongrass, thick part only, outer layers discarded, inner part sliced
10 red finger-length chili pepper, halved and deseeded
1 tablespoon dried prawns
2 candlenuts or macadamia nuts
2 tablespoons oil
1 tablespoon fresh lime juice
2 teaspoons shaved palm sugar
2 tablespoons water
$\frac{1}{2}$ teaspoon salt or fish sauce, to taste

Grind the onion, lemongrass, chili pepper, and candlenuts or macadamia in a food processor or mortar until smooth.

Heat the oil in a wok and stir-fry the paste over medium heat until fragrant, 1–2 minutes. Add the lime juice, sugar and water, mix well and bring to a boil, then simmer uncovered, stirring, for 2–3 minutes until the mixture thickens. Season with salt to taste and remove from the heat. Cool and store refrigerated in a sealed jar.

MAKES: *1 cup*   **PREPARATION TIME:** *45 mins*
COOKING TIME: *5 mins*

Lemongrass paste

Lemongrass is an aromatic herb used for centuries in Southeast Asia. It may be sliced very finely as garnish, but in this case, this interesting paste is used for many of my curries or laksa dishes, as it has the freshness of ginger and galangal, and the aroma of kaffir lime. (see photo above)

4 stalks lemongrass, thick parts only, outer layers discarded, inner parts sliced
1 in (3 cm) fresh galangal root, peeled and sliced
10 cloves garlic, peeled
$1/2$ in (1 cm) fresh ginger, peeled and sliced
12 red finger-length chili peppers, halved and deseeded
1 tablespoon dry shrimp, dry-roasted (page 207)
1 tablespoon oil
2 teaspoons shaved palm sugar
4 tablespoons water
1 kaffir lime leaf or regular lime leaf, cut into thin strips
$1/2$ teaspoon salt, or to taste

Grind the lemongrass, galangal, garlic, ginger and chili peppers in a food processor or mortar until fine. Add the dried shrimp and grind to a smooth paste.

Heat the oil in a skillet and sauté the paste over medium heat until fragrant, 2–3 minutes. Stir in all the other ingredients, except the salt, and simmer uncovered for 3–5 minutes, stirring constantly until the mixture thickens. Season with salt to taste and remove from the heat, cool and store refrigerated in a sealed jar.

MAKES: *1 cup*   PREPARATION TIME: *30 mins*
COOKING TIME: *10 mins*

Meat curry powder

Normally curry powders are freshly made by cooks who have the time to measure out each spice and dry roast it before grinding them all into a paste or powder. It may be convenient to use a commercial blend like "Baba" curry powders, but it is more satisfying to make your own and vary the ingredients as needed.

3 tablespoons coriander seeds
4 teaspoons cumin seeds
$1/2$ tablespoon fennel seeds
4 dried red finger-length chili peppers, stems discarded, broken into pieces
1 teaspoon fenugreek seeds
$1/2$ teaspoon mustard seeds
1 teaspoon ground cinnamon
1 teaspoon ground nutmeg
1 teaspoon ground cloves

In a skillet, dry-roast each of the whole spices separately over gentle heat until fragrant, 2–3 minutes each. Let them cool and then grind all the spices to a fine powder in a mortar or spice grinder. Store in a sealed jar refrigerated or frozen.

MAKES: $1/2$ *cup*   PREPARATION TIME: *10 mins*
COOKING TIME: *10 mins*

Fish curry powder

The difference between a fish and a meat curry powder is a couple of spices that add sourness and aroma to the fish curries. You may choose a commercial blend or make your own using a little less or more fenugreek seeds, mustard and some lime juice to hold the powder together.

3 tablespoons coriander seeds
1 teaspoon cumin seeds
4 teaspoons fennel seeds
4 dried red finger-length chili peppers, stems discarded, broken into pieces
2 teaspoons fenugreek seeds
1 teaspoon mustard seeds

In a skillet, dry-roast each of the whole spices separately over gentle heat until fragrant, 2–3 minutes each. Let them cool and then grind all the spices to a fine powder in a mortar or spice grinder. Store in a sealed jar refrigerated or frozen.

MAKES: $1/2$ *cup*   PREPARATION TIME: *10 mins*
COOKING TIME: *10 mins*

Sweet tamarind date chutney

This recipe was given to me by a friend who comes from a Cape Malay family from Cape Town, South Africa. They cook very interesting foods similar to our Malaysian kormas and pilaffs. (see photo above)

$^1/_3$ cup (100 g) chopped pitted dates, or chopped pitted
   dates with whole raisins
2 teaspoons fennel seeds, dry-roasted and ground to a
   powder in a mortar or spice grinder
1 tablespoon ground red pepper, or to taste
$^1/_2$ cup (150 g) tamarind pulp, mashed in 1 cup (250 ml)
   water and strained to obtain juice
$^1/_3$ cup (65 g) dark brown sugar or jaggery
Salt, to taste
1 tablespoon oil
$^1/_2$ teaspoon mustard seeds
$^1/_4$ cup (35 g) chopped roasted macadamia nuts

Process the dates, fennel seeds, ground red pepper, tamarind juice, sugar and salt to a purée in a food processor. Heat the oil in a wok and stir-fry the mustard seeds over high heat until they pop, 1–2 minutes. Add the purée and bring to a boil, stirring constantly until the chutney becomes thick, 2–3 minutes. Reduce the heat to low and simmer uncovered for about 2 more minutes. When the chutney has a dropping consistency, stir well and remove from the heat. Stir in the macadamia nuts and serve immediately. Store the unused chutney in a sealed jar in the refrigerator, after cooling.

MAKES: $^3/_4$ *cup*   **PREPARATION TIME:** *30 mins*
COOKING TIME: *10 mins*

Mint pachidi chutney

Minty and garlicky and deliciously reminiscent of coconut macaroons. Serve it as a condiment with roast meat, or as a relish with rice or roti.

1 tablespoon oil
1 onion, chopped
2 cloves garlic, sliced
$^1/_2$ in (2 cm) fresh ginger, cut into thin shreds
4 green finger-length chili peppers, deseeded and sliced
$^1/_3$ cup (30 g) dried unsweetened grated (dessicated)
   coconut, dry-roasted until golden brown
2 cups (80 g) fresh mint leaves, washed and dried
Freshly squeezed juice of 2 limes
Salt, to taste

Heat the oil in a wok and stir-fry the onion, garlic and ginger over medium heat until golden and tender. Add the chili and coconut and stir-fry for 1 minute, then remove from the heat. Process the coconut mixture with the mint leaves in a food processor until smooth. Transfer to a bowl and add the lime juice and salt to taste. Cover and chill until ready to serve. It keeps refrigerated for 3–4 days.

MAKES: $1^1/_2$ *cups*   **PREPARATION TIME:** *20 mins*
COOKING TIME: *5 mins*

Cucumber mint raita

This is an Indian side dish that is used to "smother" the flames of a spicy curry or other main dish. Use it also as a salad dressing. I often throw in a peeled banana to make an unusual dessert! (see photo below)

1 baby cucumber, peeled, cored and diced
1 teaspoon salt
1 semi-ripe tomato, diced
1 onion, finely chopped
$^3/_4$ cup (185 ml) plain yogurt
1 green finger-length chili pepper, deseeded and finely chopped
$^1/_2$ cup (20 g) fresh mint leaves, chopped

Sprinkle the cucumber with the salt and mix well. Allow to stand for 30 minutes, then drain and squeeze the liquid from the cucumber. Add all the other ingredients and mix well.

Note: For a creamier version, substitute the same amount of coconut cream for the yogurt.

MAKES: *1$^1/_2$ cups*   **PREPARATION TIME:** *20 mins*

Chili jam

The word "jam" is used in Australia to describe a thick spice paste that we call a "sambal"—but these sambals are far less sweet than a true jam. This is a favorite recipe that can be made up and heated for use later and will make a great Christmas gift when bottled. (see photo above)

2 tablespoons oil
4 cloves garlic, crushed
1 medium onion, chopped
1$^1/_2$ tablespoons Sambal Oelek Chili Paste (page 240) or other sweet chili paste
$^1/_2$ cup (60 g) dried shrimp, rinsed and dry-roasted (page 207)
1 tablespoon tamarind pulp, mashed in $^1/_4$ cup (60 ml) water and strained to obtain juice
$^1/_4$ cup (50 g) dark brown sugar or shaved palm sugar
1 tablespoon fish sauce
Salt, to taste

Heat the oil in a skillet and sauté the garlic, onion and Sambal Oelek over medium heat until fragrant, 1–2 minutes. Add all the other ingredients, except the salt, and sauté until the volume reduces to half, 3–5 minutes. Season with salt to taste and remove from the heat. Cool and store refrigerated in a sealed jar.

MAKES: *1 cup*   **PREPARATION:** *20 mins*
COOKING: *10 mins*

Fish stock

Simple to make if you have leftover fish bones or prawn shells, and certainly more authentic than using commercially prepared fish stocks which may contain MSG. I use amchoor or mango powder for a change instead of lime juice. This stock only needs $\frac{1}{2}$ hour of cooking.

$\frac{1}{2}$ cups (2 liters) water
10 oz (300 g) fish bones, or fish head, cleaned well
2 teaspoons amchoor mango powder, or 10 oz (300 g) shrimp shells
1 green onion

Bring all the ingredients to a boil in a stockpot. Reduce the heat to low and simmer partially covered for 30 minutes, skimming off the residue that floats to the surface. Remove from the heat, strain through a fine sieve and discard the solids. Allow the clear stock to cool completely before refrigerating or freezing.

MAKES: *2$\frac{1}{2}$ cup (625 ml)*   PREPARATION TIME: *5 mins*
COOKING TIME: *25 mins*

Vegetable Stock

A vegetable stock may be made from any vegetables that you can have on hand, but the root vegetables give more flavor, especially onions and carrots, and a stick of celery. I use red dal as a thickener for these stocks, as they also add flavor, but you may use potatoes as a thickener instead.

4 cups (1 liter) water
2 cloves garlic, bruised
1 onion, cut into wedges
2 carrots, peeled and chopped
$\frac{1}{2}$ cup (100 g) red (mysore) dal
1 cup (250 ml) water

Bring all the ingredients to a boil in a stockpot. Reduce the heat to low and simmer partially covered for 30 minutes, skimming off the residue that floats to the surface. Remove from the heat, strain through a fine sieve and discard the solids. Allow the clear stock to cool completely before refrigerating or freezing.

MAKES: *2$\frac{1}{2}$ cup (625 ml)*   PREPARATION TIME: *5 mins*
COOKING TIME: *30 mins*

Chicken stock

Make friends with your butcher to obtain the boned carcass of chickens or the knuckle joints and make them into a stock, using some vegetables and some ginger to add flavor. Meat stocks including chicken should be cooked for at least 1 hour, to obtain the best flavor. Remove the residue that floats to the top as it cooks.

8 cups (2 liters) water
2 lbs (1 kg) chicken bones or $\frac{1}{2}$ fresh chicken
1 small onion or 3 green onions, chopped
1 celery, sliced
6 black peppercorns, freshly cracked
5 cloves garlic, chopped
1 in (3 cm) fresh ginger, peeled and bruised
2 stalks lemongrass, thick part only, outer layers discarded, inner part bruised

Bring all the ingredients to a rolling boil for about 5 minutes in a stockpot. Reduce the heat to low and simmer uncovered for 30 minutes, skimming off the residue and fat that float to the surface. Increase the heat and return to a boil for 10 minutes then remove from the heat. Strain through a fine sieve and discard the solids. Allow the clear stock to cool completely before refrigerating or freezing.

MAKES: *6 cups (1$\frac{1}{2}$ liters)*   PREPARATION TIME: *20 mins*
COOKING TIME: *45 mins*

OTHER INGREDIENTS

Asian eggplants are generally smaller than Mediterranean eggplants. Some are long and cucumber-shaped or ovoid, while others are about 1 1/2 in (4 cm) thick and boomerang-shaped with a regal purple color. They come in a variety of shades of purple, mottled purple or green, and distinctive among them is the bright green pea eggplant which has a peppery center and is often used by the Thais in green curries. The eggplant is used in curries, pickles, sambals or mashed rather like the Baba Ganoush of the Middle East.

Asian shallots are small, round and pinkish-purple and add a sweet, oniony flavor and a hint of garlic to countless dishes. They are sliced, deep-fried and used as a garnish. Asian shallots are smaller and milder than those found in Western countries, with less juice so that they fry more easily. French shallots may be substituted, but use only half to a third as many as the recipe calls for as they are much larger.

Baby anchovies Known in Indonesia and Malaysia as *ikan bilis* or *ikan teri*, these tiny whitebait fish are ubiquitous in Southeast Asia. They are lightly salted and dried and sold either filleted, with the tiny central bone and the head removed, or whole. They are fried in a sambal with chili, onions and garlic (see Sweet and Spicy Ikan Bilis Nibbles with Peanuts, page 219) and are the main ingredient for a coconut rice dish called *nasi lemak* (page 103). Incidentally, *ikan bilis* were the main protein source for many Asians during the deprivations of the last World War!

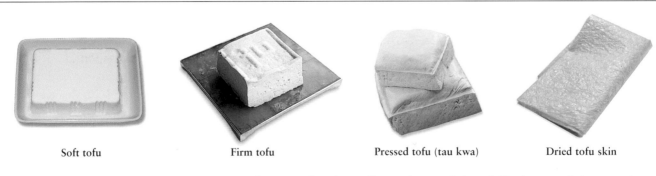

Soft tofu   Firm tofu   Pressed tofu (tau kwa)   Dried tofu skin

Bean curd or tofu comes in many different forms. **Soft tofu** is silky and smooth but difficult to cook because it falls apart. **Firm tofu** holds its shape well when cut or cooked and has a strong, slightly sour taste. **Pressed tofu** (often confusingly labeled as firm tofu) is a type of firm tofu with much of the water pressed out of it and is therefore much firmer in texture and excellent for stir-fries. Refrigerate fresh tofu enclosed in a plastic container submerged in water. **Dried tofu skin** is the dried skin that forms on top of boiling soybean milk. It is dried and sold in sheets as a spring roll wrapper.

Barbecued dried pork sheets Also known as *bak kwa*, these thin sweet slices of pork have been marinated in hoisin sauce or a sugar-honey paste and then grilled slowly over charcoal. They are eaten as a snack or cut into fine strips and used as a garnish or as the main meat component for fried rice or a rice salad (see Tropical Salad with Barbecued Pork, page 43).

Bok choy is a highly nutritious variety of cabbage with long, crisp stalks and spinach-like leaves. It has a clean, slightly peppery flavor and is a wonderful addition to soups and stir-fries. It is available in most well-stocked supermarkets.

Chickpeas Also known as punjabi channa or garbanzo beans, this dal is used in curries, boiled in stews or added cold to Indian salads with potatoes and fried onions then dressed with a tart sweet sour sauce (see Mixed Bean and Potato Salad with Herbs, page 39). Chickpeas can be stored in unopened packets in the pantry for at least 3 months.

Betel leaves This leaf is known as *paan* in India. They are the spicy and highly nutritious leaves from a vine that is related to the pepper plant. There are two varieties of the betel leaf, both growing on climbing vines. The Thai and Vietnamese variety, used to wrap finger foods, is called *chaplu* and is less bitter and softer than the tougher variety chewed with betel nuts and calcified lime. Grape leaves are a good substitute.

Channa dal is also known as Bengal gram. One of the yellow split lentils with the lowest glycemic index, these split peas have a dull yellow color and a sweet nutty flavor. They need to be soaked overnight before being cooked. They cause the most flatulence of the dals and are therefore frequently cooked with a tiny piece of *hing* or asafoetida, a well known anti-flatulent tree resin. The dried beans can be stored in unopened packets in the pantry for at least 3 months.

Chinese broccoli Also known as *kailan* or Chinese kale, Chinese broccoli has long, narrow stems and leaves, and small edible flowers. The stems are the tastiest part of the plant while the leaves are slightly bitter and are often discarded. Chinese broccoli is available fresh in all Asian markets and many supermarkets. Substitute broccoli stems, bok choy or broccolini.

Dried red chilies

Finger-length red and green chilies

Bird's-eye chilies

Chilies Many different varieties of chilies are used in Asia. The flavor of fresh and dried chilies is different, so be sure to use the type specified in the recipes. **Finger-length green and red chilies** are usually moderately hot. Red chilies are often dried and ground to make **chili flakes** and **ground red pepper**. Tiny but fiery-hot **bird's-eye chilies** may be red, green or yellowy-orange. Cut or break dried chilies into pieces and soak them in hot water for about 10 minutes to soften them before grinding or blending. If you want to reduce the heat without losing the flavor, discard some or all of the seeds.

Choy sum or chye sim Also known as chinese flowering cabbage, this is one of the most delicious members of the cabbage family, with soft mid-green leaves and stems, sometimes sold with delicate yellow flowers visible.

Dried rice paper wrappers These paper thin wrappers are made from a batter of rice flour, water and salt, then steamed and dried in the sun on bamboo racks, which leaves a cross-hatch imprint on them. Used to wrap a wide variety of spring rolls, dried rice paper wrappers must be moistened to soften them before using. Available in many Asian food markets, they will keep for many months if stored in a cool dark place.

Dried shrimp These tiny, orange-colored saltwater shrimp have been dried in the sun and come in different sizes. The really small ones have their heads and tails still attached. Look for dried shrimp that are pink and plump, avoiding any with a greyish appearance. The better quality ones are bright orange in color and completely shelled. Dried shrimp will keep for several months. They

should be soaked in warm water for several minutes to soften slightly before use. They are generally pounded in a mortar or ground in a blender to break them into smaller bits or flakes.

Dried sweet Chinese sausages Also known as *xiang chang* or *lap cheong*, literally meaning "fragrant sausage," these small sweet sausages are made with pork that is flavored with rice wine, salt, sugar and monosodium glutamate, smoked and then dried until hard. There are three varieties: one has a high fat content, another is made from less fatty pork, and a third and rarer type is made with added liver which produces a darker color and richer taste. They are sold in bundles tied with red string and packaged in plastic wrappers. To use them, slice thinly and toss into stir-fries, boil or steam them, then use in fried rice or sticky rice packets. These sausages may be steamed or boiled then sliced thinly into any salad for a sweet and spicy alternative to fresh meat. This is a good standby in a pantry, but once opened, the sausages should be refrigerated. Substitute beef jerky or any sweet sausage or salami.

| Dried black Chinese mushrooms | Enoki mushrooms | Oyster mushrooms | Woodear fungus |

Mushrooms are grown commercially throughout Asia and are highly sought after. **Dried black Chinese mushrooms** are similar to shiitake mushrooms but must be soaked in water before use. **Enoki mushrooms** are clusters of slender, cream-colored stalks with tiny caps that are available fresh or canned; the tough ends of the stems must be discarded before use. **Large oyster mushrooms** are available fresh or in cans. **Woodear fungus**, also known as cloud ear fungus, is a crinkly greyish-brown dried mushroom that swells to many times its original size after being soaked in warm water for a few minutes. They have little flavor but are prized for their texture.

Egg noodles and **wheat noodles** Egg noodles and wheat noodles are eaten universally in Asia, except India. Southeast Asians, especially Thais, Malaysians, Indonesians and Filipinos, have adapted Chinese noodle recipes to their own local tastes. Egg noodles are bright yellow in color, whereas plain wheat noodles are pale in color. Today it is possible to buy fresh Chinese egg noodles and wheat noodles in most supermarkets around the world and dried versions are also available. Fresh or dried pasta or instant ramen noodles may be substituted.

Glass noodles or **cellophane noodles** These thin strands are made by forcing mung bean starch through a sieve to produce something like vermicelli. When cooked, these noodles become glassy and slippery and because they do not have any flavor of their own, they absorb flavors cooked into them. Substitute rice vermicelli noodles if not available.

Golden syrup When cane sugar juice is reduced to produce sugar, it goes through a further refining process—golden syrup does not and still retains the flavor of the cane. Pure golden syrup is a golden brown color and is used as a sweetener for cakes and for puddings.

Jicama Also known as *bangkuang* or yam bean, these tubers came from South America but are eaten extensively in Asia now. Jicama is a close relative of the potato but is larger, sweeter and crunchier, with less carbohydrate and more vitamin C. It has a short root and a thin papery skin that can be peeled off easily to reveal a white flesh inside that tastes like a juicy nashi pear. In Asia, the peeled root is often sliced into salads as it remains crunchy without "weeping" when acidic dressings are added and does not discolor when exposed to air. It is used by the Nonyas as a spring roll filling and in the famous *rojak* salad (see Crisp Rojak Salad with Spicy Sweet Dressing, page 98). Peel the skin and slice the flesh into large pieces, then slice again diagonally. Jicama stores well without refrigeration for a few days but is best kept refrigerated unpeeled until needed. Depending on the recipe, substitute apple or pear.

it in fresh water for at least 15 minutes to remove some of the saltiness, repeating if necessary. It is available in vacuum packs from well-stocked Asian supermarkets.

Chicharon is easily made by trimming the thick layer of fat and skin from roasted cuts of pork belly or shoulder and then either frying or roasting it until crispy. Good-quality *chicharon* is found in Latino or Vietnamese stores.

Palm sugar is distilled from the sap of various palm fruits. It is usually sold as a solid block or cylinder. It varies in color from gold to light brown and has a faint caramel taste. It is used to make Palm Sugar Syrup (see page 78), which is wonderful on pancakes or french toast. Palm sugar should be shaved, grated or melted in a microwave oven before measuring it. Substitute dark brown sugar or maple syrup.

Ponzu sauce Japanese ponzu sauce is made from mirin or rice wine, rice vinegar, soy sauce, bonito flakes and konbu seaweed. When the sauce is cooled and strained, lemon or other citrus juice is added, producing a tart but pleasant-tasting sauce that is used as a dressing in Asian dishes. In Japan, it is used in the one-pot *nabemono*, both as flavoring and a dipping sauce when the dish is served. You can buy ready-made ponzu sauce in Asia markets, generally in bottles.

Preserved Chinese cabbage Also known as *tang chye*, this is made from Chinese or Napa cabbage which is shredded and then salted and dried. It turns golden brown once preserved. It is slightly moist, with a salty flavor and crunchy texture. It is often sprinkled on rice porridge and is sometimes used to garnish noodle dishes.

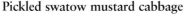
Pickled swatow mustard cabbage
Also known as *kiam chye* or *xian cai*, this is a slightly sour and extremely salty brined vegetable. Various types of salted cabbage are used in Chinese and Nonya dishes: the most common is made from mustard cabbage. Soak

Pork cracklings Also known as *chicharon*, this crispy fried pork skin is commonly eaten as a snack in the Philippines or used as a meaty addition to vegetable and noodles dishes.

Rice stick noodles Also known as *hofun*, river noodles or *kway teow*, these noodles are produced fresh in most Chinatowns in larger cities and are also available as dried noodles in plastic bags in all Asian food stores. There are two sizes, one slightly thicker and wider than the other. The larger flat noodle is used in stir fries (see Bean Sauce Noodles with Shrimp and Sausage, page 54), in soups (see Beef Noodle Soup with Fragrant Herbs, page 155) or in steamed noodle recipes, while the narrower noodle is used in Thai noodle dishes, for instance the famous Pad Thai.

Rice vermicelli Also known as rice threads, *mifen*, *beehoon* or *meehoon*, these white noodles are made from rice flour although similar noodles are also made from wheat, dried beans or tapioca. They're similar to bean threads, only they're longer and made with rice flour instead of mung bean starch. Before using, soak the dried noodles in hot water until soft (about 5 minutes), then boil them briefly (from 1 to 3 minutes) and rinse with hot water.

Sambal oelek (see recipe on page 240) This is an Indonesian term for a sweet chili paste with garlic, some dried shrimp or shrimp paste (*belacan*) and small Asian shallots as well as palm sugar. Many of these chili pastes also contain vinegar or lime juice or tamarind. Today *sambal oelek* does not necessarily come from Indonesia and the use of the term has come to be applied to any sweet ground chili paste with onions and garlic added. It is used as a "stir-fry starter" to begin a stir-fry, as a dipping sauce,

or to add spice and flavor to any curry or seafood dish.

Sawtooth coriander This herb has long pungent blades with serrated edges and a taste that is a cross between coriander, mint and basil. It is known in Cambodia as *chi bonla* or *chi barang*, *prik chee farang* in Thailand and *ngo gai* in Vietnam (elsewhere, it is sometimes referred to by its botanical name, eryngo). Sawtooth coriander is generally added to soups (see Pineapple Fish Soup with Tamarind and Tomatoes, page 107) and served as part of a platter of fresh herbs with Vietnamese food. Fresh coriander leaf (cilantro) is the best substitute.

Tempeh is made by culturing boiled soybeans in the same way that cheese is made from cultured milk solids. It is a vital and inexpensive meat substitute for Indonesians and Malaysians who live on a rice and vegetable diet with little meat. Tempeh has 40% more protein and far more vitamins and minerals than

meat. Substitute firm tofu or pressed tofu if you cannot find it.

Turmeric leaves Also known as *daun kunyit*, these leaves are highly aromatic and impart a delicious flavor to many dishes. Like turmeric root, the leaves also have many health benefits in aiding digestion, fighting bacteria and cleansing the system. The leaves are used as herb, particularly in Sumatra. There is no substitute.

Wolfberries Also known by their Japanese name, *goji* or "red berries," these dried berries have a pleasant sweet-sour flavor and are often added to soups, especially chicken soup. They can be added to stir-fried vegetables (see Beef and Black Mushrooms with Chinese Broccoli, page 233) for color and texture and are said by the Chinese to have strong medicinal properties. Available at most Chinese herbalists. If unavailable, use dried cranberries.

INDEX

DEDICATION

Aromas have seldom been explored for themselves except by vintners, sommeliers and perfumers, although they are recognized as an integral part of flavor. An Asian housewife prides herself on food that is *wangi* or *ho heong*, as my Amah used to say. Aromas intrigue when they are combined carefully into a fragrance that is difficult to analyze and yet at the edge of your senses, as they bypass the cognitive brain, going directly to the emotive. So enjoy aromas in food by breathing deeply and sitting down to eat, as you use all your senses for a complete experience.

To my family and many friends who have perfumed my life, this book is for you—with love.

ACKNOWLEDGMENTS

This book has been slow-cooking for a long time like any good dish, with spice and herb. Starting as a book on the aromatics of Malaysian food, it contained 90 traditional recipes with a working title we called "Ginger Flower."

My daughter Anushiya Selvarajah, a trained teacher of Asian cooking for over 10 years, assisted by Patricia Soosay from Perth, who wanted to gain more of an understanding of Malaysian cooking, tested recipes for months. Both girls knew the food and understood the cuisine just as much as I did, yet we found ourselves re-testing, changing and sometimes reverting to our original recipes in an attempt to improve and to simplify techniques. Finally without any murders or mayhem, the recipes were collated and I thank both Patricia and Anushiya sincerely for teasing out the best flavors with dedication and care.

When it was decided that the book take on a more general impetus with foods ranging from all across Asia, I included recipes from my travels. All Asian food is aromatic, in individual and separate ways. Most include similar ingredients, yet become culinary creations that excite the imagination as different techniques are employed. Thanks also go to Matt Lim, the stalwart in the revival and change of the book's direction and to Diane Temple for her careful recipe formatting. The help and friendship of Philippa Sandall, Andrea Rademan and Wendy Lloyd Jones have, as always, been invaluable.

I include some recipes from friends whose work I admire: Lyndey Milan and Di Holuigue, Pauline Loh, Patricia Soosay, Simon Goh and Marty Morrison. I would also like to thank Michelle Sandhu, my niece in Singapore, my brother Abel Arumugam and his wife Gomathy, and Andrea Rademan in Beverly Hills, California, for the use of their kitchens and their computers while working abroad and for their generosity, to Christina Ong for her creative eye and food-styling that has guided the book's tone and atmosphere and to Masano for his photography. Thanks also to Dr. Max Lake, OAM.FRCS, International wine judge and author of six books on flavor, taste and aroma. I would not have dared to venture into this realm had I not been convinced of Max's support and critique; to dear friends Cheong Liew for his support and David Thompson for writing the foreword.

And to Ben Cardillo, for allowing me to see my Malaysia through his eyes, when, in 1991, he wished we had smell-a-vision while we were filming for a television series in Kuala Lumpur.

The following books were used as references:
Spice Notes by Ian Hemphill
Dictionary of Japanese Foods by Richard Hosking
The Chinese Kitchen by Deh-Ta Hsuing
Thai Food by David Thompson
Taste by Max Lake
Sense and Sensuality by Max Lake
Tropical Planting and Gardening by H.E. Holtum and Macmillan, revised by Barlow Enoch and Russel

Published by Periplus Editions, with editorial offices at
61 Tai Seng Avenue #02-12, Singapore 534167.

Text and recipes © 2007 Carol Selva Rajah
Photos copyright © 2007 Periplus Editions
All rights reserved.
ISBN 13: 978-0-7946-0353-3
ISBN 10: 0-7946-0353-X

Distributed by
North America, Latin America and Europe
Tuttle Publishing, 364 Innovation Drive,
North Clarendon, VT 05759-9436 U.S.A.
Tel: 1 (802) 773-8930; Fax: 1 (802) 773-6993
info@tuttlepublishing.com
www.tuttlepublishing.com

Japan
Tuttle Publishing, Yaekari Building, 3rd Floor
5-4-12 Osaki, Shinagawa-ku,
Tokyo 141 0032.
Tel: (81) 03 5437-0171; Fax: (81) 03 5437-0755
tuttle-sales@gol.com

Asia Pacific
Berkeley Books Pte Ltd
61 Tai Seng Avenue, #02-12
Singapore 534167.
Tel: (65) 6280-1330; Fax: (65) 6280-6290
inquiries@periplus.com.sg
www.periplus.com

All recipes were tested in the Periplus Test Kitchen.

Photo credits: All photography by Masano Kawana except pages 7–11
and backcover flap. Drawing representation of my family home taken
from old photographs and created by Carolyn McCulloch, Sydney.
Page 11: Market photograph, Ray Williams Photography, Sydney.
Backflap photograph: Ronald Leong Singapore.
Design by the Periplus design team

Printed in Singapore
10 09 08
6 5 4 3 2 1